A
Handmade
Wilderness

Also by Don Schueler

Preserving the Pascagoula

Incident at Eagle Ranch: Predators as Prey
   in the American West

Adventuring Along the Gulf of Mexico

The Temple of the Jaguar: Travels in the Yucatán

A Handmade Wilderness

DON SCHUELER

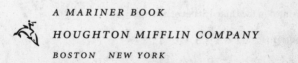

A MARINER BOOK

HOUGHTON MIFFLIN COMPANY

BOSTON   NEW YORK

For information about permission to reproduce selections from
this book, write to Permissions, Houghton Mifflin Company,
215 Park Avenue South, New York, New York 10003.

For information about this and other Houghton Mifflin
trade and reference books and multimedia products, visit
The Bookstore at Houghton Mifflin on the World Wide Web
at http://www.hmco.com/trade/.

Library of Congress Cataloging-in-Publication Data
    Schueler, Donald G.
    A handmade wilderness / Don Schueler.
        p.   cm.
    ISBN 0-395-68997-X   ISBN 0-395-86022-9 (pbk.)
1. Natural areas — Mississippi. 2. Country life — Mississippi.
3. Schueler, Donald G. 4. Brown, Willie Farrell.   I. Title.
QH76.5M7S28   1996
508.762'2 — dc20
95-40398   CIP

Printed in the United States of America

QUM 10 9 8 7 6 5 4 3 2 1

Book design by Melodie Wertelet
The map of the Place was drawn by Don Schueler.

To

Elizabeth, Theodora, Marsha, and Lane

Contents

Preface

Twenty-seven years ago, when Willie Brown told his mother that he and I had just bought eighty acres in the backwoods of Mississippi, she threw a fit. "Oh Lord Jesus!" she yelled at us. "Don't you know they still burning churches out there! You gonna get yourselves killed for sure!"

Willie and I attributed this outburst to a mother's natural tendency to be overprotective and therefore prey to needless worry; but the following evening when we announced the same news at a dinner party, our fellow guests, all old friends, made it clear that they too thought we had gone around the bend. "You mean," one of them said, "you've bought property in Mississippi? Behind the Coast, in the *real* Mississippi?"

We might as well have told him we were buying a condo in the Mekong Delta. "Well," I said defensively, "it's the only dry land within easy reach of New Orleans that isn't likely to be developed any time soon."

"And that didn't cost too much money," Willie chimed in.

"Oh, I'm sure it was cheap; and no doubt it will be safe from development," the friend said. "But have you ever wondered *why?*"

Before Willie or I could formulate an answer to this unkind question, other friends helpfully proposed their own. These touched upon everything from the poor investment prospects of the area to the problem of having rednecks in white sheets for neighbors to the scarcity of cultural activities to the likely abundance of snakes. It remained, however, for our hostess, a woman notorious for her good sense, to put all these misgivings into calm, thoughtful perspective. "You'll be outsiders," she said, "a black man and a white man in southern Mississippi. And you're city people; you don't know a thing about the area. The real problem is, you haven't a clue about what you're getting into."

That was in 1968. A year later, the same friends were coming up to the Place to picnic and even, occasionally, to camp out overnight. By the time several more years had passed, when the Place was beginning to take on the outlines of the lovely and sheltering refuge it has since become, they had forgotten their original objections to the venture. The real nature lovers among them, once they began to see what the Place was all about, would invariably say something like, "Boy, I wish I had a place like this." And I would invariably answer, "If Willie and I could do it, just about anyone can."

No doubt this response was sometimes construed as a boast masquerading as a pretense of modesty. In a way, I suppose that's what it was. After all, Willie and I were very proud of what we were accomplishing. But I meant what I said. Just about anybody who loves nature and has a certain capacity for vision and enterprise can do what Willie and I have done — namely, restore a small piece of the natural world to something like its original healthy state. The rewards can be very great. For us, commitment became a grand passion, the source of a joyful, ongoing sense of adventure that enriched our lives beyond measure.

But there is no denying that, while adding to our collection of joys and triumphs, we also shed copious quantities of blood, sweat, and tears. More, I see now, than we need have done. Our levelheaded friend had been right. We really hadn't known what we were getting into; and when we could have used some advice, there was none to be had.

So, on the assumption that there are a good many people out there who dream of one day having a place like the Place but who are worried about what they might be getting into, I decided to write this book.

A
Handmade
Wilderness

The West Seventy

The Northwest Forty

The Middle Ridge — Schaffer's Hill

The Pine Plantation

The Inde...

Pitcher Plant

Bogs

THE PLACE
CIRCA 1980

Finding it

The dream that Willie and I had was to own land in the country. But not just any land. Not, for example, some cute little cabin in a resort development, and most definitely not the sort of "secluded" three-acre lot in the wilds of exurbia that is presently gobbling up even more of rural America than suburban sprawl itself. In its specialized way, our dream was more ambitious than that. Before we got together, Willie had never seen anything greener than New Orleans's City Park in his whole life, but the idea of "the country" entranced him. He wanted to grow things, and he loved all shapes and sizes of animals (except, back then, snakes). It thrilled him that he might have as neighbors creatures he had only seen in the Audubon Zoo or on TV nature shows. Also, he had a taste for living adventurously. As for me, I was an amateur environmental activist who loved the natural world and wanted to protect it and live close to it, at least on a part-time basis. Together, our enthusiasms added up to a great yearning to have our own private nature reserve, a place that would be a haven, not just for us, but for the flora and fauna that would share it with us.

What we needed, obviously, was a pretty sizable chunk of countryside; enough space so we could be in touch with the natural world without moving it out when we moved in. But when we started our search, we didn't know how much space was enough, or where to look for it. Or, most crucial of all, how much we could afford to buy. Willie was a floor sander and I an assistant professor at a state university. Which is to say that we could be classified, at best, among the country's Taxable Poor. Moreover, like all good Americans, we were in debt. We had just finished fixing up a neglected house in one of New Orleans's many wonderful old neighborhoods, and the bills were still coming in.

It took us a while but we eventually concluded that, this side of a homestead in Alaska, we were not going to be able to afford a large slice of some scenic natural wonderland. In the Deep South, as in most of the more heavily populated regions of the nation, pristine wild land is almost nonexistent, and what little is left ought to be, and sometimes is, protected from any kind of human settlement. But, guided by real estate agents, we did find some large tracts of private land for sale that would have suited us just fine. Places that were within a couple of hours' drive of New Orleans, furnished with magnolias and mossy oaks, and usually situated along the banks of some lovely stream or bayou. But you pay extra for rustic scenery. At the going prices, the amount of land we could afford would have been barely enough to accommodate us, a pair of mockingbirds, a few squirrels, and maybe half a raccoon.

It took us a couple of months of that sort of window shopping before we decided to face reality. We could buy some tiny bit of real estate that already looked the way we wanted it to look, or we could (maybe) buy a decent-size piece of land that didn't; but we couldn't have both. From that realization evolved another: that land, like the half-wrecked old house we had restored in the city, could be rehabilitated. There was, however, one big difference: a piece of land, unlike a house, would do most of the restoration work itself if we just gave it enough time.

We adjusted our expectations accordingly. We would settle not just for any second- or third-best land, but for as much of what Willie called "the least worst land" as we could afford to buy at the cheapest price. No doubt a certain measure of sour grapes went into that decision, but we were excited by it, too. We had posed ourselves a challenge and then taken ourselves up on it. Whatever else, we were in for an adventure!

There are millions of acres of least worst land available in this country, much of it within reasonable commuting distance of large cities. It is land that wears the heavy scars of human abuse, land that is not near coastal beaches or pretty inland lakes or fashionable ski slopes — land that the developers wouldn't touch with a ten-foot surveyor's pole. It is the stony gray hills of the Northeast, covered with thin third-growth woods; the overgrown pastures and fields of abandoned farms in the Carolinas; the ravaged sites of former strip mines in the Alleghenies; the unirrigated prairie corners of the Midwestern corn belt; the near desert of expired sheep ranches in west Texas and New Mexico; the dry scrublands east of the Cascades. It is the sort of land that has to be envisioned in terms of what it once was and could be again. The sort of land that desperately needs to be loved and protected, and rarely is.

Here in the Deep South, land like that is almost always composed of pinelands or hardwood bottomlands from which virtually all the marketable timber has been stripped. There are thousands of acres of that kind of cutover woodland available for sale at any given time, but Willie and I had a hard time finding a piece of it that was right for us. The real estate agents on the Mississippi Gulf Coast never did catch on to what we wanted. They were bemused when we said that we actually preferred land that had some swampy ground on it, that we didn't care if the timber had been recently cut, that we definitely didn't want frontage on a paved road. And no, we weren't interested in a property with a dwelling on it, unless it was an old country homeplace we could fix up ourselves. They did their unimaginative best. They showed us twenty-acre pine plantations with the young trees lined up like soldiers; they showed us small farms with ranchette houses; and, inevitably, they showed us more of the streamside properties we had already decided we couldn't afford.

Finally, they and we gave up on each other with mutual sighs of relief, and we went land hunting on our own. What we did first was buy U.S. Geological Survey maps of areas that, judging from ordinary road maps, seemed to be not too heavily populated and at the same time not too far from New Orleans. These days you can purchase aerial satellite photos from NASA of any tract that interests you, blown up to whatever size you want. But those old survey maps served us well enough. They were incredibly detailed, indicating not just land elevations and main roads, but the location of every dwelling, pond, streamlet, and dirt track to be found in a given quad at the time the map was drawn. With these for guides, Willie and I, in the company of Schaeffer, our fawn Great Dane, and Sammie, our thoroughbred mutt, roved the back roads of southwest Mississippi in our Volksbus for half a dozen winter weekends in a row. We checked out faded For Sale signs nailed to fenceposts at the edge of weedy pastures and burned-over woodlots. We accosted local people in the front yards of their trailer homes, asking them if they knew of anyone roundabout who was trying to unload some property. Sometimes all we got was a suspicious look that passed from my white face to Willie's black one, but sometimes we were rewarded with a name and directions to someone's house.

During those weekends, we tramped a lot of parcels of land. We were like Goldilocks: even the most likely properties didn't quite fit; they were too large or too small or too expensive or too close to the neighbors or too ecologically bland. Yet, all along we felt that we were getting warmer, that the just-right property was out there, waiting for us, and sooner or later we would connect with it.

Meantime, we were learning just what least worst land meant in practical terms, and what it cost per acre. Even more important, we were getting some idea of how much land would be the minimum needed to create the sort of pocket-size nature reserve we had in mind. In different regions of the country, and in different ecological zones within those regions, that minimum can vary greatly. In calculating it, there are a lot of factors that have to be considered: Is the acreage for sale likely to become an island surrounded by other, more developed properties? In that case it will have to be much larger than an equivalent tract bounded, at least on one or two sides, by lands that are owned by a timber company or a government agency or a private conservation group, or that are just plain inaccessible due to the terrain. Does the tract offer, at least *in potentia,* a reasonable sampling of the area's natural habitats? Does the aquifer allow for a water source that you can tap without losing your shirt paying for a well a couple of thousand feet deep? Above all, will the configuration of the land and its eventual vegetative cover offer enough seclusion for you, as well as adequate food and shelter for at least the more adaptable species of resident wildlife? You don't have to be an Aldo Leopold to figure out that forty acres of mesquite in south Texas isn't going to give you as much biodiversity as, say, a small, well-watered dale in southern Pennsylvania. On the other hand, you can probably buy half a dozen forties in south Texas (minus mineral rights, of course), for the price of one in the Northeast. Indeed, in that open country you would want to anyway, to keep your nearest neighbor from shooting at your jackrabbits and coyotes from his front porch.

Willie and I eventually decided that one south Mississippi forty might, just barely, serve our purpose. As it turned out, however, we ended up buying twice that much. Later we would be glad we did, even though at the time it put us that much more into hock. What happened was that one chilly, rainy day in December, we were out questing once again, and we ended up on a particularly wet, muddy dirt road that snaked this way and that in its not very successful effort to avoid the many narrow creek bottoms that tried to intercept it. Now Volksbuses are not noted for their traction in slippery situations such as this, so I suppose I shouldn't have been as surprised as I was when ours embarked on a long slide while I was trying to get around an especially sharp curve.

"Uh-oh," said Willie, pressing his hands against the dashboard. Sammie, easily rattled, hopped into his lap. Even Schaeffer, usually the most imperturbable of dogs, looked concerned.

For a few seconds everything was out of control, with the Volksbus skating perilously close to the edge of a deep drainage ditch. Then the road, though not the Volksbus, straightened out, bringing into view two men standing right in the middle of it. To judge from the expressions on their faces, they had never seen a Volksbus driven sideways before. They both carried shotguns, and their first impulse, as we swooped down on them, was to point the guns in our direction rather than jump aside. Luckily, the bus came to a halt — still facing sideways — a few feet from where they stood ankle deep in mud.

"Hi," I said, giving them my very best effort at a disarming smile.

They didn't reply, but they did lower their guns.

All things considered, they were not the sort one would want one's sister to date. Low brows, sullen eyes, paleolithically slouching shoulders. For several seconds they just stood there, slowly sizing us up. No doubt we did seem an unlikely quartet to be roaming the backwoods of Mississippi: Willie, trim, handsome, black; Schaeffer, large even by Great Dane standards, pressing his dark mask against a back window; Sammie, barking ferociously from the safety of Willie's lap; myself, flummoxed and no doubt citified-looking, trying hard to think of something folksy and friendly to say.

On Schaeffer's account a bit of light finally flickered in the men's eyes. Evidently they had never seen a Great Dane before.

One of them asked, "What's he good fer?"

"Well," I mumbled, "he's, uh, sort of a pet."

The light in the two pairs of eyes went out. I might as well have told them he was an objet d'art. "Of course," I added defensively, "he's a very good watchdog." Which was not exactly true. Then, to change the subject, I asked them what they were hunting.

"Deers."

"That's great," I said. I meant it, too. It wasn't that I had any enthusiasm for deer hunting, but I was glad to learn that there was a population of deer hereabouts that was numerous enough to hunt. I had hoped there might be; but there were also a good many humans living along the back roads we were exploring and, just judging from first impressions, I suspected that even the adaptable whitetail might find it hard to coexist with them.

"Any luck?" I asked.

"Naw," they said.

As though to confirm this observation, the air suddenly turned loud with a fanfare of complaining yaps and yelps. The next instant the van was surrounded by a swirling pack of black and tan deer hounds. They ignored Sammie's yammering, but when aristocratic Schaeffer, confronted with this canine rabble, uttered a contemptuous "Woof," they did their excited best to climb through the windows.

The spectacle was too much for Willie. "They don't like him being so high and mighty," he laughed. And when Schaeffer woofed again, even the two men had to grin. "He do look like a deer," said one of them.

"You're right. Ha, ha," I answered, beginning, on that benign note, to carefully back the Volksbus around in the midst of hound-ish chaos. I figured we had had enough country motoring for one day. But when at last we were about-faced, I asked the hunters the question I had asked so many times during these last weeks: "You wouldn't know if anyone has some land for sale around here, would you?"

Pause. Then one of the men answered, "Well, you might could try Old Man Stanton. Lives about five miles south on the hardtop. He's got a bunch a pieces all out in here."

We did try Old Man Stanton, who turned out to be a spry, round little gentleman in his seventies, with a habit of appending wicked little chuckles to everything he said. And, yes, he had a few pieces of land in the neighborhood that he had acquired during the Depression as payment on defaulted loans. Right off he seemed to understand what we were looking for in the way of bargain-basement property, perhaps because that was the only kind he owned. He told us to come back the following Saturday. When we did, he donned old-fashioned army leggings ("Snakes, y'know, heh, heh") and energetically led the way on a day-long progress during which we toured a forty here, then an eighty over there, then another forty "just down the road a little ways, heh, heh."

By late that drizzly afternoon, after we had slogged across what must have been miles of beige meadows, plundered pine woods, and flooded gulleys, even Mr. Stanton admitted to being "a mite give out." The supply of his scattered holdings was giving out too. Wearily, we climbed out of the car to have a look at the last property, an eighty, that he had to show us.

It was the Place.

2

Taking an inventory

Nowadays if you are shopping around for a private nature reserve you shouldn't have too much trouble turning up some ecological information about the area of the country where you are conducting your search. There are regional guidebooks, often published by university presses, that will help you identify wildflowers, trees, birds, reptiles — even insects. And state wildlife agencies and environmental groups can give you advice about the preferred foods and habitat requirements of many wildlife species. So even before you start looking for the right place, you can begin educating yourself about how to take an ecological inventory once you find it.

When Willie and I first laid eyes on the Place more than a quarter of a century ago, much of that sort of information was unavailable. And we were such rank amateurs when it came to natural history that trying to assess the environmental value of what we were buying was largely a matter of hit and miss. Besides, it was winter. A snowless Deep South winter, to be sure, but still not the best time of year to be trying to identify obscure wildflowers on the basis of a bunch of withered stalks, or indigenous birds that were probably vacationing in the Yucatán, or a species of tree that, leafless, looked like every other scraggly old tree in sight. Considering the odds, Willie and I were pretty lucky to figure out the potential of the Place as well as we did.

God knows, our Promised Land didn't look all that promising on that dreary December day. What it did look was *big*. To a couple of city rubes, a tract one-half of a mile long by a quarter of a mile wide seemed a vast expanse of real estate. As the buzzard flies, it lay about twenty-five miles back from the Gulf Coast in a relatively narrow belt of gently rolling land known locally as the sandhills. During the Pleistocene epoch, between 1 and 1.5 million years ago, ancient rivers shaped its modest ridges and hills out of the alluvial clay and sand they had carried with them in their southward progress.

Silviculturists can't say with absolute certainty whether the upland forests that took over here as interglacial seas withdrew were dominated by hardwoods, notably the majestic live oak, or by that most durable and noble-looking of Southern pines, the longleaf. The longleaf's special genius lies in its ability to survive forest fires when it is just a little sprout, with its tufty head barely poking above ground. Young oaks are not fortunate enough to have this immunity. However, if they manage to grow tall enough to make a parasol of their dense evergreen foliage before a forest fire catches up with them, then shade-tolerant shrubs and hardwood saplings, including more oaks, spring up under them. In time, these crowd out sun-loving pine seedlings and grasses; and without dry grass and pine straw to feed upon, fires find it increasingly difficult to invade these hardwood enclaves.

Back in the old days, the frequency with which forest fires occurred would have been the crucial factor in determining whether oaks or pines got the upper hand, at least on the dry and sandy upland slopes. Given the exceptionally high incidence of electrical storms in this region, as well as the Choctaws' practice of periodically setting fires to improve habitat for deer and other game, big burns must have been pretty commonplace around here long before the white man showed up; so it seems likely that in most areas the longleafs had the upper hand, a probability supported by the few accounts left by early travelers in this region. But whether the wilderness that covered the sandhills was overwhelmingly dominated by starkly vertical barrens of towering pines, or divvied up between them and sprawling Sherwood Forests of massive oaks, it must have been something really wondrous to see.

In terms of human exploitation, these forests were, and still are, the only important natural resource that the sandhills can boast. The thin, sandy loam topsoils, highly acidic and nutrient poor, are ill-suited for anything but subsistence agriculture; and no mineral wealth has been found beneath the underlying hard clay pan. This poverty of resources explains the poverty of the sandhills' human history. Even before most of the tribes of the Choctaw Nation were deported to Oklahoma's Indian Territory in the 1840s, they apparently used this area only sporadically, preferring the richer hunting grounds of the alluvial river bottomlands that intersect the sandhills to the east and west. It was a preference shared by early white settlers in this region. Although records of white settlement along the Gulf and the coastal rivers go back to 1699, when Pierre Le Moyne, sieur d'Iberville, founded Old Biloxi, this backcountry remained largely uninhabited for almost two hundred years thereafter. No Taras, no Scarletts, no armies of cotton-picking slaves; only a few isolated homesteads with dogtrot cabins, corn cribs and rail fences, staked out by people who, for one reason or another, had no choice but to settle here. Even during the Civil War the sandhills were a territorial no man's land, not considered much worth fighting over; the most that local tradition can lay claim to is a small stream near the Place called Confederate Creek, where, it is said, a small band of Southern cavalrymen sometimes hid their horses when they weren't out raiding.

By the late 1800s, however, the epic plundering of the Deep South's pine forests — what timbermen still call "The Big Cut" — was reaching into southern Mississippi. Timber barons unleashed armies of tree cutters, both black and white, onto lands they leased or bought for next to nothing. The railroad companies (which acquired more than a million Mississippi acres as rights of way) built hundreds of miles of track for the sole purpose of transporting lumber. The first inland town in these parts was founded in 1898 when a large sawmill and turpentine kiln were set up at a crossroads fifteen miles south of what is now the Place to tap the area's seemingly limitless supply of timber and pine resin. In its heyday, during and right after the First World War, it was a bustling community that boasted a thousand homes, a fifty-room hotel, even a movie theatre. Yet within a decade this little boomtown had become almost a ghost town, surrounded by a clear-cut wasteland that by then encompassed all of southern Mississippi. When Willie and I appeared on the scene forty years later, the town survived as an eyeblink roadside hamlet, with nothing to show of the mill or hotel or any of the other monuments to greed and short-term planning that had first brought people here. Most of its former inhabitants had moved on, but there were still some old-timers around who, in their youth, had taken part in the dismantling of the local forests, including those on the very acres we now owned. They still remembered the gut-wrenching labor of bringing down pines more than one hundred feet tall and four feet in diameter; the long teams of straining oxen dragging the huge logs out of the woods; the narrow gauge railway systems on which they were hauled over hill and dale to the mills. Our next-to-nearest neighbor, Hovit Bodner, showed us the site in a hollow, marked by a few scattered bricks, where the lumbermen's camp was located. And he described how the Place had looked after they departed — the hills so utterly laid bare that he had been able to see wagons passing on the road to the Coast, then a dirt track, more than a mile away.

Since then, under the none-too-gentle management of folks like Mr. Stanton, much of the Place and the land surrounding it had been cut over whenever a stand of pines got tall enough to be converted into broomsticks, pulp, or creosote fence posts. Meanwhile, the local people were practicing a First World version of the Third World's slash-and-burn syndrome. Unimpressed by the property rights of absentee landowners, they set the hills afire every spring to eliminate dry winter grass and pine straw, thereby inducing early grazing for their free-ranging herds of half-starved cattle.

This, then, was the much-exploited landscape that Willie and I were to embrace as our own private Shangri-la. Right off, we loved it. Partly because we were already seeing it as it could be. And partly because, in the way of stray dogs, it looked as if it could use some tender loving care. I don't mean to suggest that the prospect the Place offered us was totally unprepossessing; not at all. But there was no denying that from some angles it did illustrate what least worst land was bound to look like.

Five sandy hills — ridges actually — lay wholly or partly across the Place like the fingers of a gouty hand. The knuckles of these hills, roughly aligned with the northern border of the property, were the highest elevations on the tract. The descending ridges, the fingers, tapered down to a narrow swampy creek, known as a brainch hereabouts, that lay along the southern boundary line. Of the four dales separating these ridges, the one between the broad thumb of high ground on the eastern property line and the next ridge, the index finger, was the widest. This was the hollow (which we named — what else? — the Hollow), where the lumber camp had once been located. The drainage ravines separating the other ridges were more steeply trenched by rain runoff, and varied in width from thirty feet to thirty yards. They were also wetter than the big hollow — miniature brainches, really — where rickety young stands of sweet bay and tupelo managed to survive the fires that annually swept the adjoining hills.

On the hills themselves there were some spots where the thin loamy topsoil was utterly gone, and the underlying hard yellow clay lay exposed like the top of a skull. Mostly, though, the upper slopes were covered by wild meadows of wire and bluestem grass, gallberry and briars; and wherever you looked, these open spaces were dotted by bright hairy green tufts, the irrepressible, troll-like seedlings of the longleaf pine.

Farther down the slopes, the second growth (actually third or fourth growth in most cases) was more advanced. Some of the stands of pines, though still pretty scrawny looking, would soon be eligible to end up as pages in the *New York Times*, but among them stood a few sizable longleafs, slash, and loblollies that the lumbermen had spared as "seed trees." There was also a smattering of young red oaks and a good many clumps of their rather disreputable cousin, the scruffy-looking blackjack oak, a "weed tree" that actually prefers to grow in poor soils.

None of these landscape features was unique to the Place; in fact, they were common to all the tracts Mr. Stanton had shown us, and to the sandhills generally. But there were three places on the property that, even on that first day, we recognized as being special.

One of these was the pitcher plant bog — two bogs, actually, each about an acre and a half, separated by a narrow but dense brake of sweet bay, young cypress, and titi. Back when we bought the Place, these highly specialized ecohabitats were not considered threatened, as they are now; but even in winter — maybe especially because it was winter — we were struck by their absolute apartness from everything around them. Normally, the vegetation of contiguous ecological zones tends to merge and overlap somewhat where the zones meet. But the boundaries of the open, austere bogs were as emphatically demarcated as the perimeters of fairy rings. The line they drew between themselves and the hillside pines on the one side, the gray-green wall of the brainch on the other, was determined by a combination of factors that had to be just so: a mere inch or two of difference in elevation ensured that the sandy soil would be saturated with water for much of the year but rarely flooded. This sogginess, combined with a very high level of acidity and a paucity of nutrients, discouraged most plants and trees from taking root. Some of those that did, like the ground-hugging sundews and both the parrot and frog belly pitcher plants, had evolved into carnivores, capturing and ingesting nitrogenous insects in various sinister but ingenious ways as a means of making ends meet. Even in winter, wherever cattle had not trampled them, the desiccated shells of the tubular pitcher plants and the dry blooms of white-topped sedge, like burned-out stars, were perfectly intact. In among them a few slender young cypress posed like Balinese dancers in dramatic yet delicate attitudes.

But our pitcher plant bogs were more than the sum of their parts. There was something archaic, even alien, about their severe, inhospitable beauty. Willie, eyeing the frog bellies a touch uneasily, said, "They got things here that ought to be growing on some other planet," which summed it up exactly.

The second of the Place's scenic marvels was a grove of live oaks on the crest of the index ridge. It was dominated on its northern edge by a single great behemoth of a tree that grew, regrettably, just outside our property line; but the grove itself was ours, its nucleus composed of about a dozen satisfyingly large and hoary trees whose heavy black limbs were draped with the Place's only noticeable strands of Spanish moss. Hovit would later tell us this had once been the site of a homeplace, occupied by a widow woman who had so many children (not all her own) that she didn't know what to do. At least not until she decided to set up a still and make moonshine — quite openly, according to Hovit, who was one of the stray kids she adopted for a while. It seems that the revenuers just gave up arresting her. The local judge, faced with a Hobson's choice, wasn't about to send her to jail, not with that huge brood depending on her ill-gotten gains for their beans and cornbread.

By the time Willie and I appeared on the scene, the widow woman and her homeplace were long gone. But the oaks that had once shaded her house not only lived on, they were rearing a family of their own. A troop of their older offspring, already pretty impressive, had grown up around them. And to one side, struggling to assert themselves amid thickets of waxmyrtle and yaupon, a whole new generation of adolescent oaks was colonizing the side of the ridge that sloped down toward the Hollow.

Mighty oaks from little acorns grow much faster than most people realize. This bunch still had a ways to go before they reached adult treehood, but we could see that the potential for a really imposing forest was already there.

The Oak Grove and the pitcher plant bogs would have probably sold us on the Place just by themselves. But it was the Hollow that convinced us we would somehow have to find the money to buy both of Mr. Stanton's adjoining forties, since it lay athwart their common boundary.

Over the course of a quarter of a mile, the Hollow's concave surface broadened as it dropped some fifty feet to the swampy brainch. Its northern end, where the forest of juvenile oaks was taking over, had once been cleared to make room for the widow woman's corn field, but the lower slopes supported a stand of hardwood trees that had somehow managed to reach near maturity in spite of the onslaughts of fire and axe. Under their canopy a whole second-growth woodland of water oaks, live oaks, red oaks, holly, red maple, and yellow poplar had already grown tall enough to shelter its own understory of dogwood (*dogwood!*), sassafras, huckleberry, sourwood, and, at the damp margins where the Hollow's slopes merged with the flooded brainch, a thicket of wild azalea.

Of course, we couldn't identify most of these trees and shrubs at the time. And we certainly didn't realize that what we were looking at was probably the last surviving fragment of "dry" hardwood forest within a radius of twenty or thirty miles. What we did know was that this was a special place. Even in winter, with most of the trees leafless, it had the stately if somewhat derelict air of an abandoned park on some once very grand estate. Later on, when spring was well under way, stepping into its cool shadow from the glare of the open ridges would be like entering into Hudson's *Green Mansions* for the first time.

Well, at least that's the way it would seem to us.

As I say, we were lucky. We couldn't know it at the time, but those first eighty acres contained a microcosm of virtually all the ecosystems that the Mississippi sandhills had to offer — live oak stands, longleaf and slash pine barrens, mixed pine and oak woods, upland hardwoods, bogs, bottomland swamp. To be sure, it was all battered, chewed up, scorched, and generally much put upon; but nearly everything was still at least embryonically in place. Given half a chance, it would show a Southern Baptist a thing or two about being born again.

One of the greatest joys of reclaiming a piece of the natural world is that the process of taking an ecological inventory never ends. Like that storybook king in his countinghouse counting all his money, Willie and I just kept tallying up new treasures to add to our trove. There were, for example, the young magnolias hiding in a damp corner of the Hollow that we didn't discover until we had owned the Place for more than a year. And the locally rare fringetrees that bloomed for three springs in the Oak Grove before we realized what they were. Unbelievably, it took us almost as long to notice that a stand of pines on the third ridge, which we had walked in and around a hundred times, wasn't run-of-the-mill slash pine as we had assumed but an altogether different species, shortleaf pine, here unexpectedly growing at the southernmost edge of its range! And fifteen years would pass before we found a single rare grass-pink orchid blooming delicately at the edge of the bog.

But when it came to new discoveries, it was the wildlife that delighted us most of all. We never grew tired of seeing the regulars — the familiar songbirds, the fox squirrels, the quail, the raccoons — and it was always a red-letter day when we caught a glimpse of some more elusive creature: a Cooper's hawk or a deer or a wild turkey. But best of all were those sightings that were firsts, as when I glanced up into a red oak just as a peregrine falcon alighted there; or when Willie noticed an unusual flash of color at the feeder that turned out to be the first painted bunting sighted at the Place; or when, moving aside a heavy beam, as I did a couple of summers ago, I uncovered a shiny little three-lined salamander — a species that had kept itself a secret from us for twenty-five years while living almost underfoot. Hardly a month goes by without some such revelation. It is like receiving lovely, gratuitous gifts that you didn't even know you wanted.

It's not just the Place, of course. All across the nation there are countless other places, each with its potential treasure of wonderful surprises, waiting to be claimed by people who genuinely care about the natural world.

3
Neighbors

Before getting too excited about some promising-looking tract of land you've discovered in the rural hinterlands, you would do well to size up your prospective neighbors. Don't be shy. Pay them a visit. And while you're making small talk, discreetly check out their attitudes and lifestyle.

Needless to say, Willie and I didn't do that. True, after having covered just about every back road in the area, we did have a general notion that we were not moving into an upscale rural neighborhood; but when we told Mr. Stanton we would take the Place, we had no idea who our nearest neighbors were.

We found out pretty quickly. The first time we explored our half mile of brainch completely, we were thrilled by its swampy otherness. Our very own Okefenokee, even if it was only thirty yards wide. There were a few fairly tall cypress and lots of black gum, tupelo, and sweet bay. Some picturesque little dark pools clogged with tree roots. A barely glimpsed gray squirrel. A pileated woodpecker.

And, in three or four secluded spots, rusty metal drums.

Somebody had really had it in for those drums. Some had been slashed, apparently with an axe. Others, I surmised, had been dynamited.

It took a little while for the significance of these artifacts to sink in. When it did, I was pleased to see in them the reminders of a colorful bit of local history. "Well, well," I said to Willie, "it looks like our brainch was once a hideout for moonshiners."

The only thing wrong with this observation was the tense. When we came to the next little pool, the two drums we found there were very much intact. Beside them, a crudely welded metal container sat on cinder blocks, with a butane tank and burner underneath. The whole scene exhaled an air of expectant waiting. Soon enough this little distillery would be back in business.

On the other side of the brainch, rows of dead corn stalks climbed an eroded hill. At its crest, wood smoke drifted up from the chimney of an invisible house. Willie and I exchanged a long look. Without a word we moved on, not exactly hurrying, but not dawdling much either.

We were in something of a fix. The surveyor would be coming the next day to drive stakes along our property lines. I had visions of him discovering that active still and dutifully tipping off the revenuers, who would dutifully blow it to smithereens. Even if our unknown neighbor were not caught at the scene, he was bound to be seriously ticked off at the loss of his capital investment. And he would understandably assume that the new people next door had ratted on him.

There was nothing for it but to warn him. That same afternoon I drove round to his place, which turned out to be a pretty respectable-looking establishment: A square cinder block house in a yard ornamented with azaleas instead of the customary fragments of dismembered old cars. A pickup was parked out in front, but when I knocked on the door there was no response. Another knock. Still only silence. But as I was about to turn away, the lady of the house came from around the back. She was short and stocky and wore a flowery print dress, a tight speculative smile, and a floppy, face-shielding bonnet of a kind that I had previously seen only in Western movies.

As I was introducing myself to her, the front door opened. The man who emerged was the same height she was, but as thin as she was stout. When he moved, his wiry little frame stirred inside his coveralls like a cat in a burlap sack. His face was pure Southern Gothic. The skull beneath the crinkled, papery skin was as fragile looking as an eggshell. One good eye stared hard at me from its deep socket; the other, made of glass, looked over my shoulder. A hand-rolled cigarette hung from rather pendulous lips.

This was Hovit Bodner, who would later show me the site of the lumber camp and fill me in on local history. The woman was his wife, Lurlee. When I explained that I had just bought the adjoining property, Lurlee allowed as how she'd already heard about me and a colored feller looking the place over. Then she added, with a twanging stress that suggested real conviction, "Lots of times, strangers makes better neighbors than kinfolks do, an' that's the truth!"

Although her remark seemed to be motivated more by a low opinion of some of her kinfolks than an openmindedness toward strangers, I took it as an encouraging opener, and for a few minutes she and I made small talk while Hovit, puffing his cigarette, weaved silently back and forth inside his coveralls, his good eye becoming, at times, as glassy as the glass one. When I complimented Lurlee on her azaleas, she asked with furious interest, "You like flowers? Now Hovit, he'd mow 'em all down if I didn't watch him every minute." At this, Hovit made his only contribution to the conversation. "Damn right," he muttered. "Can't mow worth a damn with all them damn flowers in the way."

After a little more chitchat about flowers, I judged the time was right to broach the reason for my visit. "Ah," I began, "this morning I, er, took a walk in the brainch down there." I nodded toward the distant wall of trees at the bottom of the hill. Three eyes looked in the indicated direction, then back at me.

I plunged on: "I just happened to come upon a still down there. You know, a moonshine still?"

The eyes narrowed, the faces became grim masks.

"Well," I blurted, "I just thought you might have heard whose it was. You see, I've got this surveyor —"

Suddenly, they were backing away from me as though I had spectacularly broken wind.

"What I mean to say is —"

Hovit was in full retreat, coveralls flapping like sails. Lurlee covered his rear. "Jus' tell 'em you don't know a thing in the world about it!" she snapped. "Can't do a thing in the world if they don't catch you on it."

"I just wanted to let you know," I pleaded. "In case you wanted to move it."

"Us! We don't know nothin' about it. Not a damn thing."

Hovit was inside the house. Lurlee had backed her way up the concrete steps. I was backing mine down toward the gate.

"Nice talking to you," I called miserably to the slamming door.

By the time I got back to the Place I was in black despair, convinced that if Willie and I stayed the night as we had planned, we would be murdered in the cots we had set up inside the van. But when I suggested that we move out before it got dark, Willie demurred. He had a boeuf provençal started on the Coleman stove he'd just bought. "Ain't nobody gonna run us off just when I'm learning how this thing works," he said.

So we stayed; and we weren't murdered after all. Schaeffer and Sammie, our fearless guardians, slept as soundly through the night as the disciples at Gethsemane. Come morning, we walked down to the brainch. Except for the cinder blocks, all traces of the still had vanished.

Later on, when we got to know Hovit and Lurlee better, we would all have a good laugh about that first meeting. But what none of us ever ventured to say out loud was that it was just as well that the encounter had taken place, even if it did end in the conversational equivalent of a train wreck. If that surveyor had found the still, if he had tipped off the revenuers about it, and if

Hovit had decided to blame us for its loss, then things could have become pretty unpleasant. Over the years, I would become cautiously fond of Hovit; he was a great character, and he generally meant well by Willie and me. We were often invited to drink coffee with him and Lurlee, and on several occasions he allowed us to borrow or rent his tractor, even though, as he more than once remarked, he was so attached to it that if it came to a choice between the tractor and Lurlee, the tractor would win hands down. But he had a dark side. He was quick to take offense; and he was a serious alcoholic, given to turbulent, weeks-long drunks that would end with Lurlee carting him off to the VA hospital to be dried out and sometimes to have a broken bone repaired. Hovit's bones were exceedingly brittle, and he was forever shattering one or another of them during his bouts with booze, including a kneecap that had not properly mended and caused him endless pain. Also, he was worried that his one good eye was going bad on him. And as though that weren't enough, he confided to us that he often had terrible dreams. No wonder, then, that even when he was sober his moods could swing from amiable to dark in no time at all.

Lurlee would later tell me that the bad dreams came of his having wielded a flamethrower as a weapon during the Second World War. "I reckon that's one reason he drinks like he do," she said. "He claims he still hears them hollerin', all them people he burned up, womens, children, soldiers, all kinds . . ."

Hovit's army career had begun a few months before Pearl Harbor, when he'd been arrested for bootlegging and an unusually strict judge had given him the choice of enlisting or going to jail; it had ended at the Battle of the Bulge when he lost his eye to a piece of shrapnel. Since then, between his veteran's disability pension and his bootlegging, he and Lurlee had managed very well by local standards; but what with his fractured bones, his fear of blindness, his stupendous hangovers, and his nightmares, poor Hovit was often in a pretty bad way.

When he was sober, however, he could still get around well enough; and one day he decided to come along with Willie and me on one of our explorations of the brainch (now christened, of course, the Brainch). We were glad he did. Although he hadn't boasted much about it, we knew by then that Hovit was the scion of one of the area's oldest and most distinguished bootlegging families, so being accompanied by him was like being guided on a private tour. At the site of each dynamited or hatcheted still we paused respectfully while he, in his somewhat meandering commentary, resurrected the functioning "outfit" from the ruin of its broken parts, dating it, explaining how it had worked, and recollecting the number of gallons of whiskey it had successfully produced before the spoilsport revenuers demolished it.

From what Hovit told us, there must have been something of the atmosphere of a mad scientist's laboratory about a still in operation, what with fires hissing, the liquid burbling and thumping through the curling pipes, and the "worm" of tubing drip-dripping the condensed booze at its nether end. In the old days before Hovit went off to war, the "fire boxes" were built of clay and the stills themselves, in which the fermented corn mash was boiled, were smallish and made of copper. The whiskey was run through the distilling process twice to double its strength and improve its taste. Then it was carefully cut with the none-too-crystalline waters of the Brainch, for it could blind or kill you if you drank it straight.

Since the war, Hovit admitted, the craftsmanship involved in moonshine making, as in everything else, had declined. Metal drums instead of open troughs were used to ferment the mash, as well as to boil it, and a butane burner pumped flames into a pipe that ran right through the bubbling brew. Sometimes, instead of tubing, car radiators were used as condensers, although Hovit insisted he never stooped to that.

In the course of our tour, Hovit also cleared up another mystery. I had wondered about the purpose of two or three small enclosures I had found in the Brainch — crude pens made by pulling a few strands of barbed wire around a closely grouped clump of trees. They were used to protect the drums of fermenting corn mash, Hovit now told us, as though nothing could be more obvious. But from what? I asked. "Hawgs," he said. "Woods hawgs." He chuckled. "Now if you ever want to see a sight, there ain't nothin' to match a bunch of hawgs after they've got into some mash. Fallin' on their noses an' runnin' into trees an' such. A while back a couple dozen of 'em flopped out on the county road an' couldn't nothin' get past 'em for half an hour. I'm tellin' you, ain't nobody can get as drunk as a hawg, not even me!"

One afternoon not long after Hovit's tour, I put together my own make-believe still beside the spring, just for the fun of it, using some of the shattered leftovers of his real ones. It was a jerrybuilt affair: a couple of hatcheted drums, a badly dented "thumper," some disconnected coils of tubing piled together in an arrangement that no one could have mistaken for the real thing. No one, that is, except a revenuer. I had made no effort to conceal my handiwork, so I suppose the feds must have spotted it on one of their frequent helicopter patrols along the Brainch. At any rate, two agents showed up one day in a car with a bumper sticker that proclaimed, MOONSHINE KILLS. When I blithely explained that I had set up the still as a lark, you would have thought from their cold-eyed looks that they were listening to the confessions of a serial killer. For several minutes, while Willie and I waited apprehensively, they debated whether or not we were worth arresting. Finally, with a great show of regret, they decided not, and settled instead for a grim lecture on the illegality of setting up *any* kind of still, no matter how dysfunctional. After which they rudely kicked ours over and carried the thumper and tubing away with them, giving us a last suspicious look by way of farewell.

When I told Hovit of their visit, he allowed that "Feds ain't exactly known for their sense of humor," and consoled us by promising that one of these days he would set up a real outfit for us, "jus' for show, y'know," so we could see how it worked. But he never did. Not for us, anyway, and certainly not for show.

The Janier family lived half a mile closer to the Place than Hovit and Lurlee. From the first, Roddy Ray Janier, his wife, Eloise, and his easygoing mother, Cora, went out of their way to make us welcome. Possibly they felt the need of friendly neighbors as much as we did, since Roddy Ray and Hovit did not get along too well. It seems that Roddy Ray, while still in his teens, had made a stab at getting into the moonshining business himself, but Hovit, who felt the local brainch could support only one operator, had persuaded him to give up on the idea by promising to kill him if he didn't. Roddy Ray had switched his career choice to welding and was doing very well for himself, but neither he nor Hovit had forgotten their territorial dispute.

I remember our first meeting: Willie and I were sitting on the slope of the most easterly of our five ridges, the thumb, which we had named the Pasture because Hovit, to provide grazing for his woods cows, had burned it so often that it was virtually treeless.

After a brilliant beginning, the Saturday morning had become morose and gray; but we had not. Our land was still new to us, and we were happily taking it in, piece by piece — which on this occasion meant gazing out over the open slope, watching the tall bluestem grass bend and blow in a stiff February wind. We were deeply immersed in this contemplative exercise when, above the whispery singing of the grass, we suddenly heard the thumpety-thump of galloping hooves. We looked behind us, and there was Roddy Ray charging down on us astride a plug-headed palomino (rightly named Joker, as I would later discover), which he reined in with a dashing flourish when it was almost in our laps.

"Mother seen you comin' in yesterday," he said. "She heard

you bought this place, so I figured I better come say hello." This
he did, when he had flung himself off his horse, with a wide,
boyish grin and handshakes all around. He was in his mid-twen-
ties, dark haired, thickset, and, like most people hereabouts, of
French extraction. At the time I supposed that Janier was a Cajun
name, and that Roddy Ray and his neighbors must be an offshoot
group of the French Acadians who settled in southwestern Louisiana after the English drove them from Nova Scotia. Later, however, I would learn that the name derived from one of the crew
members who accompanied Bienville when he explored the Mississippi coast. The descendants of that early Janier must have
flourished procreatively, if not otherwise, for now the name belonged to half the families in the sandhills.

From the first, Roddy Ray came across as a good-natured,
outgoing sort of person. We talked about our plans for the Place,
even though we didn't exactly know what they were yet. Roddy
Ray was all for cattle raising and he spoke, ironically as it would
turn out, of what a fine pasture this big wild meadow would
make. Though he owned only an acre of land, he had several head
of cattle out roaming the woods, as well as a herd of goats that we
had already ruefully noticed devouring every leaf and blade of
grass in sight. *Our* leaves, *our* blades of grass. In fairness, they had
every right to do so; for in those days, our adopted county had a
no-fence law. If a landowner didn't want other people's livestock
on his property, it was up to him to fence it out. Not that it would
have made any difference, but this was just one of those little
details we hadn't checked out before we fell in love with the Place.

Roddy Ray was much more in sympathy with Willie's floor-
sanding profession than my academic one. "English!" he hooted.
"Hodamighty damn how I hated English!" Nor did his opinion of
me as a good ol' boy improve when he asked me if I hunted and I
told him no. He let out a disbelieving grunt and said, "Well, I'll
teach you! Willie too, if y'all want."

Yet, notwithstanding the shortage of shared interests, it seemed to me that, compared to my first disastrous session with Hovit and Lurlee, Willie and I were doing just fine conversing with Roddy Ray. If our answers to his questions — Were we going to build a house? Were we going to have a pond? Did we have wives or girlfriends? Were we going to move up here full-time eventually? — sounded equivocal, he didn't seem to mind.

Finally, there was a pause during which the three of us just sat there side by side, staring at the waves of bending grass while Joker banged his thuggish head against Roddy Ray's shoulder. I guess we were all trying to think of something else to talk about.

Then Roddy Ray did indeed think of something else: "You see on TV where George Wallace is running for president? Whatta you think of that?" It wasn't clear whether the question was directed at Willie or me.

I held my breath while Willie answered in a quiet voice, "He don't like black people like me, so I don't see why I should like him. I hope he loses."

The wind turned suddenly colder. I know Willie felt it too. In the silence following his reply, I was thinking: *Now the shit hits the fan. Just when everything was going so well!*

But I had not given Roddy Ray enough credit for fair-mindedness. After mulling over Willie's response, he admitted, "I reckon I wouldn't neither if I was a — if I was colored."

Inwardly I gave a sigh of relief. But then, not content to leave well enough alone, Roddy Ray asked, apparently of Willie, "Well, what you think of this Martin Luther King fella?"

Willie gave me a sideways It's-your-turn look. I took a deep breath and said, "Well, I think he's a pretty brave man."

It was obvious that Roddy Ray wasn't used to the sort of responses he was getting from us. For quite a while he scuffed dirt with the pointy toes of his cowboy boots. Finally, however, he leaned forward, flashing a grin from under his slightly drooping cowboy mustache. "Y'know, you're right about that," he declared. "Just between us, he's got some guts. I will say that for him.

Course, so does Wallace. They got that in common anyways; they both got guts!"

He laughed delightedly at this reconciliation of opposing views. "Now me," he went on, "I like Wallace, but he ain't gonna win; what I'm hopin' is that Kennedy's brother, that Bobby fella, runs for president. He's who I'd vote for. He's for the little man."

"Yeh," Willie ventured, "and *he's* got guts too!"

At that, all three of us began laughing our heads off. As though the idea of three such very different men all having guts were a colossally funny joke.

Now, thinking back on it, that day seems even longer ago than it actually was.

Anyway, it marked the beginning of a friendship between us and Roddy Ray. That same evening, at his invitation, we went over to his trailer to meet his wife, Eloise, their year-old daughter, Baby Gladys, and his mother, Cora. Eloise was a frail-looking woman, thin as Popeye's Olive Oyl, with wire-rimmed glasses, a reedy voice, and mousy brown hair. In her dealings with other adults, she came across as a rather unassertive, even timid young person who had never outgrown the shy, homely little girl she must have been not all that long ago. Whereas her mother-in-law — "that widow woman," as Hovit's wife, Lurlee, always referred to her — was the exact opposite: raven haired, Rubenesque in her proportions, as outgoing as her son, with a taste for racy jokes and a husky, easy laugh that put men, especially, at their ease. Yet, different as the two women otherwise were, they had in common a warm-heartedness and generosity of spirit that Willie and I found very welcoming, especially at that early date when we still knew so little about our country neighbors.

They insisted that we share their supper of pork chops, black-eyed peas, and cornbread, and so we did. We were a little nervous at first. After all, we were not what the Janiers were used to in the way of dinner guests; but if there was any sense of social unease concerning the color of Willie's skin, or mine in combination with his, while we were crowded elbow to elbow around the tiny kitchen table, it was never allowed to surface.

It helped, of course, that Willie just happened to be the most likable human being God ever made. He had no illusions about the white world, having been made to sit at the back of buses and drink from segregated water fountains when he was a little boy, but he carried no chip on his shoulder. And he had a smile that reflected his soul, so radiantly beautiful it could make a granite rock smile back. Eloise in particular was much taken with him, and was determined to see that he got his fair share of attention — which meant his fair share of food. Every time his plate reached half-empty, she shoveled another helping of pork chops and cornbread onto it. When Willie protested that he was stuffed, she scolded him: "If you don't eat, Cora and me'll think you don't like country cookin'." Cora chimed in by swearing that we were both so skinny she could see light through us; and Roddy Ray, patting his stomach, declared, "Ain't neither one of you gonna be able to do any country kind of work unless you put more meat on your bones."

By the time Willie and I got back to the Place, we were so bloated and drowsy we could hardly get out of the Volksbus; but we were vastly pleased with how well the evening with the Janiers had turned out. We agreed that, without doubt, Roddy Ray and his family were the very flower of sandhills society, and that we could count ourselves fortunate to have them as our neighbors.

In all honesty, I couldn't say the same for Vera Combe and her common-law husband, Wilbur, the only other people living within a mile of us. It wasn't that they were unfriendly — at least not toward us — well, not Vera at any rate — but they were a little unsettling to have around. They looked to be in their sixties when we came to the Place but they must have been much younger than that, considering how long they've lasted since. Wilbur had large, bulging blue eyes, a nose the color of bruised plums, and a serious speech impediment which made it difficult to carry on a conversation with him. His problem was not so much that he stuttered but that he stuttered so wetly, spraying out a veritable cascade of slobber that was tinged an unattractive shade of brown by the chaw of tobacco he always kept wadded in his cheek. Even with the best intentions in the world, it was difficult to ignore his affliction since one couldn't help flinching whenever he tried to say something, which fortunately was not too often. Vera, who didn't always have the best intentions in the world, would sometimes tell him to "jus' stop that spittin' and shut up."

Vera herself had the trembles, a palsy that was more pronounced when she was sober than when she was drunk, which perhaps explains why she was so often in the latter state. She was no beauty, with her crinkled skin and toothless smile, but she was an outrageous flirt, deliberately inciting Wilbur to fits of flaming jealousy. According to Roddy Ray's mother, Cora, this was the reason for their frequent late-night lovers' spats, during which they traded pistol shots while chasing each other in and out of their little shack and from tree to tree outside.

In a way we were relieved to learn this. More than once during our first months at the Place, Willie and I had been disconcerted and mystified by this exchange of gunfire in the not-so-distant distance — punctuated by dreadful shrieks that were actually curses heaped by Vera upon her too-possessive swain. At least now we knew we were listening in on a more-or-less ritualized domestic duel rather than an ongoing guerrilla war between feuding local families.

On the negative side, however, I couldn't help noticing that Vera behaved in an aggressively coquettish way whenever she came by to hit me up for a small loan or pay back a previous one, which she always did as soon as her welfare check arrived. Whenever she stroked my cheek or called me "honey" or told me what a "cute, kind thang" I was, Wilbur's eyes tended to protrude even more than they normally did. Since the last thing I wanted was to arouse his jealous ire, there was nothing for it but to discourage their country habit of just dropping in on us. I began not to have any cash on hand when they showed up, and always something urgent to do at some far corner of the Place. In time, the visits became less frequent and eventually ceased altogether.

I'm sure that Wilbur, at least, was pleased by this distancing, and apparently Vera took no offense either. According to Cora she still referred to me as that "cute, kind thang" even when the only communication between us from one end of the year to the other was the bottle of vodka we left on their doorstep at Christmastime.

Wilbur and Vera were the most colorful social liabilities that Willie and I incurred during our first year or two at the Place, but not the only ones. We made the mistake of trying too hard to develop good public relations with the local folks we met through Roddy Ray and Hovit. I can see how others in our situation might welcome the chance to get to know the sort of "good country people" that Flannery O'Connor wrote about, but for us it became a pretty wearing business after a while, attempting to build relationships with people, even nice people, with whom we didn't have much in common. We hadn't come to the country to extend our social horizons, and we weren't cut out to be social anthropologists; so it was a relief, really, when we finally acknowledged that no matter how at home we were at the Place, we would always be outsiders in the sandhills of Mississippi; and that suited us just fine as long as we were left in peace. We decided that except when dealing with trespassers and poachers — about which, more later — the best policy was to keep a low profile with most of our neighbors. Roddy Ray and his family, Hovit and Lurlee, and our old friends from the city were company enough when we were in a gregarious mood. For the most part, though, Willie and I were content just sharing the Place with each other, the dogs, the livestock menagerie that we gradually acquired, and the wild creatures that had lived there all along.

4

Starting out

At the beginning of our first April at the Place, without giving the matter as much thought as perhaps we should have, we set out to build a small self-contained wing of what was to be a much larger house. We chose the middle ridge on which to build it for the aesthetically perverse reason that the site, wide open except for clusters of stripling slash pines, had little to recommend it in the way of scenic charm. The way I figured it, the more obvious settings for a dwelling, such as the Oak Grove and the Hollow, were better off being left in their natural state, innocent of our meddling, whereas the middle ridge, which could use all the landscaping it could get, offered us the challenge of creating a beautiful setting more or less from scratch.

At first Willie was a bit skeptical of this not very practical line of reasoning — "Why can't we pick someplace that at least has a little shade?" he wanted to know — but I won him over with visions of a fast-growing orchard and a garden crowded with vegetables and flowers, as well as a pen full of industrious, cheerful chickens (Willie wanted some chickens badly) laying eggs like mad. Even before we began work on the house, we planted the orchard, a very small orchard to be sure, composed of four each of the varieties of peaches, pears, and plums that were supposed to do best in the sandhills. We also made a start at landscaping the site. On one side of the driveway-to-be we set out a row of azaleas, and on the other some crape myrtles we had discovered being overwhelmed by underbrush in what had once been the yard of the moonshining widow's homeplace.

The house itself would be positioned so that it overlooked the gully that lay between the middle and the fourth ridge. With the help of Roddy Ray and the county supervisor, we planned to span this wide, almost treeless swale with an earthen dam, impounding behind it a small lake filled with rainwater runoff.

Innocence is the better part of arrogance. In designing the house, I was as naively cavalier about practical considerations as I had been in choosing the site. I was teaching Malory's *Le Morte D'Arthur* that semester, a work I dearly loved, so it seemed perfectly logical that I should be inspired to build the first installment of what would eventually be an unpretentious little castle made of wood. This initial unit, though small, would be towerlike, with a steep peaked roof, twelve-foot-high walls — the height enhanced by vertical siding — and French doors on all four sides. These would enclose a single room large enough to contain our cots, the Coleman stove, a folding table, and two chairs, with enough spare floor space left over for the dogs to stretch out comfortably. Later on, this first wing would be linked by roofed decks to two others we planned to build, one of them a two-storied structure that could qualify as a real tower and provide us with a view of not just the pond-to-be but the land beyond. When the whole thing was assembled, it could be categorized architecturally as a cluster house; but what I was really aiming for was a rather airy modern version of Sir Lancelot's Joyous Garde — with lots of French doors. Anyway, something like that.

This was the first time in our lives that either Willie or I had ever attempted to put together anything more ambitious than a bookcase, so it was very much a matter of learn-as-you-go. Just buying the lumber and nails and shingles and tools and getting them to the Place was an endless hassle, and when we did, we invariably discovered we had forgotten something else we needed. During the actual construction we made any number of mistakes figuring out measurements and angles. Getting the beveled beams to fit together at the roof's peak was a day-long struggle, and it took hours and hours of planing and realigning to fit the old French doors we had bought at a demolition site, each with its slightly different measurements, to the frames we had built for them. Muscles ached and fingers cramped from sawing all the lumber by hand (there being no electricity yet). And there were accidents. On one day, Willie was literally knocked off his feet when he was stung by an aptly named cow-killer wasp. On another, a hammer I had carelessly left atop a ladder landed on the bridge of my nose, producing two full-blown shiners that kept my students spellbound and speculative for the whole of the following week. And for good measure, we and the dogs were regularly persecuted by Hovit's mean red bull.

What can I say about all this? Only that it added up to a wonderful and productive spring; and that Willie and I were as happy as any two humans have a right to be.

While we were cementing and hammering and sawing away, there were a lot of small creatures on that middle ridge whom we had not yet had time to notice, but who were already noticing us. It came as something of a revelation to find that at every stage in the construction of the little house we had would-be tenants ready and eager to move in. We had hardly begun laying the foundation when the first boarders turned up. The house was to rest on twelve piers, each containing three tiers of cinder blocks, which meant that we had to bring some seventy blocks and half blocks to the Place in our brutally overloaded van. By the time we had figured out how to get the corner angles of the house aligned and stretched strings on which to suspend bubble-levels so we could line up the piers evenly, and then practiced the by no means easy trick of troweling a layer of cement — just the right consistency, not too wet, not too dry — onto the edges of one block long enough to press another one against it, the weekend was used up and we had to head back to New Orleans, leaving most of those seventy blocks still lying in the grass where we had dumped them.

The following weekend we started in earnest to cement them into place, picking them up, naturally enough, by the cross section that divides the interior of each block into two separate compartments. We first discovered that some of these chambers were inhabited when an exquisite little green treefrog, alarmed at being so unceremoniously relocated, hopped out onto the back of Willie's hand. After that we checked the blocks before grabbing hold of them and found two or three more openings that were occupied by the little frogs, which we gently evicted before their nice new apartments could become their cement-sealed tombs.

In the course of this examination, we noticed that the interiors of most of our brand-new cinder blocks were already heavily laced with spider webs. Spiders, however, did not stir our protective instincts the way small emerald green frogs did, and so we rather heedlessly thrust our fingers into their webs whenever we picked up another block. Several times I felt the feathery movement of delicate legs traipsing across my gripping thumb or index finger — not exactly a pleasant sensation, but, since I knew it was just a harmless little spider scurrying about, I paid it no mind. Until, that is, one such harmless little spider, more adventurous than its sisters, crawled up my thumb and out onto the broad daylight of my knuckles where I could see it clearly.

It was a black widow. I knew the creature only from pictures in books, and I couldn't see the bright red hourglass on its abdomen; but its plump shiny black shape left me in no doubt about its identity. With more consideration for its feelings than I had thus far shown, I set the cinder block ever so carefully on the ground and slowly spread my hand out beside it. The spider, after a second's hesitation, abandoned my knuckle for a blade of grass, and I began to breathe again.

I got the flashlight from the van and started peering into the shadowy interiors of the dozen or so blocks we hadn't yet cemented into place. Almost every one of them had at least one, and sometimes two, black widows in residence. As casually as I could, I remarked to Willie, who was about to pick one of the blocks up, that from now on we had better use both hands to carry them, making sure our fingers didn't probe inside. When I told him why, his eyes widened a bit, but he took the news pretty calmly, observing that if they hadn't bitten us by this time, they probably never would.

They never have. I've had many run-ins with black widows since: moving a portable toilet box from one spot to another, filling and refilling a big watering can while the poor spider that lived inside kept running up the handle each time she was flooded out, and then back down again as soon as the can was emptied; and, yes, toting cinder blocks on later occasions when I simply forgot the advice I had given Willie; all this without mishap. The bite of a female black widow is said to cause agonizing pain, very like that of an appendicitis attack, which lasts for several days. So it is fortunate that, except when dealing with its natural prey, including would-be suitors of its own species, it seems to be a remarkably easygoing creature, willing to live and let live. Neither Roddy Ray nor Hovit nor anyone else I asked had ever known anyone who had been bitten — even though black widows were common enough in these parts to colonize a pile of cinder blocks in a matter of days. *That* — the wonderfully opportunistic way they moved in on the bonanza of man-made housing we had inadvertently provided — was the most remarkable thing they had to teach me.

The lizards, in three varieties, were attracted by the lumber we brought in and the things we did with it. Fence swifts were the first to show up, using the stacked two-by-fours (as they also use wooden fences and rotting logs) as vantage points from which to survey the ground roundabout. They are primitive-looking little things, with blunt noses and downturned mouths that give their faces a discontented cast; and their skin is very noticeably scaly, resembling rusty chain mail. Not only are they swift, but their eyesight is very keen; one minute they would be basking on the sun deck provided by our lumber pile, and the next, dashing madly through thick grass to snap up some unlucky grasshopper or beetle twenty feet away — the equivalent, for you or me, of spotting something at a distance of a quarter of a mile and catching it within a matter of seconds.

Once we had the floor joists in place, and covered by a platform of plywood flooring, the anoles moved in. These slender, beautiful lizards, which look like elfin dragons, are often called chameleons, although the only thing they have in common with the Old World lizards that rightfully claim that name is that they can change color — from dull brown to bright green to brown again. These are natural hues, of course, yet as far as I can tell, anoles seem indifferent to the idea of camouflage. Regardless of what the background color may be, they usually turn brown when they are basking in the sun and always turn green when they are having a territorial dispute with another anole. The rest of the time, they switch back and forth for reasons that only anoles understand.

I spent a lot of time watching anoles when I should have been working; and one day I discovered that their epidermis, besides being changeful, is also nutritious. I noticed an anole with what appeared to be a terrible case of sunburn, which signified that he was shedding an old, outgrown skin. But instead of just wriggling out of it like a snake, he was neatly peeling it off and eating it with apparent relish. It was a salutary demonstration of Nature's waste not, want not principle, but in practice it was a little weird to watch.

In common with the fence swifts, male anoles do pushups to advertise their sexual availability and assert their territorial rights. It is a marvelously comic exercise to watch, but unlike the swifts, which are fairly sociable creatures and don't mind sharing a two-by-four with others of their kind, anoles are deadly serious about these athletic exhibitions, which they reinforce by incessantly extending their pink throat wattles even when there is no potential mate or rival in sight. If a rival does show up and fails to be impressed by these displays, a no-holds-barred fight ensues. It can be a surprisingly serious, even awesome experience to watch, close-up, while a couple of anoles trade jaw holds for a half hour or more. In their miniature but furious combat I had no difficulty discerning the sort of titantic struggles their huge Jurassic ancestors must have once engaged in.

The five-lined skinks were the most salamandrine of the lizards that moved in on us, their glistening, streamlined bodies held close to the ground, their movements sinuous and rather snakelike. So various was their coloring that when I first began seeing them wriggling across the floor platform, I supposed that we were playing host to three or four different subspecies; but my reptile book soon set me straight: the ones with cobalt blue tails were juveniles, those that looked to be a uniform shade of dusky bronze were old gaffers whose stripes had faded, and the fellows with bright orange heads were breeding males. Evidently, these variations were a skink's way of compensating for not having a throat fan with which to semaphore its intentions, or front legs strong enough for pushups.

Although the skinks tended to be more secretive than the anoles and fence swifts, none of these species was particularly shy. Until we browbeat him into not pestering them, Sammie sometimes ran them off, but they accepted our construction activities with equanimity, going about their business while we used the floor platform to saw two-by-fours and hammer together the frames of the walls. No doubt they were curious to see just how far we would go in providing them with a habitat diverse enough to suit them all. And indeed, by the time the walls were up, the joists laid across their top plates, and the converging rafters of that infernally difficult-to-build roof painstakingly beveled and braced and joined at the peak, our lizard families had pretty well sorted themselves out. Representatives of each were often in view at the same time, but the skinks were partial to the dark undersides of joists and flooring; the sun-loving fence swifts stayed topside, using the edges of the platform floor as lookout posts; and the anoles, as at home on vertical surfaces as on horizontal ones, spent most of their time running up and down the studs in pursuit of flies. There was nothing about all this lizardly niche-finding that would surprise anyone who possessed even a casual acquaintance with ecological concepts, yet until then it was the sort of thing I had only read about in books or seen in nature films. I had never before had the chance to observe, on a day-to-day basis, wild things adapting to an alien habitat in much the same way that human pioneers might colonize a new world. I was enthralled by their enterprise; and when I found that our tree frogs, undeterred by their earlier expulsion, were lurking behind folded camp chairs or anything else we left leaning overnight against a wall, I laughed aloud in wonder and delight. It was so nice to know that creatures other than roaches and Norway rats could take such cheerful advantage of the human presence!

The lizards and frogs and spiders were at least willing to let us share the house we were so considerately building for them. Not so the pair of Carolina wrens that claimed it as their own when the exterior work was almost completed. The outside paneling was all in place, and the steeple roof finally covered with felt and shingles. All that remained was to fit the French doors to their frames, a task which, as noted earlier, proved more arduous and time consuming than we had anticipated. It was while all four of those door frames were still gapingly wide open that the wrens decided to move in.

Other birds are more renowned for daring: kingbirds dive-bomb hawks ten times their size; mockingbirds send cats and mailmen running for cover; but for sheer cheeky chutzpah on an everyday basis, nothing beats a Carolina wren. Humans don't faze them at all. While reading in a hammock, I've had them inspect my bare feet on the off chance that a tick or two might be hiding between my toes. And they are just as brazen in their dealings with larger birds; they will even peck holes in the eggs of species foolish enough to choose nest sites too close to their own. Given that sort of temperament, it seems only natural that when they sing their pretty tweedling song — and they sing in all seasons — the loudness of their voices should be out of all proportion to their small size.

When this pair started zipping in and out of the doorless doorways, arranging twigs and leafy odds and ends in one of the shelflike spaces where the roof rafters lay athwart the supporting wall plates, we were at first amused. We were taking a break at the time and, not knowing anything about wren psychology, we assumed they would desist when we went back to planing French doors right under their noses. Not a bit of it. While we went on with our house building, they went on with theirs, flying under *our* noses as we worked. By the time we were due to leave for the city that Sunday evening, with only one set of doors in place, I was becoming seriously worried that before we could get the rest of them installed and the house secured we might have a wren sitting eggs inside. Not knowing what else to do, I took down the half-finished nest and stuck it in a nearby tree. But the wrens ignored the hint. When we returned to the Place five days later they had a tightly woven nest, all ready for occupancy, in the same spot where they had built the first one. This time I brutally destroyed it even as the little wrens looked on. Though plainly outraged, they seemed to get the message, and we saw no more of them during the next two days.

We had the best intentions of getting all of the three remaining sets of doors in place before we left, but on Saturday Cora and Eloise and Baby Gladys came by, Cora bearing a couple of pounds of freshly fried bream and hushpuppies wrapped in newspaper. What with the picnic that ensued, which lasted half the drowsy afternoon, and then a rainy Sunday morning, and then the walk we could not resist taking through the wet green Hollow once the rain had stopped, one side of the house still remained open when it was time for us to leave. Although the wrens had apparently given up on us, I nailed a couple of pieces of plywood across the doorless doorway just to play it safe.

Not safe enough, however. Wrens are not only small but compactly built; when we returned we found that they had managed to squeeze themselves and the makings of yet another nest through a crack I had carelessly left between the plywood and the top of the door. When I pried the plywood loose, one of them flew in, the other out.

By now, Willie was on the side of the birds. "If they want to live in our house all that bad," he argued, "why don't we just drill a hole through the wall by their nest? That way they'd have their own door and wouldn't need to use ours."

Even though little white droppings were beginning to show on the beam where the nest sat, the birds had so daunted me that I would have gone along with Willie's idea if it had been feasible. But it wasn't. There wasn't enough room in the angled space beneath the eaves to turn the hand-operated drill; and in any case, we lacked a bit large enough to do the job. So, once again, the wrens' nest was dismantled and, without any more delays, we trimmed and fitted the last of the French doors to its frame. Then and only then did the stubborn little birds admit defeat.

Without knowing anything about the saga of the wrens, a visiting friend likened our newly finished dwelling to an oversize birdhouse. But what it really resembled more than anything else, especially when viewed at a distance, was an oversize gazebo. A beautiful, stately, *medieval* gazebo, as I remarked to Willie. Admittedly, it looked somewhat stranded sitting out there on the bare ridge with only our sticklike fruit trees and other plantings to serve as a garden setting; but that didn't bother us. We were already seeing the house and its surroundings as they would look a few years hence.

Only one pair of the French doors was needed as a doorway. In front of one of the three others we put the folding table and on it we set the Coleman lamp. Not counting the moon, the stars, the fireflies, and a flashlight, this was our only source of light once the sun went down. Inevitably, its yellow-white radiance proved an irresistible beacon to every moth and Junebug that happened to be anywhere in the neighborhood. Whenever it was lit, they thumped their heads and wings against the glass panes, apparently wanting more than anything else in the world to immolate themselves in its hot glow. While they heedlessly tried to fulfill this ambition, two or three of our resident treefrogs, noticeably larger and fatter than when we had first encountered them, scrambled across the panes on adhesive toe pads, gobbling some of them up. And when others, exhausted, fluttered toward the ground to rest, they came to an equally dismal end in the gullets of our latest boarders: a burgeoning population of common Southern toads. Here again, I was amazed at how adeptly wild animals learn to take advantage of a good thing. The first night that the lantern's light shone through the French doors, I found a single toad stationed under it. A week later there were two; two weeks later, five. The fact that we were absent much of the time, and the lantern unlit, didn't seem to bother the patient toads a bit. The minute the light went on, they hopped out from under the house, looking plump and self-satisfied, ready for another feast. During daylight hours we almost never saw them.

Early in June, the next link in what was becoming a household food chain introduced itself — much to the dismay of Willie, who almost stepped on it. Willie could take black widow spiders in stride but, like most people, including most country people, he was afraid of snakes, and the demeanor of the one that lay stretched out at our doorstep was in no way calculated to put such a fear to rest. It was an Eastern hognose snake, otherwise known as a puff adder, and its timing in showing up just when it did could hardly have been worse. A week earlier we had taken a short exploratory stroll, as we often did during work breaks; this one through the Hollow and across the index ridge. It had lasted no more than half an hour, but in that little while we were treated to close-ups of six snakes of five different species, all of them intent on making Willie nervous. There was a black racer shedding its skin, a green snake trying to look inconspicuous on a branch a foot from Willie's shuddering shoulder, a long thin coachwhip with black scales lightening to gold-green at its nether end, a gorgeously patterned five-foot-long corn snake sliding into an armadillo burrow, another black racer, and, at the edge of the pitcher plant bog, a small cottonmouth taking the sun. This was a snake-watching record we would never again equal, and at every encounter, it was Willie who first gasped, "Look!"

As far as I was concerned, this evidence that the Place hosted an impressive variety of reptile species was cause for celebration. But by the time we got to the coachwhip, number three in the lineup, poor Willie was already groaning, "Oh Lord, another one!" That afternoon, for the first (and next-to-last) time, he'd had doubts about whether buying the Place had been such a great idea after all.

And now here was this new snake, as fearsome-looking as a pit viper, seemingly so eager to scare Willie that it had sought him out rather than wait, as the others had, to be discovered in the woods.

The reality, of course, was that Willie could hardly have been more frightened of the hognose snake than the hognose snake was of Willie. The problem for both of them was that this quite harmless reptile's way of dealing with a threatening situation was to bluff — to open its mouth, inflate the front part of its naturally thick body into a rather cobralike hood, vibrate its tail, and pretend to strike. In its encounters with man, the hognose's strategy works only too well; most people in the sandhills are convinced that puff adders are poisonous and go out of their way to kill them. This is all the more regrettable since, when pushed a little further, hognose snakes reveal themselves to be touchingly vulnerable creatures; if their fake bellicosity doesn't impress whatever is frightening them, they turn belly up, open their mouths, and play dead. Which is what this one did when I came out of the house and stood over it. Even Willie, his initial alarm subsiding, had to smile when I rolled the snake right-side up and it immediately flipped over on its back again. Only when we moved away did it cautiously right itself and slip under the house, probably congratulating itself on how successfully it had fooled us.

Hognose snakes specialize in hunting toads, and this fellow was on our doorstep because it had somehow gotten wind that we had a supply of them available. For most predators, toads make a risky meal; they have glands on their necks that, when they are attacked, secrete a poison capable of making a cat or a raccoon awfully ill. But hognoses can swallow toads, poison and all, with no ill effects whatsoever.

A week later I checked the side of the house where the light of the Coleman lantern fell. Although I like hognose snakes, I also like toads, so I felt a little sad, though unsurprised, to find not one of them in sight.

The armadillo didn't move in with us until much later. On the evening he introduced himself, he couldn't have done so even if he had wanted to, since we had only just got the piers of the house in place. We were lounging beside the Volksbus — Willie with a beer, me with a martini, admiring a fine sunset while a coq au vin simmered on the Coleman stove, Mozart played on the battery phonograph, and nighthawks bonked overhead — when up from the lower reaches of the ridge came this ridiculous-looking little oddity trotting through the grass, an animated gray football with a long tail attached to one end and a tiny jackass head to the other, heading straight for us, quite as though he had been invited to stop by for a drink.

Their peculiar appearance aside, nine-banded armadillos have many interesting, even extraordinary ways about them. They are, I believe, the only animal besides humans that can have sex face-to-face. Unlike humans or most other animals, however, when they become pregnant they can defer the development of their embryonic young until they are good and ready to bring them into the world. More remarkable still, when they do deliver them, their offspring turn out to be quadruplets of one sex or the other, almost never both. But the peculiarities of armadillos are not limited to their reproductive activities. They can detect a grub deep underground and with their powerful claws dig it up in seconds. They can cross rivers either by swimming or by walking along the bottom, depending on whether they feel like inflating their stomachs with air or not. And they have a remarkable aptitude for contracting leprosy, which makes them useful to scientists studying that disease.

Having lavished so many unusual traits and attributes on armadillos, Mother Nature must have decided it would be *de trop* to give them anything as ordinary as a brain. At any rate, they show little sign of having one. I am continually astounded that they manage to survive as a species at all. If cars pass over them — they are always wandering out onto roads — and the wheels miss them, they jump up in the air so the axle can break their backs. If someone decides to shoot them because they are tilling up his garden in an unauthorized search for grubs and worms, or, more likely, because the someone in question just feels like killing something, it never occurs to them to run away until it's too late. And if dogs grab hold of them, they simply scrunch up, hoping, often mistakenly, that their maillike hide will protect them. They are, in fact, so heartbreakingly dumb, and nearsighted to boot, that they will walk right up to you while you are sitting in plain view on the side of a hill, drinking a martini or a beer.

Yet, despite the seeming odds, these absurd little creatures have managed not only to survive but, in marked contrast to most wildlife species in the Age of Modern Man, to expand their range. Starting out from Mexico they have colonized, first Texas, then all of the Southeastern states in just a few decades. According to Hovit, they turned up at the Place only about a dozen years before Willie and I did.

And now here was one of them, coming to pay us a social call like any nosy neighbor curious to meet the new folks on the block. Although their gory remains were an all-too-familiar sight on Mississippi highways, this was the first live armadillo either of us had ever seen.

Willie was enchanted. "Let's catch him for a pet," he said. "No, no," I exclaimed, "no wild pets!" But Willie was already on his feet, lunging for the little beast as though it were a fumbled football. Luckily for Willie, for those digging claws are sharp, the armadillo popped out from between his extended hands and dashed down the slope. Whooping happily, Willie took off after him while I was still struggling to my feet, ineffectually yelling "Stop!" and sloshing martini all over my shirt and pants.

Enter Schaeffer and Sammie. Sammie hopped out of the Volksbus as soon as the ruckus began and, seeing that the armadillo was small and in full retreat, joined cheerfully in the chase. Schaeffer, however, had been sound asleep in the bus's shadow, and when he was roused by all the hullabaloo, he banged his huge head hard against the tailpipe. Taking in the scene — the armadillo scuttling down the hill, Willie and Sammie in hot pursuit, me yelling — he must surely have thought: "This is what comes of moving to the country!" He was a city dog born and bred, and if he had been consulted about buying the Place, he would have certainly vetoed the whole idea. Unlike Sammie, he was brave and stalwart; but he was also the most fastidious dog I've ever known.

He didn't like getting his feet wet, or sleeping under vehicles instead of in air-conditioned rooms, or doing his business in unmown grass, or having his rear end stung by insolent deer flies. The country, as far as he was concerned, was a cross to bear for Willie's sake and mine.

Now his worst fears were being realized: Wild beasts were on the loose and one of them had struck him on the head while he slept. Willie and Sammie had obviously rushed to his aid, so now he must rush to theirs.

Off he went in great loping bounds, as oblivious as Willie to my protests. I wasn't worried about Willie overtaking the armadillo, but either Schaeffer or Sammie might, and might do it harm. So, cursing, I went running after the three of them.

In a beetling dash the armadillo dove down the steep slope and into its burrow at the bottom. Willie, knees and elbows pumping, paying no attention to where he put his feet, tripped over a root that sent him sprawling. Sammie, right behind him, scrambled along the length of his prostrate body as though it were a log. Schaeffer, unable to brake as Willie started to get up, slammed into his rear, knocking him flat again. And finally, yours truly, galloping headlong to the rescue — of the armadillo, that is — was launched into flight by the same mischievous root that had snagged Willie.

Willie and I lay there in the grass, the wind knocked out of us. Schaeffer circled around, looking worried, while Sammie barked insults into the mouth of the armadillo's burrow. Willie, facing away from me, was lying so still, his sides heaving, that for a scary instant I thought he might be hurt. But then I heard a muffled hoo-hooing sound and relaxed. Willie was laughing into the curve of his arm.

"It's not funny," I growled, already composing the lecture I meant to give him on why we mustn't harass wild animals.

"Oh yes it is," said Willie, turning his dirt-smeared face toward mine. "Can't you see that poor armadillo down there in his hole, trying to tell his folks about who all was chasing him," he exclaimed between hoots. "They ain't ever gonna believe him, least of all about Schaeffer! They're gonna send him to bed without his supper for telling such a lie!"

"Just great," I sighed. "All this time I've been living with Uncle Remus and didn't know it."

I couldn't help smiling, though; for, as clearly as Willie, I could see that unfairly chastised armadillo, stomach empty, glumly marching upstairs to his burrow bedroom.

5

The track

As I say, these were happy days. Busy as we were with building the house, we found time enough to savor our first spring at the Place: maples glowing with scarlet seed; dogwood and wild azalea blooming in the Hollow; quail plaintively calling on the slopes; yellow butterwort, sunbonnets, and exquisite little birdsfoot violets peeking out from under the collapse of dry winter grass; longleafs shedding clouds of green pollen and sprouting candlelike buds. And in the Oak Grove and the Hollow, songbirds undertaking the melodious if also acrimonious business of competing for mates and territories. Willie had set up feeders around the house, and he was having a grand time identifying cardinals, towhees, blue grosbeaks, and the dozen other species that came to them. Even when I knew the birds' names, he wouldn't let me tell him, preferring to match them up with their likenesses in our field guide himself.

However, not everything the spring had to show us was on the order of birdsong and green burgeonings. We never went very far on our walks without finding abundant evidence of the human presence and its impact on our weathered hills and dales. Hundreds of deep holes marked where the taproots of tall pines, cut down decades earlier, had finally rotted out. Beside some of them, buried in the grass, lay rusted fragments of the curved tin basins in which turpentine gatherers had collected resin for turpentine. Along the edge of the pitcher plant bogs were the stumps of young cypress that Hovit and Roddy Ray had cut — cypress being a preferred wood in the construction of corrals and hog pens because it is shunned by termites. And scattered everywhere, but especially in the Hollow and the Brainch, were bottles, beer cans, and a dismaying abundance of spent shotgun shells, some dating from years before, some from as recently as the winter just past. Also everywhere, there were tracks. Clodhopper tracks of cows; round, splayed tracks of pigs; stapled tracks of goats; padded tracks of free-roaming dogs.

To me, those ubiquitous tracks, more than anything else, were a constant reminder of the abuse to which the land was still being subjected; yet I was so accustomed to finding every patch of damp or sandy ground scored by them that I never gave them a second glance. Not, that is, until a day late in spring when, walking along the entrance trail, I chanced to notice the tracks of one of Roddy Ray's goats sharply superimposed on those of Hovit's herd of woods cows — and suddenly did a double take. Goats, I told myself, were sociable animals; it seemed very odd that one of them would be taking a stroll by itself. So I gave the tracks a closer look and realized at once that a deer had made them.

It was an indication of how overhunted the sandhills were that I should find myself marveling at the track of an animal as common as the whitetail deer. But even Roddy Ray, who considered a passion for deer hunting an indisputable proof of manhood, and the killing of his first buck the climactic moment of his life thus far, conceded that deer were by no means abundant in the area. I myself had never seen one on the Place, nor expected that I would; its overgrazed meadows and stands of thin young pines seemed incapable of sheltering anything larger than a rabbit or an opossum; and even the Hollow and the Brainch, heavily browsed by goats, offered little cover. Yet through this unpromising habitat a deer had wandered, leaving behind a memorandum of its passing.

From that moment I was hooked on wild animal tracks. I began reading those I found scrawled in the sandy soil with the same avidity that some people reserve for the *New York Times* or the *National Inquirer*. At the time, not only the deer but all the Place's huntable wildlife, with the exception of an occasional squirrel or quail, were keeping out of sight; so it was a great thing to discover that, even though they hid from me, I was able to keep track (literally) of their secretive lives. Tracks could name a species: the crippled-looking handprint of an opossum; the neat little pug marks of a fox (or a small dog?); the side-by-side tracks of a raccoon; even — now that I could believe in their presence — the occasional knife-sharp hoofprints of a deer. Tracks could tell me the direction an animal was heading, whether it was walking or running, if it was alone or with others of its kind, whether it was immature or fully grown. And if I made the same rounds often enough, they sometimes disclosed the pathways an individual animal regularly traveled, or the relative abundance of a particular species.

To this day, there are few pursuits that give me more pleasure than deciphering the scripts that wild animals inadvertently trace in the Place's sandy soils. It is an enthusiasm too intensely linked with my love for the Place itself to qualify simply as a pastime, a delightful hobby. It's hard to explain, but discovering that first delicate toe print of a deer on ground churned up and trampled by my neighbors' unfenced livestock was like finding a line from Donne or Auden among the graffiti inscribed on a tenement wall. It spoke movingly of the resilience of this plundered bit of the natural world that Willie and I had so chancefully acquired, its gallant determination to survive everything that people had done to it.

Willie with his birds, me with my tracks. It wasn't something we talked about, or even thought about consciously, but during that first spring a bonding was occurring between us and the Place. We had started out by buying some property; now it seemed that, as the Venetians had wedded themselves to the sea, so had we to this worn and scruffy piece of land. For better and worse, we would love, honor, and protect it — if we could just find out how — until . . . well, until death should us part.

6

The fence

H ovit's mean red bull was the ostensible reason for the fence. Whereas most of the bulls I've known, including the one we would own later on, have been placid animals that liked to have their foreheads scratched, Hovit's bull was a cartoon version of what bulls are supposed to look and act like. All his weight and size, scrotum excepted, was up front in his head, horns, and shoulders. From there on back, where most of the meat was supposed to be, he quickly tapered down to narrow gristly flanks and hindquarters that a butcher would need a chain saw to dismember.

He and his undernourished harem regarded the Place as their private grazing ground, so I guess it was only natural that he should be incensed when Willie and I began building a house in the middle of his favorite pasture. Whenever he was nearby, he reacted to the sound of our hammering as to a red flag, thumping across the ridge with head and stringy tail held high, intent on confrontation. Willie, in the manner of Sammy Davis, Jr., would say "Heah come d'bull," and he and I would ascend ladders if we weren't already on them. Sammie, meanwhile, would discreetly take to the woods. Which left Schaeffer to man the field alone. In fairness to Hovit's mean red bull, it must be said that the Great Dane did his best to aggravate the brute's natural contentious-

ness. He might loathe the bucolic scene, but he was the descend-
ent of dogs that had once brought boars and aurochs to bay; and
he was also very protective of Willie and me. So whenever the
bull descended on us, he would go to meet his horn-tossing,
wild-eyed advance and proceed to waltz around him in elegant
bounds, ducking his angry lunges, now and then woofing in mild
excitement — while Willie and I, from the safety of our ladder
perches, begged him to desist. After a few minutes of this, the bull
would do one of two things: give up temporarily in disgust and
swagger back to his lady friends (who were devastatingly unimpressed by these exhibitions) with Schaeffer escorting him part
of the way, or, ignoring the dog, head straight for us, circling
the cagelike frame of our half-built house, huffing and puffing
as though he really might blow it down. Fortunately, his attention span was very short. Having made his point, he would forget what it was and turn away, leaving us in peace for the rest of
the day.

Except for one time when he slammed against my ladder and
almost dislodged me, Mean Red posed no real danger to us humans as long as we saw him coming. As for Schaeffer, although
not particularly light on his feet, he was so much less clumsy and
more intelligent than his adversary, and so obviously having a
good time playing matador, that we eventually decided not to
worry about him.

Which was a mistake. One day, as Mean Red was leaving the
scene of battle, Schaeffer, overconfident, persisted in nipping at
his fetlocks and the bull caught him a lick in the ribs with a
hind hoof. Schaeffer gave a startled "arf" and backed off. When
we checked him over immediately afterwards, he seemed un-
hurt, but an hour later we were horrified to discover a hideously
sagging bulge on his rib cage that was getting larger by the minute! We rushed him to the nearest vet, some fifteen miles away,
where we learned to our great relief that the injury, a hematoma,
was not as serious as it looked. Indeed, Schaeffer seemed as be-

mused as the elderly country vet by our alarm. But after that we took no more chances. We kept him on a leash during the afternoons, which was when Mean Red usually showed up; and as soon as the bull came trotting down the ridge we hustled Schaeffer into the Volksbus before ascending our respective safety ladders.

There was no way Hovit was going to admit that Mean Red was a dangerous animal that ought to be penned up. "Now, Don," he would say in a soothing, quasi-fatherly voice, "you just got to show that bull who's boss. You just stand your ground; let 'im see you ain't scared of 'im, an' after a little bit he'll go off about his business."

Of course I had no intention of standing my ground, as Hovit well knew. But I couldn't admit that to Hovit, as Hovit also knew. Which left me with only one course of action: Since Hovit wasn't going to fence Mean Red in, we would have to fence him out.

Had the bull been my only concern, the problem could have been solved by enclosing the house and a couple of acres around it with a few strands of barbed wire. But once the idea of a fence had planted itself in my mind, it grew and grew until I had convinced myself that it must surround the entire eighty acres. A fence would protect the Place from the forays of Roddy Ray's goats, Hovit's cattle, trespassing hunters, the world in general; it would give our poor worn-out land a chance to rest. That was what I told myself, and it made perfectly good sense. But I have no doubt that on a less conscious level I was also driven, like the anoles on the rafters of the house and the singing, quarreling birds in the surrounding woods, by an instinctive need to stake out a territory and defend it against all comers.

The way it turned out, I was the one who did most of the work on the fence. I wasn't teaching summer school at the university that year so I had the free time. Willie, on the other hand, had to stick with his floor-sanding job just to "make the groceries," as they say in New Orleans. On weekends he came up from the city to help me, bringing the dogs with him, but the rest of the time I was on my own.

If I do say so myself, the fence I undertook to build was pretty impressive as farm fences go — one and a half miles of stout hog wire mesh, four feet high, stapled to sturdy six-foot-long creosote posts, with two strands of barbed wire to top it off. The first stage in the project was to dig the post holes two feet deep along the boundary, then distribute the posts, set them up, and tamp in dirt around them until they were unbudgeable. Afterwards, the rolls of wire would be unloaded at the appropriate intervals and, one by one, unrolled, stretched, and stapled. It seemed such a nice orderly procedure in theory; but carrying it out would be something else again.

I can think of several periods in my life when my physical endurance was pushed to its outer limits: when I was a Marine Corps boot at Parris Island, for instance, marching in the blazing sun until enough members of my platoon had collapsed from heat prostration to satisfy our sadistic drill instructors; or when I worked as roustabout on an offshore oil rig where we sometimes had to unload pipe and drilling clay for thirty-six hours at a stretch. But none of those times could compare with the pain-through-strain that went into building the Place's equivalent of the Great Wall of China during that scorchingly hot summer of 1968.

Digging the first few dozen post holes with the long, tonglike diggers was an invigorating, even enjoyable exercise, and I could tell it was doing wonders for my pectorals. But then the blisters started, even though I wore gloves, and when I persisted with the digging, they became raw, painful wounds. From then on it was a matter of bad going to worse. What with the shock of slamming the diggers into the brick-hard earth on the ridges, and the strain of pulling them out of the gluey mud in the Brainch, my back started to give out, and all those muscles in my arms and chest that had begun by feeling so nicely exercised now felt as if they'd undergone a few warm-up sessions on some inquisitor's rack.

Even so, the aches and pains that the digging entailed were nothing like as fearful as the murderous heat in which the work was done. Temperatures that August ranged from the mid- to high nineties. Every half-hour or so I paused, stripped, and wrung a veritable stream of muddy sweat out of jeans, shirt, even my socks. I gulped down salt tablets and quarts of tepid water, and still I had frequent bouts of heat prostration. The sun poached my brain. After two or three days of that sort of punishment I converted into someone more elemental than the person I normally thought of as being me. Life became a matter of getting the next post hole, just the next one, dug.

By the time all those hundreds of holes had been excavated my body had hardened considerably; but there was no way it could become accustomed to the heat. And now there were new problems. The logistics of getting materials to where they were supposed to be were pretty daunting. When Willie arrived one Friday with the Volksbus loaded down with fence posts — its springs already shot to hell from all the lumber and cinder blocks it had carried — it took us most of that weekend to maneuver the poor old crate across pocked fields and gullies, trying to distribute the posts as close by as we could to the places where they would be used. Which, unfortunately, was usually not all that close. The posts weighed about twenty pounds apiece, and after Willie left for the city, I had to carry them, three or four at a time cradled in my arms, through long tangled stretches of briers or swamp. They had been freshly dipped in creosote, which can burn off skin, and although gloves protected my hands, sweat carried the corrosive stuff through my frayed shirt. By the time I had placed all the posts along the boundary line, my stomach and forearms looked as though they'd been brushed by Hovit's flamethrower.

Setting up the posts and tamping them was a lonely drudgery; but it was fun and games compared to dealing with the rolls of hog wire. Once again the groaning van was coaxed through an obstacle course of rotted stumps, scrawny stands of pine, eroded washes, to get the wire as near to the boundary line as possible. Which, as with the posts, still left a ways to go. The rolls of wire weighed about one hundred pounds each, and when I rolled them cross-country they had a fiendish way of catching on every branch or root in their path. The half-mile of the Brainch was the ultimate trial. The wire had to be dragged through a labyrinth of roots, sloughs, cypress knees, and mud to the place where it was needed, then unrolled — hooking itself on every snag along the way — and finally pulled taut against the posts by a rope and pulley contraption called a "come-along."

Sometimes the come-along snapped under the strain. Sometimes I did. After hammering my thumb instead of a staple for the dozenth time, I would freak out and start bashing the post in an ecstasy of sun-crazed rage. When a swarm of deer flies, waiting until I had my hands full, would start stinging my face and neck, I would drop whatever I was carrying and slap myself silly trying to kill them. Toward the end of the third week I had a sort of fever; whether the result of saturation sweating, a chill, or just plain exhaustion, I couldn't guess. I felt downright tropical, shaking and quaking as though I had malaria. Sometimes I would throw myself down on the ground, heart pounding, my head ready to spin off my neck like a defective piston valve. There I would lie for long minutes, mindlessly staring at a crenelated colony of lichen on a rotting stump, or a beetle foraging in a clump of grass, or maybe a toadstool, orange-white, mysteriously fleshy, poking out of the sphagnum a few inches from my nose. Then, when the pounding and spinning had slowed down, I would get up and go back to work.

I never considered why I was forcing myself to the limits of endurance. If I had, the obvious answer would have been that I was obsessed. I had promised myself that the fence would be finished by the end of August, when the fall semester began, and time was running out. But it was also true that building that protective barrier around the Place had become more a test than a task. There were plenty of times when, sick with fatigue, I wished I hadn't undertaken it, but some part of me wanted the challenge and knew all along that I would be outrageously pleased with myself if I saw it through.

Even during the worst of those Devil's Island days, I could look forward with pleasure to the hour consecrated to the Evening Dip. Tucked away between one of the pitcher plant bogs and the Brainch was a small rainwater pool a dozen feet wide and maybe twice that long, that Hovit generously called a spring. Over the years he had deepened it during periods of summer drought in order to ensure a supply of water for his stills if the Brainch gave out. It was a pretty place, and to it I repaired each evening for a bath. Usually I was in a zombie state of stuperous, dehydrated calm after a day of fence building, and this was the case on the evening of my third or fourth visit. In the bog, along with the pitcher plants, rafts of yellow sunflowers, meadow beauty, white-topped sedge, and black-eyed Susans were blooming away, with here and there a stunning leopard lily or delicate pogonia for an accent mark; but I scarcely noticed. I stripped, searched myself for ticks, and then stretched out in the deepest part of the pool, sighing with the pure animal pleasure of being enveloped by something as exquisitely simple and refreshing as water, however tepid. This was better than all the bathtubs in the world. I felt that I could almost fall asleep.

I did close my eyes. But not for long. I don't know what it was, maybe that sixth sense people talk about, but somehow I suddenly knew that I was sharing the pool with more than pollywogs and water spiders. And indeed, when I reopened my eyes I found myself staring into the eyes of the grandfather of all cottonmouths, the largest specimen of his kind I have ever seen at the Place before or since. He was at least four feet long and almost as thick around as my wrist; and he was lounging on the bank so close by I could have reached out and touched him.

It is a trait of cottonmouths that, quite often, they do not slip away as other snakes usually do when people approach them. This one had obviously been there all along, watching me with its strange, elliptical stare while I undressed and settled into the water almost next to it. It had been in plain view. I just hadn't bothered to look. And it had chosen not to budge.

One of the things that Willie and I — especially Willie — had to get used to during that first year or two at the Place was the squirmy fact that cottonmouths were not only present on the property; they were abundantly present. Somehow we had assumed that venomous snakes would just naturally be less numerous than their nonpoisonous brethren, and, in fact, this was the case with copperheads and pygmy rattlers, which we only rarely encountered. But with the possible exception of racers and gray rat snakes, cottonmouths seemed to be our most common reptile neighbors. Fortunately for all concerned, they stuck pretty close to water as a general rule, and the Brainch was their preferred habitat. Their bite, though not usually fatal, can make one horribly ill; yet, during the last quarter of a century, I have come within inches of stepping on cottonmouths a dozen times at least, and the worst I've been dealt — other than the cold chill that Emily Dickinson neatly described as "zero at the bone" — was an uncomfortably close-up look at their gaping white mouths and flared, scary-looking fangs. Indeed, considering the cottonmouth's abundance in the Deep South and its stubborn way of holding its ground when it feels threatened, it surprises me that so few human encounters with the reptile end badly. For the human, at least. The snake is usually not so fortunate if the human has the means at hand to kill it.

On this hot summer evening when I and the grandfather of all cottonmouths had our encounter, the only thing I had at hand was a bar of Lifebuoy soap. But that was all right with me. The heat, the sun, the long hours of brute labor, the solitude, had contrived to make me so spacy that, for all the fear I felt, I might as well have been a snake charmer at a Calcutta bazaar. From just above the water's surface — I was submerged up to my chin — I gazed at the snake with what was, in someone as rational as I considered myself to be, a pretty close approximation of primitive awe and respect. As best I could tell, the snake gazed back with a look of primitive distrust and disapproval. To soothe it, I said quietly, "If you don't bother me, Snake, I won't bother you." I was not so far gone that I heard the cottonmouth reply, but I did have the distinct impression that it relaxed a little, as though agreeing to go along with my live-and-let-live proposition (the more willingly, no doubt, because ingesting me was not an option). That settled, I continued to soak, and it continued not to move. When I finally evacuated the pool (very, very slowly), it was still there, tongue flickering, watching me as I dressed and took my leave.

Each evening after that, in the usual exhausted trance, I returned to the spring to bathe. Twice again the cottonmouth was on the bank watching me, although not at such close range as at our first meeting. Of course it was there the other times, too, in the water or under a root where I couldn't see it. But that was all right. The heat and the solitude had made a pagan of me. I was certain the snake knew I was harmless, not to mention unswallowable. It would not waste its venom on me.

Needless to say, I mentioned not a word to Willie about these rendezvous at the spring.

It was almost worth feeling lonely and bone tired for five days just to feel so good on Friday evenings when Willie came driving across the ridge. His glad-to-see-you smile shining through the windshield, the dogs jumping out of the van and bounding toward me, the mail to open, clean clothes, the chest full of ice for martinis, a good hot meal to look forward to — it was like a birthday party every weekend, only better.

Ironically, the best of all those reunions was one during which Willie and I had a stormy argument — stormy being the operative word. One of the few things in the world that really scared Willie, other than snakes, were electrical storms. The dogs ardently shared this fear, though it was the unfathomable roll of thunder that reduced them to cowering wrecks, whereas Willie was more pragmatically concerned that somewhere out there was a lightning bolt that had his name on it. Or mine. As luck would have it, atmospheric conditions in coastal Mississippi churn up more electrical storms than anywhere else in the nation except northern Florida. And on Saturday of this particular weekend we were treated to a real sky-cracking dilly. When it came up on us, Willie and I were wrestling a roll of hog wire through the Brainch on the southern boundary of the Place. This was the last stretch of fence that remained to be completed, and now that the end was in sight — just a few more days to go — I was more than ever obsessed with getting the job done. When black thunder rolled directly overhead and drops began to fall, I decided there and then that no maliciously inconvenient storm was going to slow me down. Meanwhile, Willie had straightened up from the wire we were unrolling, looked up at the sky, looked at me, and looked up at the sky again.

"We better be getting back to the house," he said.

"You go," I told him.

His voice firmed up: "We're both going."

The rain was really coming down now. The thunder was thundering. In the north, a white jagged line split the sky in two. "I don't give a damn if I get wet. Storm or no storm, I'm going to finish unrolling this wire this afternoon."

"No you ain't."

"Oh yes I am."

It was that sort of stupid argument, ending with Willie stalking up the ridge to the house with the panicked dogs at his heels, and me cursing and muttering, trying to unroll the uncooperative hog wire over a tangle of slippery, wet roots and stumps. In minutes I was drenched to the bone, the lightning was coming down nearby and the barrage of thunder was sounding suspiciously like an artillery battery trying to get my range. For an uncomfortable minute I had a look at myself from the outside. The view — of a small-time Lear having a pettish snit — wasn't much to my liking. But I had boxed myself in; and the obsession was telling me that I couldn't give up now.

I had gotten maybe a thirty-foot length of the wire unrolled along the streaming posts when a glimpse of something — a deer? — moving through the sheets of rain made me straighten up. Another look and I realized it was Schaeffer, struggling in and out of deep pools and over the slippery logs with which the Brainch was choked. I figured that his sturdy Danish loyalty had overcome his fear; he must have pushed open one of the French doors and headed back to the Brainch in search of me. He was soaked and trembling when I called him over. "Well, poor old pup," I said, crouching beside him, "at least *you* care what happens to me." For — I am ashamed to say it — along with feeling guilty and obsessive, and also a bit scared now by the flares of lightning going off all around me, I was also feeling as sorry for myself as for Schaeffer. Even though I knew how these storms unnerved Willie, I found myself blaming him for deserting me.

I was still indulging this mean little thought when, a few seconds later, I looked up and there was Willie to make a lie of it. He was a few yards away, up to his knees in the flooding Brainch, looking exasperated and worried and half drowned.

Whether it was shame or pure pigheadedness, I still couldn't quite give in. "You and Schaeffer start heading back," I yelled above the noise of what might as well have been a waterfall. "I'll come along as soon as I get a few more feet of the wire unrolled."

I had barely gotten the words out when the storm, apparently fed up with my refusal to submit to it, unleashed a bolt of lightning that struck a bay tree about twenty yards away with the force and noise of a howitzer shell. I watched half of its crown collapse, as though in slow motion, behind the intervening columns of wet black trees. At the same instant I remembered that water was an excellent conductor of electricity, and that all three of us were standing in it. Hugging terrified Schaeffer, I hissed, "Okay, okay, dammit; you win." Then the dog and I headed toward Willie. He waited for us, looking badly shaken, and together we slogged and stumbled our way back to the Volksbus, which Willie had driven as far down on the ridge as he dared without risking its getting stuck.

The rear of the bus was filled with the last of the rolls of wire, so we all scrambled into the front seat, Willie and me distributing huge, quaking Schaeffer across our laps. Sammie, who had not quite managed the courage to face the storm with Willie and Schaeffer, crouched on the floorboard at our feet. Fear had loosed poor Schaeffer's anal glands, so the bus stank to high heaven. Normally this would have embarrassed him, but he was too glad to be safe to care about the smell. The same was true of Willie and me.

Willie was in charge. "We ain't moving until this is over," he said. "I don't think that lightning can get at us as long as we got rubber between us and the ground, but there's no point attracting its attention by driving around." Schaeffer and I accepted this decision without argument, and for the better part of an hour we remained squashed up in the reeking Volksbus with the windows barely cracked, hardly able to move, while around us the storm raged and howled until it wore itself out.

When at last it had, Willie said, "Now if this old bus can make it back up the hill, we can get ourselves dried off and make some fresh hot coffee."

"Sounds good," I said; and indeed it did.

Now, remembering that storm, I marvel — not very originally, I admit — at the mysterious and unpredictable way that happiness is allotted us. If I were obliged to list the very best hours I've experienced in my life, that cramped hour in the smelly, rain-lashed Volksbus would have to be one of them. The person who mattered most to me in the world, as well as the great-hearted dog I loved most after him, had overcome their very real fears enough to come out into the storm to rescue me — not just from the lightning and thunder, but from my own nutty, egotistical obsession. And they had. We had ended up snug and safe, with me suitably chastened, but also gladdened by the gift I'd been given of undeserved love. For once in my life I knew how lucky I was; and I felt that nothing bad that might happen in the future could ever take that hour away from me.

I still feel that.

However, one year later, something bad would happen that would take away damn near everything else.

7

The country night

During our first years at the Place, fox hunters frequently loosed their hounds on or near the property at night. They would sit in their cars on the county road, drinking beer or moonshine, listening to what they called the "music" of the baying pack as it pursued its quarry through the woods roundabout, making comments like: "There's ol' Jackson out ahead'uv the others; I'd know his voice anywhere," and "Yeh, but that ol' bitch Milky is a-catchin' up fast." After a couple of hours, they would toss their empty cans and bottles out the window and head for home, leaving their dogs to be collected in the morning. Meantime, the dogs would go on ransacking the woods all night, literally hounding foxes and occasionally young deer to death, and keeping hard-working folks from getting a decent night's sleep.

We were not popular with this fox-hunting set. For one thing, there was Schaeffer. After we had been rousted out of our sleep a couple of dozen times by hounds coursing the Hollow, he decided he had had enough of their carryings-on. One night he got to his feet with a disapproving "woof," pushed the French doors open, and bounded out before I was awake enough to stop him. Sammie would have followed if Willie hadn't collared him — although, given his part-hound ancestry, there was no telling whether he meant to backup Schaeffer or join the pack.

The middle ridge was bathed in cold moonlight. Schaeffer

positioned himself out there, motionless as a cast-iron lawn statue, looking noble and heroic. For two or three long minutes he held that pose, staring off in the direction from which the increasingly loud houndish ruckus was coming. Then, suddenly the pack was in view, swarming up the slope — an eerie loping drift of about a dozen gray-white shapes, howling their heads off.

Schaeffer waited until they were perhaps a dozen yards below him. Then he launched himself from the ridge and came down on them like the proverbial wolf on the fold.

"Oh no," Willie cried. "He's gonna get all torn up!"

I was already running toward him in my bare feet, hollering "Come back, Schaeffer! Come back!"

Before I got anywhere near him it was all over. The hounds, fixated on the hot scent of the fox they were running, had been taken by surprise and utterly routed. They scattered in all directions, yelping with a hysteria that, even granting Schaeffer's huge size, struck me as a bit excessive. Especially since, having made his point, Schaeffer didn't deign to pursue them. He calmly accepted the fuss I made over him and then accompanied me back to the house, while in the distance the hounds regrouped and, belling woefully, headed back the way they had come.

After that, I not only allowed Schaeffer to disrupt any hounds that were coursing close to the ridge, I helped him do it. Whenever a pack was moving toward us, we would go trotting off in the direction they were headed, me armed with a flashlight if the night was dark. Then, while Schaeffer did his "Charge of the Light Brigade" routine, I would roar at the top of my voice, "Get outta here, you goddamned mutts!" — yelling not so much at the hounds as at their owners, who were sure to be parked somewhere nearby. Both Schaeffer and I relished our spoilsport roles: he as scourge of a canine rabble; me as champion of the Place's foxes, which obviously needed all the championing they could get.

Usually after one of these interceptions we and the foxes would be left alone for a while, at least when the fox hunters knew we were at the Place. However, one winter weekend a couple of them turned the tables and did some intercepting of their own. Willie had to work overtime so I had driven up to the Place alone. It was evening, a cold and dreary one, when I arrived. Just outside the gate, a beat-up pickup was parked in the entrance road with two men sitting in it. Even before I pulled up next to them, I guessed that they had been waiting for me.

There was no time to deliver the noncommittal smile I had ready, or ask the obvious question about what they were doing there. The older of the two, a thickset, overalled fellow in his mid-sixties with a choleric red face, leaned out the window as I came abreast and shouted, "Why the hell ain't you livin' on the fuckin' road like regular people? What right you got livin' way back here in the woods?" His breath steamed and swirled in the cold air. "You and that colored fellah!"

Taken off guard, I snapped back, "What business is it of yours where we live?"

"Because your damn fences is ruinin' the huntin'! Them foxes slip under 'em and the deers can jump 'em, but my dawgs gotta climb over and they get their feet all cut up. Slows 'em down! You got no business puttin' up fences back here where you don't belong. I believe you done it deliberate. Don't think I ain't heard you a-hollerin' at my dawgs!"

"You were supposed to hear," I said. "I work hard for a living and I don't need your dogs waking me up in the middle of the night just so you can listen to them running some poor little fox to death."

"Poor li'l fox," he snarled. "I been runnin' foxes in these parts since before you was born, so don't tell me what you don't need."

I snarled right back, "I'll tell you anything I damn please if it concerns my land!" With a little shock, I realized that I was actually *enjoying* being angry.

The fox hunter seemed to realize this too. The red drained

from his face; the expression shifted from belligerent to merely sullen. "You ain't got no right," he muttered, but with less conviction than before. "That gawddamned fence —"

"Is on my property," I cut him short, "and I'll build it ten feet high if I want. In fact I just may do that."

Throughout this exchange, the driver of the pickup, who wore a week's worth of stubble and a curiously vacant look on his lined face, had said not a word. But when I seized my advantage to launch into a lecture on property rights, canine noise pollution, and the questionable ethics involved in allowing a dozen hounds to pursue one small fox, he suddenly let out a weird little barking laugh, not at all nice-sounding to my prejudiced ear. Then he switched on the ignition, turned the truck around, and without further ado drove off, his friend still hanging out the window looking bitterly back at me.

After they had gone, I remained where I was for a considerable while. I no longer felt very brave or angry. I was remembering the furious look on that old man's face, and hearing again his buddy's unpleasant laugh. In the sandhills, good fences obviously didn't always make good neighbors.

In the distance I could see the pointed outline of our one-room castle. It looked awfully vulnerable, sitting out there on the winter ridge. How could we defend it — or ourselves — if matters took an ugly turn?

Deliberately I put aside that uncomfortable line of thought and focused on the fence instead — my good sturdy hog wire fence with its two strands of barbed wire on the top! — stretching away from the locked wooden gate in both directions until it was lost in the shadows of trees and the gathering dusk. In building it, my intention had been to protect the Place from depredating livestock. It had never occurred to me that it might also help the neighborhood deer and foxes escape their persecutors. My spirits rose, thinking about that.

Still, I was troubled. Back in the city I told Willie about my run-in and suggested that maybe he should stay away from the Place for a while, just in case there were repercussions. But he wasn't having any of that. "Those kind of people ain't gonna bother us," he said. "You stood up to them, and they know you know who they are, or leastways what they look like. They'll figure if they try anything, you might try something back." He gave me a grin. "Besides, two of us is better than one."

Although Schaeffer and I continued to harass the hounds that harassed our foxes, and the fence continued to slow them down, there were no more confrontations with angry fox hunters, nor did they try to get even with us for interfering with their sport. But during those first couple of years we had other reasons for sometimes feeling uneasy when night descended on the Place.

We didn't live *way* back in the woods, as the red-faced fox hunter had claimed; but we were pretty isolated. Our eighty acres were "landlocked" — that is, without any frontage on a public road — which is one reason we got the land at a price we could afford. Years later we would buy the intervening property from its absentee owners, but even when we did, our only link to the outside world — by which I mean the unpaved county road and our nearest neighbor, Roddy Ray — was the half of a mile of rutted logging trail winding past the site of the old widow woman's homesite and on through the woods. Until we moved in, this track had been used only by coon and fox hunters, moonshiners, and back-seat Romeos and their dates; and since we had no electricity during those first years and therefore no porch light to warn people off, it was quite a while before they all got the word that someone was living back there where the track ended.

Until they did, it could be a pretty unsettling experience to be sleeping out on that exposed middle ridge, first in the Volksbus, then in the little house, and be awakened by the growling dogs to the sight of headlights advancing toward us in the small hours of the night. Or, somehow more sinister, the beam of a flashlight probing the darkness. Once the fence was up, these interlopers usually turned around when they came to the gate; but until then, they were likely to keep right on coming until my loud "Who's there?" and the dogs' barking brought them to a halt. There never was a response; just the flashlight about-facing, or the sound of gears shifting and headlights sweeping the pines as a car or pickup turned around.

The unease induced by these nocturnal visitations, augmented by the quarrel with the fox hunters, was reason enough to make me feel a bit jumpy sometimes during our first full winter at the Place. But on Willie's account, I also found another cause for worry. Up until then, Roddy Ray and his family and even Hovit and Lurlee had taken such an apparent liking to Willie, and he himself seemed so unconcerned about being the only black person for miles around, that I had put aside my concerns about how he would fare in the insular world of the sandhills, where apartheid still ruled. Now, however, I was beginning to wonder if all was as well as I had supposed.

One day, Roddy Ray had invited me to accompany him and his "hawg dog" in a search for his band of half-wild hogs, the idea being to catch one of them and fatten it for butchering. In those days, everybody in the area laid claim to a dozen or so of these lean razorbacks, although the animals fended for themselves and roamed the piney woods at will. Ownership was defined solely by ear marking. While shoats were still small and manageable, their "owner" notched their ears in a distinctive pattern that henceforth identified them as his. In theory, you were only supposed to mark the offspring of your own similarly marked sows; but in practice, just about everyone, Roddy Ray included, notched any young pigs they could get their hands on.

Now that the shoats Roddy Ray had caught last year were

grown up and anything but manageable, it was the job of his burly hawg dog to run one of them down, grab it by its snout or ear, and hold on while Roddy Ray and I roped its legs and trussed it up. First, however, we had to find one to catch.

We were crossing an oddly out-of-place little clearing in a plantation of pines when I stepped on something hard and flat that could have been a rock if this weren't the sandhills, where rocks were nonexistent. When I picked it up, it proved to be an old brick, one of several lying close together under a layer of moldering pine straw. "Must have been an old homeplace here," I said, holding the brick up for Roddy Ray to see.

Roddy Ray glanced over his shoulder. "Naw," he said. "That's from an old niggah graveyard that used to be here."

"A graveyard for black people? Out here? But there aren't any blacks anywhere around."

"Used to be. There was still some when I was real little."

"What happened to them?"

Roddy Ray shrugged impatiently, wanting to move on. "I dunno," he said. "They was runned off, is what I always heard."

I couldn't get any more out of him during the rest of that afternoon's unsuccessful search for his hogs. All he would say was that he didn't rightly know what had happened; and he sounded pretty testy saying even that.

A few days later, on a gray December morning, Hovit paid us a call. He was in one of his drying-out phases, so he was feeling rather under the weather. He sat slumped in one of the folding chairs, moodily drinking coffee and chain smoking while Willie and I constructed a doorstep for the little house. I considered asking him about the graveyard — if anyone knew the story, he would — but I was afraid of what he might say, especially with Willie there to hear, so I held my peace.

What he did say, without any prompting from me, was troubling enough. We were almost finished with the doorstep, and he had been silent for some time, when out of the blue he turned to Willie and said, "Y'know, Willie, a bunch of mens in the neighborhood has been talkin' about you . . . [long pause] and they say they're goin' to show up one of these days and *he'p* you."

Willie replied, "That's nice," in what sounded like an offhand way.

None of us pursued the subject, but after Hovit had left Willie said to me, "I know what you're thinking, but what I think is, he was just trying to say I don't have nothing to worry about from his friends."

I wanted to believe him. But that night I couldn't sleep. I remembered how during the last two or three weeks both Roddy Ray and Hovit had independently asked Willie — Hovit two or three times — whether he was "fixin' to get married" any time soon; and how Willie had told them no. Now I was suddenly convinced that both men had been trying to find out if Willie was planning to start a family up at the Place and eventually populate the neighborhood with a crop of little Willies. I began to wonder if that might have something to do with Hovit's vaguely threatening reference to a "bunch of mens" coming to "he'p" us, or even, now that I thought about it, with those headlights and flashlights that sometimes seemed to be deliberately searching us out in the middle of the night.

Willie did not lie awake as I did; but next morning he admitted that while he slept he had had a dream in which "all these men came and tore down our fence." During the month that followed, headlights still sometimes appeared at the gate at night; and two or three times I had to order groups of trespassing hunters off the Place; but no bunch of mens showed up either to help or harm us. When, eventually, I asked Hovit about the graveyard, all he would tell me was that some turpentine workers were buried there, and their families had moved away " 'cause they knew they wasn't wanted."

With no more than that to feed on, my fears gradually subsided.

Until, in the small hours of a close-to-freezing February night, I was awakened by Willie's hushed voice:

"Don, lookit; there's a light. A fire."

He was sitting up in bed, facing the French doors on the east side of the house, which, like the others, were shut against the cold. I got up and came around behind him. Even before I was in position to see what he was seeing, even while I was still half-asleep, I didn't doubt who the light, the fire, belonged to. Surprisingly, I felt ready for them, not in the sense of having any course of action planned, but ready to be calm, to think clearly about what needed to be done.

When I did see what Willie saw, it only confirmed my expectations. A reddish orange light — a fire, surely — was glowing in the depths of the Oak Grove. When I tried to make a burning cross out of it, I couldn't quite. On the other hand, it was safe to assume that Boy Scouts weren't toasting marshmallows around it either.

It was quiet out there. The dogs, inside with us, hadn't barked; if they stirred now it was only because we were awake. For a second, a part of my mind focused on them. Willie and I could take off into the woods if we had to, but what about the dogs? They wouldn't understand that they too were supposed to hide.

All the while, I was staring at the light. So was Willie. Just as the same realization came home to me, he said, "It can't be a fire. It don't move like fire does."

Quietly we opened the door, stepped outside, and advanced in our cold bare feet a few steps toward the Oak Grove.

It took us a long minute and some sidestepping, first this way, then that, to get a clearer perspective before we were ready to believe that what couldn't be, was.

Our Klansmen's council fire, our burning cross, was in fact a bright orange crescent moon just above the horizon, broken by a cloud and a grid of tree trunks. Neither of us had ever seen the moon in such a guise before, and only very rarely since.

I realize this would have made a much better tale if we had indeed been besieged by hordes of torch-waving kleagles and Grand Dragons, but I recount it as an example of how a few stray signs and portents, a measure of isolation, and the country night can combine to work on one's imagination in nervous-making ways. Granted, Willie and I were a pretty offbeat pair of outsiders to be settling in the Mississippi sandhills, and we knew it; moreover, we hadn't imagined those intrusive headlights in the wee hours, or the import of Hovit's and Roddy Ray's pointed questions, so it wasn't surprising that paranoia found in us some fertile ground to sow a seed or two. But, our special circumstances aside, nighttime in the rural countryside is not at all the same thing as nighttime in a "safe" national park or forest, and its special effects can assail even experienced campers with a case of the heebie-jeebies. On several occasions, perfectly sensible, reliable friends of ours have asked us if they could spend a few days at the Place while we weren't there, only to return to the city after a night or two of mysterious noises and unnaturally natural silences, exclaiming, "How do you guys stand being up there all alone? You can't tell what the hell's *out there!*"

They say *what* but they mean *who.* Out there in the rural boondocks, it's people going bump in the dark, not ghouls or savage beasts, that we fear. A falling pine cone can sound like someone's stealthy footstep; a cow in the underbrush, like a lurking prowler; a barred owl, like a maniac serenading the moon. It doesn't take much for the imagination to go hog wild.

Most people, of course, soon learn to come to terms with the rustic night's lively repertoire of false alarms, but some, even some people who have lived in the country all their lives — Cora, for example — never do. So, if you are planning to buy property in a backwoods area, it might be a good idea to decide beforehand just how much privacy you really want. Lots of people believe they want as much as they can get; but it can't hurt to put the notion to the test over a few country nights before you start building a house too far from a proper road.

As for Willie and me, it never occurred to us, even on the occasions when we were really spooked, to regret the relative isolation of the Place. God knows what Thoreau would have made of us, but in our amateurish, part-time, mostly self-reliant way, we traveled widely in our eighty-acre kingdom — at night as well as in broad daylight. Just before bedtime, if the moon was bright, we often took a stroll along the entrance road. Especially in later years when the oaks loomed tall and hazy blue as clouds above us and threw great splashes of shadow across the moon-drenched track, it was like stepping into a Barbizon painting of a scene too impossibly romantic and lovely to be real. If the night was dark, we sometimes went exploring with a flashlight along the edge of the Hollow, harmlessly jacklighting opossums, rabbits, spiders in their dewy webs, even, once in a very great while, a deer. Mostly though, after the dishes were washed, if the weather permitted and there were no baying hounds on the loose to disturb the peace, we sat outside the house, beers in hand, and just took it all in, that nighttime world "out there." We learned to identify the calls of barred owls and screech owls and chuck-will's-widows, the different voices in our choir of frogs and toads, the different constellations in the sky overhead. We watched heat lightning flicker horizontally across the horizon and made quite serious wishes on falling stars.

In short, we made friends with the night and increasingly felt at home in it, not unlike the wild creatures roundabout us who relied on it to shelter them.

8

Camille

By our second August at the Place, our plans for the middle ridge were coming along nicely. The little gazebo house was painted and furnished with chairs and comfortable cots; and we had constructed a sort of passageway deck that would link it to the next unit we planned to build. The fruit trees and shrubs were doing well; and with the help of Cora and Eloise we had made an attempt, though not a very auspicious one, at getting a vegetable garden going. On the lower reaches of the ridge we had started a reforestation project, planting a couple of hundred pine seedlings — slash pine, as the county forester had advised — that were successfully taking root. Where the entrance track passed through the fence, the gate I had set up was impressively flanked by sections of telephone pole seven feet high; and Mean Red, who had attended the building of the fence with thick-witted interest the previous summer, occasionally chasing me around a tree, was now officially banished. He still stopped by now and then and looked in at us — rather forlornly, it seemed to me, as though he couldn't understand why we were making him feel unwanted.

But the greatest change of all was in the gully that the house overlooked. Roddy Ray had prevailed on the county supervisor, a buddy of his, to have a twelve-foot-high dam dozed across it. The work was finished just before Willie and I were due to take off on a vacation we felt we richly deserved. Looking down at the ugly two-acre gash of raw red earth, Roddy Ray pounded our backs and we pounded his in mutual congratulation. We had no doubt that by the time we returned the huge cavity would have become a little lake filled with rain runoff. Each of us had his own some-what different vision of its function — Willie seeing it as home for the ducks he planned to buy; Roddy Ray, as a fishing hole stocked with bluegills and bass; me, as a new wildlife habitat patrolled by herons, kingfishers, and raccoons — but we were as one in our certainty that it would be the perfect centerpiece for the entire property.

With Roddy Ray promising to keep an eye on things while we were away, and with so much to look forward to when we got back, we set off on our camping trip out West with light and carefree hearts.

Willie was thrilled by his first mountains, elk, waterfalls, can-yons. For other campers, he was something of a thrill himself. This was still the '60s, remember, and a black man camping out in the national parks — with a white man, no less — was a rarer sight than a bighorn sheep. But that made the trip all the more agreeable, for most of our fellow campers were the sort of peo-ple who had had their consciousness raised during that tumul-tuous decade, and so they reacted to us with almost excessive friendliness.

We kept to the parks and national forests as much as we could in our journey northward through the Rockies; and we made a point of not knowing what was going on in the world at large. I doubt that we would have heard about Camille until we got home if I hadn't noticed the "Killer Hurricane" headline on a newspa-per at the checkout counter of a Montana store where we stopped for supplies. When I looked at the map on the front page, with its hurricane arrow plunging right through southwestern Missis-sippi, and read the accounts of the havoc the storm had wreaked, I knew we might be in trouble. But I also knew there wasn't much we could do about it. Willie and I talked it over, and decided to go on to Glacier National Park, the last destination on our outward journey. We were glad we did. We had such a fine time gaping at mountain goats and moose and miles of vertical scenery that we managed not to think much about the hurricane until we headed for home. Which was just as well; for we would think of little else once we got there.

Camille was one of the most vicious hurricanes ever to come ashore in North America. By the time it had spent itself, it had killed hundreds of people, smashed the Mississippi Gulf Coast flat with a stupendous tidal wave, and left a wake of almost unbelievable destruction across hundreds of inland miles. The Place had been directly in the path of its 200 mph winds.

Good friends of ours who were looking after Schaeffer and Sammie while we were away had managed to skirt around the National Guard roadblocks on the Coast and check the Place out. They tried to forewarn us about what we would find there, but it wasn't until we drove into Mississippi ourselves that we began to realize just how bad things were: mile after mile of blasted pine forests and pecan orchards, snapped utility poles, houses with their roofs ripped off, demolished barns, trailers strewn about like crushed aluminum cans, stunned-looking people standing in heaps of twisted wreckage.

Even then we weren't really prepared for what awaited us at the Place. There were trees down all along the entrance track, so we left the Volksbus at the county road and walked in. The gate was still intact; but to either side I could see sections of my proud sturdy fence pulled loose from the posts and flattened by fallen pines. And on the middle ridge where the little house had stood — nothing!

We found the steeple roof lying like a crumpled party hat in the bulldozed gully, which should have been filled with water but wasn't. Everything else — walls, shattered French doors, cots — was scattered all over the ridge.

It had been so difficult and so much fun to build, that little medieval gazebo! Yet if that had been all we had to deal with, I believe we could have accepted its loss stoically enough.

It was everything else that really undid us. I had seen hurricane damage before, but never anything like this. Camille had been very focused as well as powerful, more like a giant tornado than a hurricane; and what it had done to the Place was what a tornado might have done. We walked across the ridges in shocked silence. Tree after tree after tree was down. Of the taller pines — there hadn't been all that many to begin with — every other one had been snapped in two or twisted round and round at the base like a green twig that a kid has tried unsuccessfully to break. Even the young pines had been bent down in waves, like flattened grass.

In the Oak Grove, although most of the trees still stood, they had an indecently naked look. Broken branches hung raggedly against their trunks. Nearly all their foliage had been stripped away, and the little that remained was turning the orange brown of an unseemly final autumn.

The Hollow, our beautiful Hollow, was the worst of it. It was the ruin of its former self, bays, maples, yellow poplars piled on top of each other in an impenetrable tangle, like a giant's game of pick-up-sticks. The trees that still stood looked mortally wounded, leaning every which way, their boughs ripped out at the sockets, the sap leaking from open wounds. Sunlight poured in where before there had been deep shade.

It was then, while we were staring at what was left of the Hollow, that I noticed the silence. I'd always thought that one of the saddest lines in literature had to be the requiem-refrain in Keats's "La Belle Dame sans Merci," "And no birds sing." Well, Camille was *la belle dame sans merci,* all right, and there were no birds singing now.

In the years we'd known each other, the only times Willie and I had ever had occasion to cry were when we watched a rerun of some old tearjerker like *Dark Victory* or *Love Is a Many Splendored Thing*. But now, contemplating the shambles that the Hollow had become, it was all too much. First he, then I, sat down on the branch-littered ground and wept.

Later, passing Roddy Ray's on our way back to the city, we saw Eloise standing forlornly in the middle of what had been their yard. The trailer was about fifteen or twenty yards away from where it had once stood, wrapped around a couple of broken trees. Eloise, always frail and a little lost looking, looked more lost than ever now. The first thing she said was, "Oh Don! Oh Willie! I've looked and looked, but I just can't find them." She and the family had salvaged what clothes and furniture they could from the wrecked trailer and moved in with Roddy Ray's sister, "But little Gladys's baby pictures is still missin'," she wailed, "and I don't have no others!" She began to sob. "I come back here every chance I get to look for them. They got to be around here somewheres!"

"We'll find them," Willie said confidently; and after an hour's determined searching through tangled windfalls and under scattered fragments of the trailer, we rather surprisingly did — not only a torn and bedraggled album, but a framed blowup as well. Eloise's smile, when we handed these treasures over to her, was the one good thing we had to take away with us from that otherwise miserable day.

We went to the Place only five or six times during that post-Camille fall and winter. During these visits, we burned the remnants of the little house, we straightened fruit trees that didn't look too dead, we repaired some of the flattened sections of the fence, we wandered around a lot, feeling dazed and disoriented. Mostly, though, we turned-to with a chain saw I had bought, dismembering as many downed trees as we could so their orangy crowns of dead leaves or needles wouldn't look so horribly conspicuous lying on the slopes all around us.

As much as possible, we averted our eyes from the view that our vanished house was intended to overlook. Although we had refused to believe it at first, we finally had to face the fact that, instead of being transformed into a great big beautiful pond, our gouged-out gully was going to remain what it presently was: a great big ugly eyesore. A deep vein of sand running under the dam was draining off rainwater almost as fast as it collected. If anything, the gully looked even more hideously raw and wounded now than when the bulldozers had just finished with it. We could hardly blame the hurricane for that, but somehow our aborted hopes concerning the pond merged with and became part of the overall mood of dejection that lay upon the sandhills in the wake of the great storm.

Early in the new year, that mood darkened even more when a stricken Cora phoned to tell us that Eloise had been killed in a hideous accident. She and several of her relatives — Roddy Ray and Gladys were not among the group — were driving home from a family gathering on a rainy evening when, at a crossroads a few miles south of the Place, a drunken driver ran a stop sign at high speed and slammed his pickup into their car. Seven people had died, Eloise among them.

Willie and I hadn't seen Eloise since that afternoon when we found Gladys's photos in the wreckage of the family's trailer. When, two days after Cora's call, I gazed for the last time at her small face, unnaturally rouged and waxy looking, pretending sleep in a shiny satin-lined coffin, I remembered with real anguish the glad look she had given us back then. The loss of this simple, gentle woman, who had been so kind to Willie and me, cast one more deep shadow over the world of the Place, which already seemed sunless enough.

9

A new beginning

I n late March 1970, Willie and I came out to the Place in the company of two friends, neither of whom had been there since before Camille had struck. Buddy was from New Orleans's lower ninth ward, which meant that he was bluff and loud-voiced and talked ("tawked") with a "yat" accent (as in "Where y'at, man?"). But notwithstanding the tough-guy facade, he was a compulsively openhanded sort of person, so much so that his friends, including Willie and me, had to be careful not to take too much advantage of him. Brian was also a good and helpful friend, but he was Buddy's opposite in style: soft-spoken and rather reserved, obviously well educated, very "uptown." We had known both men for years, but at the time they had only a nodding acquaintance with each other. In hindsight it might seem that something more than fortuitous chance was required to explain their presence at the Place on that cool and sunny day; but I swear that when I invited them I hadn't consciously given thought to the fact that Buddy just happened to be a supervisor for a construction firm, and Brian an architect.

As soon as we arrived we ate a picnic lunch under a decapi- tated but still upright pine near where the little house had stood. Afterwards, while Buddy and Brian talked about architecture, Willie and I wandered over to the index ridge, past the Oak Grove, down to the Hollow. It was odd; at first we were reluctant to acknowledge what we were seeing. We were like people who have been ill for so long that even when they start to mend they are afraid to hope they are getting well. But there could be no doubt: Last summer's naked, lifeless-seeming oaks, though still awfully battered looking, were aglow with the furry little catkins that signify, in live oaks, a discreet flowering. In the Hollow, birds were singing. A gray squirrel made its perilous way along a fractured bough. Listing trees that had lost half their crowns — even some that were on their sides — were setting forth a brave display of new foliage that looked oddly tufted and askew, but also rather gallant; and everywhere catbrier, ferns, wild muscadine were hastily covering the prostrate trunks and boughs with which the ground was strewn. The Hollow still looked a wreck — but a cheerfully verdant, bedlam sort of wreck, aquiver with the blind furious energy of millions of things determined to survive and grow.

Almost in spite of myself, I began for the first time to see the violence that the hurricane had inflicted on the Place in a not altogether pessimistic light. The soils of the Hollow, enriched by layers of humus, were the most fertile that the Place had to offer, but the thick canopy of its maturing trees, combined with the incessant browsing of local livestock, had greatly inhibited the growth of young saplings and shrubs. I was no expert on plant succession; but I knew enough to realize that, with livestock banished and the forest canopy now opened up — to put it mildly — the conditions were right for a more diverse community of understory plants to flourish; indeed, the evidence that this was happening was already there. And such a habitat, interesting and worthwhile in itself, was certain to benefit the many wildlife species that needed dense undergrowth for food and cover.

Willie, his head tilted back, interrupted these reflections.

"Look," he said. He was gazing at the branches of a dogwood directly overhead, blossoming away as though this was the world's first spring.

When we got back to the middle ridge, Brian and Buddy were pointing this way and that, talking animatedly, on occasion vigorously nodding or shaking their heads.

Brian said, "You can't possibly rebuild here." He waved in the direction of the huge red gully that was supposed to have been a pond. "You don't want to have to look at *that*."

"This ridge was never much to start with anyway," Buddy chimed in.

"Buddy and I are agreed," said Brian, "that over there would be a better site." He pointed toward the east, to the slope of the index ridge.

Undeniably, this area had more going for it in the way of scenic possibilities even in its post-Camille condition than had the middle ridge. Although it was no beauty spot, there were a fair number of young trees still standing, mostly slash pines and homely blackjack oaks, but also several red oaks and live oaks, looking pretty wind blasted, to be sure, but of a fairly decent size. And down in the protected swale between the two ridges was a little cluster of dogwood saplings, already shaping itself into the magical glade it would become in just a few years' time.

"The grade is fairly steep," Brian went on. "Can you use a transit level, Buddy?"

"Hell, yeah," Buddy said. He turned to me. "This time we're gonna build the damn thing so it don't blow away."

"And while we're at it," said Brian, "we should reconsider the sort of house you want. I never was too fond of that cluster house idea."

"It was supposed to look like a castle," I said.

"I know," said Brian, sounding pained.

"Anyway," I went on, "we're not even sure we'll keep the Place. If we do, I was thinking we should probably settle for a tent or something."

But as an ally, Willie was already lost to me. "A house," he was murmuring, "a real house."

"I know you won't allow me to design the house for you," said Brian, pausing long enough for the universe to take note of what was being lost, "but when you decide what you want, I'll at least put it into a proper set of plans for you."

"Will there be a kitchen?" Willie asked.

"A kitchen *and* a bathroom," said Brian. "No more of this outdoor toilet nonsense."

"We haven't the money," I wailed.

"Borrow it," said Buddy. "And don't waste time. We gotta get started before it gets too hot."

"A real kitchen!" Willie beamed. "A real bathroom!" He loped over to the index ridge, scouting out the precise location for the house-to-be. Brian and Buddy began discussing how best to align the foundation piers.

I decided not to bother calling for a vote.

And that is how we started to start over. While all around us the Place was starting over too.

10

The second house

Although everything turned out dumbfoundingly well on our second try at building a house, I still think that living out of a tent or camper is a good idea when you are just beginning to develop a relationship with the land you've bought. Once you lay the foundations for a permanent dwelling, you can't count on a Camille to change your plans for you, so you might as well take your time deciding where and what to build.

If, that is, you decide to build at all. My own feeling is that unless you are able to spend a considerable amount of time at your place each year, it makes sense to camp out indefinitely. A van or camper, or a tent on a deck, plus an outhouse (with a real toilet seat) — such accommodations might not suit persnickety souls like our friend Brian, but for more outdoorsy types they should be all that is needed for an occasional weekend or week. Time enough for you to build when there is time enough, which may not be until the kids are grown. Meantime, there will be the pleasure of intermittently watching your land become more ecologically rich and beautiful with every passing year — without the inevitable hassles that building and owning a house entail.

But for those who, like Willie and me, buy land within reasonable commuting distance of their permanent address and who spend a lot of time there right from the start, some sort of permanent shelter can become a necessity. Let's face it, we live in a soft age; sooner or later we begin to miss the little creature comforts like electricity and a flush toilet. Weather gets too hot or too cold or too wet, deer flies or mosquitoes lust for our blood, the ice in the ice chest melts or the drinking water freezes, and after a while even an inventive genius like Willie gets tired of cooking on a Coleman stove.

Even so, you should take your time — doing as I say, remember, not as we did. Selecting the right site is terrifically important. You need to consider whether there is the risk of flooding or erosion or, in some areas, wildfire; whether adequate insurance coverage is available; whether soil subsidence will be a problem when you build; whether the direction of prevailing winds will keep you cool in summer without freezing your tail off in winter; and whether it will be a lot of trouble and expense to maintain a driveway if you build far back from a county road.

There are less obvious concerns as well, ones that in the long run may turn out to be just as important. Try imagining what the surrounding landscape will be like ten or fifteen years down the line. Will the maturing forest on the skyline block out what is presently your fine view of the setting sun, and will you care if it does? Is the site especially rich in the sort of habitat that the local wildlife needs for their housing more than you do? Or, like the Place's B.C. (Before Camille) Hollow, is it such a pretty spot that the presence of a house would only detract from its beauty?

Even on this second go-around, Willie and I didn't consider all the questions I've been raising here; but this time we did think long and hard about the design of the house we meant to build. All around us, Roddy Ray and hundreds of other people in the county were providing us with models of what we didn't want. Helped by generous government disaster loans, they were replacing their bashed-in trailers and cinder block dwellings with the sort of American Dream houses one sees in every subdivision from coast to coast. This assembly line suburban style — low pitched roofs and low ceilings, functionless cement porches, small windows in small rooms, often fronted by a treeless lawn — ignored all the important considerations that should go into building a home: regional climate, environmental setting, architectural tradition, the need for privacy, the lifestyle of the inhabitants. In fairness, Roddy Ray's new suburban-type brick house couldn't help but be an improvement on his old trailer, even if it did look just as out of place in the piney woods of southern Mississippi; but in a predominantly warm climate it collected heat and shut out every summer breeze, making air conditioning mandatory even when the temperature outside was pretty balmy. Worse, from my point of view, it managed, despite a picture window, to shut the outside out.

The design we finally came up with borrowed heavily from a traditional type of rural homeplace, once common all through the Deep South, but now as rarely seen as a mule. This was a yeoman style of architecture that called for a house to be built up on piers, with a steeply angled roof to deflect the sun, porches front and back, vertical board siding, and, in the very early models, a "dogtrot" — an open breezeway dividing the house in two. Our adaptation of this old style was just that, an adaptation, not at all a carbon copy. The steep grade of the new site dictated two stories and two levels. The front and back porches (both upstairs and downstairs on the back) would be supported by the extension of the floor beams rather than by posts, so that the house would seem to be suspended above the tilting ground. As a variation on the old-time breezeway, glass-paneled sliding doors would be lined up with each other to create a similar see-through effect and allow air to circulate when they were open. There would be a fireplace, but we would have to for go a brick one. The living room was so high above the ground that a massive foundation would have been needed for the hearth to rest on; so we settled for one of those contemporary freestanding fireplaces, a black metal affair that looked handsome enough and worked fairly well.

As for the interior space, it really would be *space* — divided more by levels than by walls, with the exception of the bathroom, kitchen, and, much later, a bedroom in the upstairs loft.

From my rough sketches, a surprisingly uncritical Brian drew up beautiful plans, and Buddy started making out long lists of the materials and tools I was to order, while Willie and I began digging the ditches for the cement slabs on which the house's piers would rest.

Believe me, unless one is a professional builder, it isn't easy to build any sort of dwelling oneself, not even a small, medieval-looking gazebo, much less a 1,400-square-foot split-level house, half of it two-storied, with a 24-foot elevation, on a 30-degree slope. But what kept hitting me again and again during the construction of that second house was the fact that the principles involved — once one got past the leveling of the foundations — were ones that even a college professor could grasp. One needs to know how far apart the studs should be spaced, and how many are needed to corner a wall, that sort of thing; and one has to use a lot of simple arithmetic to calculate the lengths of beams and the angles at which they should be cut. But actually putting together the frame of an essentially rectangular house is a very commonsensical, down-to-earth business; and the same is true of putting on a roof, installing insulation, nailing on the siding. Not easy to actually *do*, you understand; one is always miscalculating measurements or hammering one's thumb instead of the nail or misplacing the level or spraining one's back or just feeling sick and tired of the whole damn thing. But compared to trying to grasp the way computers or cars or washing machines or stereos are assembled, figuring out how a house is put together is a piece of cake.

As Buddy had promised, when we put this house together, we did it right. With an eye to future hurricanes, we built it according to the principle laid down in the old chorus song: the foot bone is connected to the ankle bone is connected to the leg bone, and so on. To the maximum degree possible, each building unit — pier, stud, beam, whatever — was securely tied to those it abutted. Thus, for example, after cement had been poured into the foundation trenches, we inserted a row of steel rods into the slabs while the cement was still wet. Then, when the pier walls of cinder blocks atop the slabs were in place, the hollows in the blocks containing rods were filled with cement — the effect being not only to reinforce the pier walls themselves, but to make them virtually inseparable from the foundation slabs on which they stood. The rods had been measured to protrude about nine inches above the walls — enough to pass through holes drilled in the support beams we placed atop the piers, with an inch or two to spare for attaching the heavy washers and nuts that would hold the beams in place. Next, the joists were fixed to the beams with metal hangers designed to make it almost impossible to pry them apart. Using hurricane and framing anchors, we applied the same principle of inseparable linkage all the way up to the roof rafters and the roof itself. Theoretically at least, even if the hurricane to end all hurricanes were to come along, it would almost have to pull the foundation slabs from the ground in order to budge the roof. (Happily, the house has not been put to so extreme a test; but it has been tested. When moderately severe Hurricane Elena passed directly over the Place in 1985, with winds gusting to 100 mph, some of our neighbors suffered a lot of damage to their homes, but ours came through without a shingle out of place. Nor has the passage of time taken any noticeable toll. Structurally, the house is still as sound and solid and plumb as it was when we finished building it a quarter of a century ago.)

It still amazes me how quickly the frame of the house went up during the spring of 1970. Especially considering the help we had. Buddy had a thoroughly professional attitude, but the construction crew he was obliged to work with had to be one of the strangest ever recruited since mankind first made the big move from cave to hut.

I don't suppose Willie and I had ever considered what a diversified — some might even say motley — collection of friends we had, until some twenty of them were assembled in the alien woods of Mississippi for purposes other than a picnic, looking dazed at the thought of being where they were, doing what they were doing. The only thing most of these people had in common, aside from their friendship with Willie and me, and, to varying degrees, with each other, was the fact that none of them had any carpentry skills whatsoever.

Like many secretly shy people, Buddy was happy being in a role — that of grouchy Egyptian slave driver — in which he felt sure of himself. He liked to stand on the platform that would eventually be our first floor, alternately bellowing orders and scribbling pencil calculations on a scrap of wood. Brian wandered about with a level almost as tall as he was, making certain everything was plumb. Willie, the only one Buddy felt was competent to operate the electric saw (we had rented a portable generator), bit his lip in concentration as he cut his way through stacks of two-by-fours. Everybody else — professors, male and female, whose idea of exercise was a nice little jog along St. Charles; an uptown lawyer and his socialite wife; a young med student and his sculptress girlfriend; a *bon vivant* of the old school grown somewhat slack in jowl and waist; three or four bearded and/or bangled delegates from the then still vital Age of Aquarius; a French Quarter waiter so airily delicate that a falling leaf might have struck him down; and assorted others, including me — hammered at nails, carried heavy sheets of plywood, climbed ladders, and lifted the frames of walls into place.

The climax of all this group effort was the raising of the roof's highest ridge beam, along with the wall frame that supported it. At this stage, the stud frames of the first-story walls and the floor of the second story were in place. On this floor platform, about fifteen feet above the ground, it was now necessary first to build, then elevate, the frames of the second-story walls. The tallest of these would provide the support for the roof at its highest point, which was very high indeed. Buddy decreed that this wall must go up first, which meant that we had to lift a heavy frame — a twelve-by-thirty-foot rectangle of studs and crossbeams — into thin air on the very brink of the platform and hold it suspended there while Buddy leveled it and hammered on enough braces to keep it in place.

At Buddy's command, we stationed ourselves along the edge of the recumbent frame. "Awright, you coolies, now lift it straight and even."

Slowly, waveringly, the frame began to rise amid grunts and gasps.

"I said straight and even!" Buddy bellowed. "It's gotta stand plumb."

"It's too high; I can't control the way it leans!"

"It's leaning out *too far!*"

"Straight and even, goddammit! *Straight and even!*"

"Nail the damned thing or I'm going to let it go!"

"If I fall off, I'll sue your ass!"

"What the fuck are you doing, Buddy! Admiring the god-damned view?"

"My toe! It's *on my toe!*"

And so it went, back and forth, both the swaying wall and the spirited exchange, for three or four perilous minutes — more than enough time to induce trauma in those of us who had an aversion to things like heights and pain. At last, however, there came the rescuing sound of nails being hammered into braces, and then Buddy's voice saying above the groans and whimpers, "All right, you weaklings, you can let go."

It was close to noon when that high second-story wall was nailed into place. Incredibly, by evening the whole frame of the structure was complete. All of us gratefully subsided into the shade of nearby trees to nurse bruises and beers. After a while, however, I got to my feet and limped off a little distance to get a better view of what we had accomplished. First Willie, then Buddy and Brian joined me.

"It's shaping up pretty good," said Buddy.

Brian conceded that, all things considered, the proportions were not too bad.

I was in no mood for professional understatement. For the first time I could actually see the dimension and scale of the house I had sketched on paper two months earlier. "It's going to be beautiful," I said flatly.

Willie exclaimed, "It already is!"

Everyone had brought sleeping bags or inflatable mattresses, since there was still much to be done the next day, a Sunday. After that, our volunteer work force would disband and go back to spending their weekends in presumably less rigorous ways. Now that the frame of the house was in place, Willie and I were confident that with a little advice from Buddy now and then, we could do the rest of the work ourselves during the summer and early fall.

That night, after a sandwich and salad supper, we had a party. The raw beams and studs of the house were draped with an improvised bunting of brightly colored sheets and blankets. Ellin, the sculptress, hung artfully arranged pine boughs above the windowless windows. Perforated aluminum cans were transformed into makeshift shades for candles. Willie's record player drowned out the generator with the music of Simon and Garfunkel, Moody Blues, Crosby, Stills and Nash, King Crimson. Out of the ice chests came bottles of beer, wine, vodka. Out of some people's pockets came small plastic bags and packets of cigarette papers. Ward, the guru of the hippie contingent, sat in a corner and told stories about his boyhood in Pine Bluff, Arkansas: how he had accidentally blown up the fireworks store and almost set the whole town on fire, how he had scandalized the Baptist preacher during his born-again baptism by deciding he didn't want to get his hair wet, how he had run away from home with a go-go dancer. Arlan, who taught the mentally handicapped and had thoughtfully brought along his soap bubble equipment, sat on a ladder blowing astonishing cascades of iridescent bubbles, some filled with smoke, some enclosed within larger bubbles, some joined together like Siamese twins, that settled on people's heads and shoulders. Willie gave everyone a pleasant fright by cavorting through the woods wrapped in a ghostly sheet with a flashlight under his chin. Everybody danced on the stage-like floor platform, even Buddy, who didn't know how.

The party lasted a long time. When most of the revelers had finally fallen asleep, Willie and I walked over to the Oak Grove and rounded up the last three or four strays. They had become transfixed by the light of a half-moon falling through the branches and were standing about helplessly, stunned by The Beauty of It All.

New Orleanians are connoisseurs of parties. But if I say so myself, I think every person who was there that night still remembers that particular party as one of the best of the best.

11

The mystery bumper

During that summer and fall, Willie and I learned to our sometime sorrow that putting up the superstructure of a house is the easy part. It's when one is doing the detail work, like nailing up each cedar board along the living room walls so it aligns perfectly with its neighbor, or building cabinets in the kitchen, or floating sheetrock in the upstairs loft so that it comes out looking fairly smooth, that one's patience starts wearing thin. In the course of a typical day, I normally used up my short supply of that virtue coping with humans and animals, so I had none left over to deal with inanimate objects such as tools and building materials; their obduracy, their frequent sheer spitefulness, worked on my nerves, as Willie would say. Fortunately, Willie was a more equable person than I could ever hope to be; and from long practice, he knew how to defuse me even when I was in the act of blowing up. Once, when I was trying to hammer an expensive cedar board to pieces because the nail I was nailing had bent once too often, he threatened to report me to the SPCW. I paused long enough to ask him what the hell he was talking about. "The Society that Prevents Cruelty to Wood," he said. "You keep on like that and they're gonna lock you up." He kept a straight face, I grudgingly laughed, and the board was saved.

Progress was slow, but we did progress. By mid-October, all the doors and windows had been fitted, the work on the interior walls was finished, an electrician had wired the house, the well had been drilled, and the plumbing, which we installed ourselves, was in place. In less than a week the Coast Electric Company would be running a line from the county road, and we would have all the light we wanted, not to mention running water, at the flick of a switch. After two and a half years of changing the wicks on Coleman lanterns and filling heavy water bottles at Roddy Ray's, it was something to look forward to.

Late one night during that final week of waiting, we were awakened by Sammie's low growling.

"You hear that?" Willie whispered.

"I'd be deaf if I didn't," I whispered back.

We were in the loft. A ghastly clumping sound, not unlike the club-footed tread of Frankenstein's monster, was coming from the floor below.

Sammie continued to growl fiercely — from under the bed. Schaeffer stood at the landing, dimly visible. He was alert but silent, and strangely reluctant to go downstairs.

I thought ambivalently about that electric light we didn't quite have yet. Even if it was available to us, I wasn't sure I would have wanted to turn it on, being equally leery of what we might see and what might see us. Still, it seemed advisable that someone should investigate. Since I was the only white male around (and there was still that hypothetical image of a burning cross lurking in the corner of my mind) I reluctantly volunteered. Sotto voce, I told Willie that if someone started murdering me he should jump off the second-story porch and run for the woods. He sotto voced back that although he thought it more sensible for us both to stay where we were, he wasn't going to let me go downstairs by myself; and anyway, if he jumped off the upstairs porch he would un-doubtedly break his legs, which would make running for the woods difficult to say the least. The upshot of this brief discussion was that Schaeffer went down the stairs first, with me following him and Willie following me. Sensible Sammie remained under the bed.

As we slipped through the living room to the kitchen, the thumping and clumping seemed to be coming from everywhere around us. Even Schaeffer was at a loss to pin it down. Whatever it was couldn't help but hear us, but it didn't seem to care. Finally, groping around on the kitchen counter, I found the flashlight. The three of us went back to the living room, where I turned it on.

Nothing! Yet still those frightful sounds.

Schaeffer was sniffing the fireplace, and Willie was gingerly peeking behind the secondhand sofa, when at last it dawned on me that the noise was coming from under the floorboards. Running outside, I knelt on hands and knees and probed under the house with the flashlight's beam. Sure enough, there was our little monster, digging away.

It was the Downstairs Armadillo, as we came to call him. Willie was absolutely certain it was the same animal — "I can tell from the way he acts" — that had come to call when we were building the first house. Now that this second house was finished, he had dug a burrow under it and moved in without so much as a by-your-leave.

The Downstairs Armadillo would keep the same address off and on for more than a year. During that time he sometimes made a nuisance of himself by digging for grubs in the mulch surrounding the shrubs we had just planted. Indeed, once when he was about to upend a small azalea, I was sufficiently annoyed to run down the slope in my bare feet and, to his indescribable consternation, smack him hard on his mailed behind. He learned nothing from this experience, however, and the next night resumed his digging where he had left off.

Yet for all his bothersome ways, we were fond of him. And to Willie it was a source of smug satisfaction that he had finally got an armadillo as a pet — well, a sort of yard pet — in spite of all my earlier lectures and objections.

We became so used to the Downstairs Armadillo's noisy under-the-house bumping that after a while we ceased to notice it. Which explains why we forgot to mention him when, having to stay in the city ourselves one weekend, we turned the Place over to a couple of our friends and their two sons. In fairness to us, and the Downstairs Armadillo, the boys to this day glowingly remember that weekend as one of the most thrilling of their childhood. But their parents, who never did discover what was making those hideous noises and spent a sleepless Saturday night wondering when whatever-it-was would come upstairs and kill them all, were quite cool to Willie and me for a long time afterwards.

12

The pond

During those months when Willie and I were filling in the skeletal outline of the second house, our new pond was filling in as well, its waters rising with every summer downpour, anywhere from a couple of inches to a foot depending on the storm's duration. So linked were the house and pond in our hopes and plans that we took as much satisfaction in the progress of the one as we did the other.

On this second try we had hired a private bulldozer operator to dam the lower reaches of the dale that the house we were building overlooked, and he had conscientiously packed its core with clay. But after the first rain it was obvious that our new pond, like its much larger predecessor, had a sandy bottom as porous as a sieve. It seemed that, this side of the Sahara, our least worst land had to be the most worst on the planet when it came to holding water. We were in despair. The prospect of having to live with the ghastly view of yet another gouged-out gully was so depressing that even Willie, usually an uncontrollable optimist, glumly suggested that maybe we should hope for another hurricane so we could move the site of the house once again. Roddy Ray, who came by now and then to supervise our house-building efforts, theorized that crawfish and moles were responsible for the leakage. Hovit helpfully proposed that we should pen up twenty or thirty hogs in the empty pond for a few months, the theory being that their trampled droppings would become as impermeable as cement. But even he didn't sound too convinced his idea would work.

Finally, after a couple of weeks of cursing the gods and wringing our hands, it occurred to us that it might not be a bad idea to seek professional help from the local county agent. As it turned out, this gentleman didn't know much about leaky ponds (or anything else as far as I was ever able to determine); but, having exhaled a great many heavy sighs to convey how overworked he was, he did ease himself over to an old file cabinet from which, after five or six minutes of searching, he extracted a pamphlet on the subject. And, wonder of wonders, it did in fact suggest a plausible remedy: Plastic!

Three weeks later we were unrolling several hundred square yards of thick-gauge polyethylene across the dry, yawning cavity of our would-be pond. When it was in place, we dusted it liberally with bentonite, a powdery white clay that becomes a gluey paste when exposed to moisture. (Normally the stuff is used to plug up oil wells, but we discovered that it works every bit as well on nostrils, pores, and lungs.) Finally, as a protective covering, we shoveled a couple of tons of bulldozed dirt back onto the plastic lining until the whole of it was buried several inches deep.

Then, in a state of almost unbearable suspense, we waited for the next rain.

It was a great day when that rain came, I can tell you. Every hour or so afterwards, we would trot down the slope to measure the foot or so of water that had collected below the dam. It was hardly more than a deep puddle, but when we finally confirmed that it was actually *staying* a deep puddle, we took off our shoes and danced around in it like kids.

By September it was a puddle no more. At the time we were nailing down the last shingles on the roof. The work went more slowly than it should have because we paused so often, happily looking down from our high vantage point at the gleaming half-acre of rainwater collected below us. We could still hardly credit it, but there it was: Our very own honest-to-God pond!

Believe me, if you have a place in the country — and if there is no compelling ecological consideration that prohibits it — you have got to have some sort of pond. Even if, as in the dry Southwest, it amounts to no more than a pool not much larger than a bathtub filled by the garden hose. Or even if, in wetter regions, you are lucky enough to have a brook or streamlet running through your property. In the latter case, a simple weir or diversion channel may be all that is needed to create a quiet water surface; in the former, one or two of those huge galvanized cattle troughs sunken in the ground (equipped with sloped ramps so toads and other small things don't get trapped in them) will serve. In between, there are all sorts of other possibilities. Depending on the amount of rainfall, the topography, the makeup of the soil, you may want to try a pump-fed pond in a flat field, a series of flushable catchments in an arroyo, an artificial backwater fed by a stream or drainage culvert, or the sort of pond that Willie and I finally achieved, with rain runoff backed up behind a dam.

Siting is important, of course: You'll want the pond near enough to your house to be comfortably in view, but not so close that your presence will keep wading birds and other wildlife away. And if it is any size at all, you will need to check out state and federal laws concerning wetlands and do your own survey to make sure you won't be harming some significant biological feature of your property — a bog or a swallow nesting bank or something like that. When Willie and I blocked off first one, then another, of the Place's drainage ravines with dams, we were so taken with the idea that we were creating new ecological habitats that we never paused to consider whether we might be messing up ones that were already present. Luckily, our thoughtlessness seems not to have had any serious consequences. Rain runoff drains out so quickly from our first fiasco of a pond that the dam might as well not be there; and the second one is so high up on its drainage ravine, and so frequently overflows at its spillway, that the pitcher plant bog a couple of hundred yards below is in no danger of drying out. Still, it's no thanks to us that our finagling with the Place's natural drainage system has done no apparent harm.

Although it's not nearly as much trouble as a swimming pool, a pond usually does require maintenance from time to time. It may start to leak or silt up or get choked with dead leaves or aquatic vegetation. Over the years ours has tried to do all of these things at one time or another. We solved the silting problem by re-excavating, every two or three years, a shallow trap at the back of the pond that catches most of the sand washed down the slope by sheet erosion. Where the silting problem is more serious, a landowner would do well to install a culvert with a valve in the base of the dam so sediment can be periodically flushed out. Such an outlet will also come in handy if eutrophication sets in or fish populations get out of balance.

As for the problem of too much aquatic vegetation, there are herbicides available that are supposed to be harmless to fish and water birds and people, but I don't trust them. If you have a fairly small pond, like ours, it is much simpler and cheaper to weed it occasionally, just as you would a garden. Not that I had any luck selling that analogy to Willie, whose slowly acquired tolerance of the reptile world still had its limits. "No indeed," he said. "There's no way I'm gonna go grabbing around underwater and come up with a fistful of snake." Which is why the job of pulling out bushels of pennywort, a small, self-introduced waterlily with a spaghetti-like root system, always fell to me. I complained on principle, but in fact water weeding was much cooler work than garden weeding. And I never did pull up a snake, although on one occasion a bemused diamondback water snake swam up to within a few feet of me and hung around for a while, apparently trying to figure out what the devil I was doing.

As for the pond's natural disposition to leak like a sieve, its polyethylene lining, even after all these years, continues holding water as securely as a stoppered bathtub — except in the shallows along the banks. There the upward pressure of tree roots, the rambunctious cavorting of Sammie and our friends' kids, and, most disastrous of all, the incessant plucking action of the ducks and geese we presently acquired, had the eventual effect of shredding the plastic pretty badly. As a result, during dry spells the water level dropped a foot or two, exposing a narrow black band of mud along the banks. It was no big deal ecologically, but aesthetically that oozy, unsightly rim offended my Platonic Ideal of what the perfect pond should look like. So I eventually splurged on a second well and pump — the one we used for the house couldn't handle the job — that had no other purpose than to keep the water at a respectable level even during the longest drought.

It took a while, but I believe that Plato himself would have conceded that what we ended up with was a pretty close approximation of the Ideal House Pond. I could write a book just about that, our pond, the many ways in which it gave us pleasure. Pines and live oaks and, later, the sweet gum and water birch we planted, mirrored themselves in its dark surface. Wild iris, day lilies, and palmettos lined its perimeter. Chicken turtles, which colonized it on their own, after accomplishing unimaginably heroic overland treks, sunned on logs especially arranged for them along its banks. Our first livestock, a pair of mallards, quickly made themselves at home in it. Stocked bass cruised back and forth along the dam like miniature sharks, checking out schools of perch and minnows for a prospective meal. On spring nights the amphibian set made the shallows ring with their courtship music: chorus and cricket frogs singing tenor and countertenor respectively, bullfrogs weighing in with their constipated bass, and the toads, loudest and most penetrating of all, trilling their wanton little hearts out like hundreds of small burglar alarms going off all at once. And, on quiet mornings when we and the dogs were inside, green herons and little blue herons sometimes stalked the banks.

The herons loved the pond. The turtles, bass, frogs, and ducks loved it. Willie and I most certainly loved it. Even Schaeffer, who enjoyed watching the frogs eek and jump when he poked his nose at them, loved it in his quiet way. But no one loved the pond more than Sammie. He was constantly plunging in and out of it like an otter, dragging so much water up the slope with him in the thick lining of his fur — to be shaken onto the first fully dressed person he could find — that he alone could account for drops in the water level. Although in all other respects unheroic, he had a fixation about saving Willie and me from drowning. If we were swimming, or just floating about on an air mattress, he would come paddling out, grab the most handy arm or leg in his jaws, and proudly tow it and its attachments back to shore. Schaeffer worried about us drowning too, and while Sammie was busy rescuing us, he would anxiously pace the bank like a lifeguard that doesn't know how to swim, ready to resuscitate us with a few slurps to the face when we were reluctantly hauled ashore.

Usually we found these antics pretty funny, especially since Sammie would get bored with his hero role after the third or fourth rescue and leave us alone, at least until next time one of us decided to do a few laps or float around a bit. But there came a day — it was the summer of our fifth year at the Place — when this canine obsession with rescue missions loused up an otherwise thrilling and memorable event.

Long before that day came round, I had discovered that wild animals and birds do not seem to recognize us humans for the dangerous creatures we potentially are as long as we look like a piece of flotsam floating on a pond. I had made this discovery under rather regrettable circumstances. Our pair of mallard ducks had settled down so satisfactorily by the time the pond was filled and the house more or less finished, that when spring came around they decided to raise a family. The hen sequestered herself in the dogwood grove at the back of the pond, sitting a clutch of eggs, while Willie and I and the drake kept our fingers crossed and hoped for the best. Then, one Sunday evening, just an hour or so before Willie and I were to drive back to New Orleans and our weekday lives, the proud mother came sailing down the pond like a royal barge with eleven animated bits of yellow fluff bobbing in her wake. It made for an exciting sendoff, and we headed for the city in a happy mood.

Alas, however, our joy was not to last. When we got back to the Place the next Friday evening and rushed down to the pond to see how our mallard family had fared in our absence, the answer was all too obvious. Only three of the ducklings were left.

The list of potential suspects was fairly long, and since some of them might be abroad that night we decided to take no chances. While the parents squawked in outrage, we herded their surviving progeny into the shallows, scooped them into a box, and carried them to the house. Willie, who found baby anythings irresistible, was especially upset about what had happened. We went to bed still speculating about who the mystery predator might be.

The following afternoon we found out. We had taken a break from working our first vegetable garden at the new site and were cooling off in the pond. The dogs, having gone through their saving-us-from-ourselves routine a few times, were asleep in the shade of the porch, and Willie and I had settled down to a nice, relaxing float, he on an air mattress and me in an inner tube. Suddenly the peace and quiet was broken by the hysterical gabbling of the adult mallards, who until that moment had seemed to be accepting the disappearance of their offspring with a fortitude that, in my opinion, bordered on callousness. Since Willie and I were floating on our backs, we didn't even have to turn our heads to see the cause of the commotion. A pair of red-shouldered hawks, wings outspread, were coming in low over the pines below the dam. As we watched, they twice glided back and forth along the entire length of the pond, no more than ten feet above the surface, their fierce yellow eyes searching the beds of iris, the palmetto shadows. The white of their breasts, the bands across their tails, the curl of their talons — every lovely detail was vividly distinct. We held our breath. The ducks fell into a panicked silence. And then with a sad wild cry, the one hawk said to the other, "Let's go; they're not here," and away they sailed, never realizing that they had been within spitting distance of the species that, more than any other, they had reason to fear.

Not that they had any reason to fear me; but Willie was another story, at least to hear him talk. He was not at all as thrilled as I was to have had such a close-up view of the birds that had done in his ducklings. "I've been trying to think positive about snakes," he fumed, "but don't go expecting me to do the same with those mean-eyed buzzards! Next time they come around, I'm gonna borrow Roddy Ray's gun, see if I don't!"

I figured there was no point in arguing with him just then. It was part of the central goodness of Willie's character that, regardless of race, creed, sex, or species, he would automatically side with whomever or whatever he perceived to be the underdog in a given situation. With that kind of bias, I knew it was just a matter of time before he would conclude, with little help from me, that in the sandhills of Mississippi as in the world at large, glamorous but occasionally inconvenient predators like these hawks were the real underdogs. How could they understand that they weren't supposed to feed *our* duck babies to *their* hawk babies? Which was, in fact, what was going on: the red-shoulders, presently to become *our* red-shoulders, were raising their young in the Hollow, as they and their descendants would continue to do for several years to come. Before long Willie would be every bit as willing as I was to share the Place with them; with the proviso that he, not the hawks, would collect broods of ducklings as soon as they were hatched.

When it came to wildlife viewing, the pond became my blind. And a very comfortable one it was, with me having nothing to do but float around on an inner tube or a rubber mat like a bump on a log. Doing that, I could eyeball basking turtles and leopard frogs from a foot away. Perhaps a dragonfly, chewing gruesomely, would make a meal of a damselfly while sitting on my knee. Several times I had such intimate views of green herons catching tadpoles that when they swallowed, I gulped. A belted kingfisher, a regular, dive-bombed bream that came to nibble on my toes. Once a great blue heron alighted softly on the bank just three or four yards away. In the evenings, swallows, nighthawks, and bats zapped flies and gnats out of the air above my head.

But of all the close-ups that the pond afforded me, the most glorious and most frustrating had to do with a set of visitors so unexpected and unlikely that even now I can hardly believe they actually did — literally — drop in.

It was late June. To escape the mid-nineties heat, Willie had taken to the house for a siesta, and I, to the water. Not that the pond offered much relief; at the surface, it was about as cool as a warm bath. Even Sammie, after one halfhearted attempt at dragging me and my inner tube ashore, gave up on the whole idea and joined Schaeffer in a snooze under a shady tree. The heat made me sleepy, too. I had shut my eyes and was just dozing off when I became aware that, at intervals, a dark shadow was eclipsing the red glow of the sun behind my closed eyelids. When I opened them and squinted upward, I expected to see a vulture cruising overhead, but right away I knew I was looking at something else. It was hard to see in that glaring sunlight, but when I shaded my eyes I could make out a huge white bird with long trailing legs, an outstreched neck, a curving bill. Unmistakably a curving bill. At first I supposed it must be a white ibis — which seemed unlikely enough, the Place being far removed from the bird's usual marsh-land habitat. But just when I was deciding that it *had* to be an ibis gone astray, even though it seemed much larger than it ought to be, the bird changed direction; its broad wings, the undersides shadowed until then, were now tilted toward the sun so that the striking black trim along the flight feathers was clearly visible. Years before, in Florida's Corkscrew Swamp, I had seen those splendid saillike wings banking in just such a way, and I had never forgotten the sight. It was impossible, yet I had to be looking at a wood stork, an extremely rare and endangered bird. Although it was known sometimes to visit Mississippi's river swamps and bottomlands, the upland sandhills were the last place I would have expected to see it. I could hardly have been more surprised if I had seen a phoenix.

The stork circled above me once or twice, as though reconnoitering; then it sailed off, and I assumed I had seen the last of it. But a minute later it came into view again — with six friends and relatives in tow!

Now all seven were circling overhead, losing elevation with each slow turn. Before long I could see the dark wrinkly skin on their necks, the black gleam of their curved bills. There could be no doubt about it. They were going to alight on the pond! They were already putting down their long legs like landing gear.

The recollection of that moment still moves me. Imagine the small arena of the pond with my basking self at its center; and just overhead, gyring round and round like fantastical creatures in some dream carousel, those huge, magnificent birds. I held my breath. They were coming in; the first of them had actually broken the water's surface with its long toes . . .

And then, bedlam. Before I quite realized what was happening, the storks were frantically fanning their wings to gain altitude, putting distance between themselves and the pond as quickly as they could.

It was the dogs, of course. Awakened from their afternoon nap by that large stir of stork wings, they had come charging down the slope to save me from what must have looked to them like a flock of monstrous avian carnivores about to make a meal of me. Their mission accomplished, they approached me with tails wagging, wearing huge self-congratulatory grins on their faces — but something in my own expression stopped them on the bank. A second later they were in full retreat, pursued by a string of maledictions that touched on everything from their unpedigreed origins to their certain fate at the dog pound, to which I swore I'd send them. Schaeffer, even as viewed from the rear, was clearly assuming his St. Martyred Canine role as he headed up the slope. But Sammie, when he was at a safe distance, shot me back a look that said, plain as words, that hell could freeze over before he came to my rescue again.

Of course, it is easy for us to forgive dogs, and even easier for them to forgive us. But for months afterwards, Willie, as well as any house guests who happened to be around, had to listen to me retell in the manner of Yeats how seven mysterious, beautiful wood storks had almost but not quite graced our little pond with their presence, how I had heard the bell beat of their wings above my head, and how, at the last minute, they had scattered, wheeling in great broken rings, and flown away.

13

An evening interlude

One evening in July of 1971, Willie and I were sitting on the upstairs porch, enjoying the view of the pond, the shaggy middle ridge, the distant backdrop of blue pines, and the western sky aglow with the flamboyant pinks and lavenders the setting sun was trailing in its wake.

We hadn't been there long when Griswold, who had been watching out for us, came swooping around the corner of the house. Wings fluttering almost soundlessly, he hovered like a gigantic moth above our feet, which were propped up on the railing, and finally chose one of mine to land on.

We had acquired Griswold several months earlier, when a student of mine had come into my office carrying a cardboard box. He explained that he had salvaged its occupant from a nest in a deserted, soon-to-be-demolished fishing camp and, knowing of my interest in wildlife, had brought it to me. When I peered into the box, a baby barn owl peered back at me. One look at him and I started laughing, and agreed to adopt him on the spot.

Unlike baby mammals, which are almost always appealing to look at, nestling birds — especially young birds of prey — tend to be seriously homely. But even in that unprepossessing league, owlets win the Ugly Duckling contest hands down. When I brought this one home later that day, Willie shook his head and said the poor thing looked as if he'd just been tarred as well as feathered. So unsightly was he, with his goofy Muppet eyes and oversized yellow feet sticking out of a mussed, scruffy blob of down, that it was impossible not to love him.

We soon discovered that feeding a baby owl was not a simple matter. Griswold's appetite was voracious, so much so that we had to carry him back and forth to the Place with us for fear he'd starve to death if we left him unfed for a couple of days. But the real problem was that we couldn't just stuff him with ground horsemeat and be done with it, as we originally intended. When we called the zoo for advice, we were told that baby owls had to be fed the same sort of rodent prey their parents would have brought them in the wild — bones, fur, tail, and all. Indeed, according to the zoo person, the frequent regurgitation of fumets — neat little balls of animal fur and bone — was absolutely essential to the healthy functioning of an owl's digestive system.

Faced with the necessity of providing our new pet with a reliable supply of rodent meat, I had a bright idea: Psychology majors at the university used hordes of white rats in their mostly inane and repetitive behavioral studies, and since the hapless creatures, after being conditioned to one student's maze, were unfit for anyone else's, they were summarily dispatched. Why, I asked myself, should all that rat protein go to waste when we had an orphaned owl that could put it to good use? So, that very afternoon, while the lab was briefly unoccupied, I surreptitiously collected a dozen euthanized rats that a cooperative graduate student had agreed to leave out for me, and stuffed them in my briefcase. When I got them home, I chopped them into pieces that Griswold could comfortably swallow, put them in plastic bags, and stored them in the freezer compartment of the fridge. I suppose I just blanked out the Willie factor. At any rate, when he came home that evening, I forgot to mention my ingenious solution to Griswold's dietary problems. Only later, when I heard him rummaging in the freezer, did I realize there was something I'd meant to tell him; but by then it was too late. One second Willie was debating whether we should have chops or sautéed chicken livers for supper; the next, you would have thought from the way he carried on that he'd opened the meat locker in *The Texas Chainsaw Massacre*. His "Oh no! Not *rats!*" must have been audible three blocks away.

I tried to explain to him what nice clean rats these were, how hygienically packaged, how inoffensive to the eye once one put aside one's outdated bourgeois prejudices; but Willie was not to be reasoned with. He agreed that Griswold should have his rat dinners; that was not the issue; but henceforth they would be kept in an ice-packed cooler, not sandwiched between the frozen ground beef and the Sealtest ice cream. The problem with this arrangement, of course, was that in a cooler their shelf life was limited to a few days instead of several months. Which meant that I had to make the trip to the psychology lab a lot more often than I had planned. Inevitably, this increased the number of times that I might be, and in fact was, caught by colleagues and students in the act of helping myself to handfuls of rats. The first time this happened, I did my bumbling best to explain about owls and fumets and all that, but while I jabbered on, the psychology professor whom I was addressing just kept staring in horrified fascination at my open briefcase crammed with lecture notes and dead rodents. So after that, I simply grabbed the rats, grinned sheepishly at whomever might be looking on, and fled.

Griswold was as unmoved as Willie by the mortifications I endured on his behalf, but he flourished on his white rat diet, growing with phenomenal rapidity into a beautiful, mature-looking (if not acting) barn owl with a soft dishlike face, and plumage in which shades of russet brown and black and white were exquisitely combined. By late spring he was spending most of his time perched on the edge of his nest box, flapping his wings experimentally. He regarded anything that moved as a potential food dispenser, so whenever anyone passed by, even Schaeffer or Sammie, he would squeak excitedly and come hopping after them, demanding to be fed some morsels of rat. Then, one evening I arrived home to find him sitting atop the doorway transom like Poe's raven, quothing his usual owl equivalent of "I'm starving!" while roundabout the furniture displayed a day's worth of fumets and splashy excrement. That same evening Willie and I agreed it was time to transfer him permanently to the Place, where he could begin learning to hunt rats for himself.

The problem was, he didn't want to. I did my best. I tried to hack him by tying strings to dead rats and dragging them at a run across the lawn. But instead of swooping down on them, Griswold would hop along behind, flapping his wings and hissing petulantly. Sometimes, exasperated, he would fly up, alight on my head (which I quickly learned to cover with a cap), and ride along until I came to a panting halt. Only then would he do a little swoop and land on the cooperatively motionless prey.

In desperation, I took a stricter line with him. While we were at the Place I stoked him with as much rat meat as he could eat. Then, when we departed, I left him at first with two rats, and later, only one, draped atop fence posts where fire ants would not too quickly find them. We felt like heels, abandoning him like that, but it seemed the only thing to do if he was ever to learn to make it on his own.

For the next two months he was always there waiting for us when we returned, flying out of the shed or a nearby tree, plaintively demanding his dinner. It was difficult to tell whether he was having any luck at all hunting for himself. Sometimes it seemed to us that he was just going through the motions of asking for food; he would peck a few times at the rat we put out for him and then carry it off instead of devouring it on the spot. But other times he acted as though he was really famished, and with his squeaking and hissing he let us know it was all our fault.

He didn't hold grudges, however. Usually he stuck around and socialized for a while even after he'd been fed, which was what he was doing on this particular evening. While Willie and I di-

vided our attention between him and the sunset, he did his usual
owl things: bobbing his head and swiveling it around, blinking
one huge eye and then the other, fluffing out the creamy feathers
on his breast, hissing softly now and then. At one point, to show
he wasn't playing favorites, he hopped over to sit on one of
Willie's feet.

Then, as quietly as he had arrived, he flew off.

It was the last time we would ever see him. Willie, always the
optimist, would insist that he had simply decided he was old
enough to manage on his own. I wanted to believe that too. It was
possible, after all, that Griswold had gone off in search of the
fertile, rodent-rich grasslands that are the preferred habitat of his
species. But I couldn't help feeling he was still too dependent on
us, that his departure was too abrupt. Hovit and Roddy Ray had
promised to leave him alone if he descended on them in search of
a handout, but that was no guarantee of his safety in an area
where most of the male population wouldn't hesitate to shoot an
owl just for kicks, especially one that looked different from the
familiar barred and great horned varieties. When he failed to
show up the next time we arrived at the Place, I couldn't help but
suspect that he had come to a bad end.

On this resplendent evening, however, we didn't know that Griswold had flown softly out of our lives for good. After his departure, we sat there quietly on the porch for some time. Finally
Willie let out a musing sort of sigh.

This was an invitation for me to ask him what he was thinking,
which I did.

"Oh," he said, "just that it's sort of strange."

"What's strange?"

"You know; the way everything has happened. How bad the
hurricane made us feel. Only, if it hadn't come along, we'd still be

stuck over there on the middle ridge, looking at that old dried-up pond. And probably we still wouldn't be finished building that first house. Whereas now we have this nicer house over here, and a pond with water in it."

"It's an ill wind that doesn't blow somebody some good, eh?"

"Something like that."

Willie was the Pollyanna, not me. Objectively, at least, I knew even back then that life can sometimes deal us a blow from which we never fully recover. All the same, Willie was right. There are some disasters — the medium-size kind that don't absolutely cripple one's mind or heart or body — that actually do turn out to be, as the cliché has it, blessings in disguise. We knew people for whom that had proved to be the case: the bright young instructor, turned down for tenure, who went on to make a fortune in the business world; the middle-aged woman friend, betrayed by a faithless spouse, who later met and married Mr. Right. So why not also a pair of naive landowners, demoralized when their first ambitious efforts came to nothing, who had managed to create on the second try what they actually wanted in the first place?

It was something to keep in mind if any more medium-size disasters came our way.

After we had again fallen into a reverie for a while, it was Willie's turn to ask what I was thinking.

I told him: "I want a deer."

"Humph! And you're the one always telling me we can't have wild animals as pets!"

"Not a pet deer. Just a deer."

A few weeks earlier, an artist friend of ours had had a showing of his latest paintings, mostly big impressionistic landscapes of the Louisiana marshes with swatches of yellows and blue-greens denoting grass and water, and blurs of blueish lavender in the background representing trees. They were impressive but brooding things, silent, empty of life.

When I dropped by the gallery, the artist told me about a rich Texan who had come in the previous day and hovered for some time around one of the paintings, looking fidgety and indecisive. Finally the fellow had approached my friend and rather shyly asked him, "If I buy that painting, can I . . . can I have a duck?" It took my friend a second to realize what the Texan meant. "I suppose he hunts waterfowl or something like that. He felt the picture wasn't complete, you see. So, way down in the right-hand corner, I painted him a little bitty duck. And I made the sale!"

I felt a little like that Texan. I was staring out at the middle ridge and its centerpiece, a tall, rather sculptured-looking dead pine left over from Camille. The sun had reached the horizon and was casting a golden light almost horizontally across the rough meadow grass on the spine of the hill, leaving the slope below in shadow. The scene was very quiet and beautifully composed. Yet something, I felt, was missing.

And so, at the moment when Willie asked me what I was thinking, I was asking the Artist, whoever He or She was: "Can I have a deer?"

I didn't expect to get one, of course, and that evening I didn't. But the next evening, same time, same station, someone must have waved a magic wand. At any rate, I got three: A doe and her two yearling offspring came up the ridge, pausing now and then to browse, moving languidly across our field of vision, posing briefly together at the base of the dead pine. Their sleek bodies were exquisitely outlined in gold.

After a long moment, the deer moved out of sight. But they had been there, I had seen them. I knew that from then on, whenever I looked at it, the picture would be complete.

14

A morning
with Hovit

Hovit could be very generous in an impulsive way, especially when he was drunk. He was just a little bit in that condition — we could tell from the blurriness in his voice and the way his good eye sometimes crossed with the glass one — when he came over to visit one afternoon not long after work on the second house had been completed. He found us putting up a fence along the perimeter of a roughly rectangular area we had marked out that would encompass the house, the pond, and the shed we had recently built, as well as the dogwood grove and a couple of acres of trees and grassy slope that we planned to landscape. When I mentioned to him that we were going to dedicate a corner of this compound to a vegetable garden, he shook his head doubtfully. "I remember that sorry garden y'all planted on the other hill when you first moved here. You ain't gonna do no better this time if you don't break up the ground right. Y'all better come get my tractor and disk; it's the only way you're gonna get that soil turned over good."

We agreed that the tractor and disk would indeed come in handy, and promised that as soon as we were finished with the fence we would pass by his house to pick them up.

A week later, when we turned into his driveway, Hovit was sitting on the cement ledge of Lurlee's neatly swept porch. Right away, we could tell this was not the best time to be paying him a call. He was leaning forward in an awkward way with his head between his knobby knees, very like a puppet when its strings have gone slack. And, very like a puppet, his head snapped violently back at the sound of the approaching van, as though one of those strings had suddenly been pulled taut. Then he struggled to his feet and, arms outstretched for balance, flung himself toward the door of the house.

"Poor guy," I said to Willie. "I guess he doesn't want us seeing him like this." Obviously he had been on a week-long bender and was in no condition to be dealing with visitors. As fast as I could, I started backing the Volksbus out of the yard.

"Lookit," Willie said, "he must have changed his mind."

Hovit had managed to get himself inside the house, but he had no sooner disappeared than he was back out again, whacking the screen door against the wall as he stumbled forward. For a moment he stood there at the edge of the porch, holding on to the back of a rocking chair, looking as dazed and unhappy as an amateur actor who has forgotten his lines.

Willie said, "Maybe he didn't want us thinkin' he was being unfriendly."

But whatever Hovit had been thinking, he evidently changed his mind once again and decided to get back inside the house. Again there was the lurching, headlong retreat, only this time his foot caught on the rocker. Instantly, his small, frail body became a sort of human projectile, spinning out of control toward the cinder block wall beside the door. When he hit it head-on, we could hear the thud of the impact from where we sat in the van.

It was all too much for Hovit. He plunked himself back down on the edge of the porch in an attitude of abject misery, rocking to and fro, holding his poor bashed head in his hands. As I backed us over the cattle guard at the entrance to the yard, I caught a glimpse of Lurlee barreling out of the house. To judge from the look on her face, she was ready to go the cinder block wall one better.

"Well," Willie sighed, "I guess we can forget about the tractor, leastways this weekend."

But he was wrong. Next morning we were awakened by the chug-chug of Hovit's tractor as it advanced across the gray, misty ridge with spectral Hovit aboard, looking like Life-in-Death in *The Rime of the Ancient Mariner*. He was using the whole of his scrawny body to turn the wheel, clinging to it not just to steer but to keep from falling off the seat.

Willie got some coffee going, and I helped Hovit to climb down from the tractor and into the house, where he propped himself, half sitting, half lying, on the old sofa we had lately acquired. His forehead was black and blue where it wasn't skinned raw, and he was sickly pale and weak; but to judge from his elfish smile, he had already had an anesthetic hair or two of the dog that had bit him, early as it was.

While the coffee brewed and Willie went off to examine the tractor, I tried to make conversation by asking Hovit about the old days and, in particular, about his life and times as a bootlegger. At first the old outlaw in him gave me a wary one-eyed stare as though to ask why I wanted to know. But once he was launched on his reminiscences, he seemed to enjoy himself, no doubt glad to be distracted from his aches and pains.

At that time, Hovit's mother was still alive, though just barely. Usually she kept to her room, but I had once glimpsed her sitting on the porch when Willie and I were driving by — a tiny, dried-up old lady who, from a distance, looked exactly like Hovit in sunbonnet drag. About his father, however, I knew nothing except that he had died when Hovit was still a child. Now Hovit filled me in on the unexpected way he had met his end:

"Him an' his best friend was at this joint one day, drinkin' — they was just young fellas, y'know — an' after a while my paw's friend got to feelin' pretty good, so him an' this other fella got in a fight. Well, before you know it, he grabs this big Stilson wrench —"

"The other fellow?"

"No, my paw's friend. Anyways, he rears back and hits him with it."

"Hits the other fellow?"

Hovit looked annoyed that I couldn't follow a simple story. "No! Hits my poor paw! He was meanin' to hit the other fella, y'see, but when he swung back real hard, he hit my paw instead. Broke his head just like that."

Hovit rubbed his own sore head in empathy. "And him his best friend too," he sighed.

From there, Hovit went on to speak wistfully of the days when he himself was a young man; how a bunch of the fellows would load up a keg on an ancient flivver and head down the dusty roads toward some roadside joint where they would find, perhaps, unattached women and, almost always, a chance to brawl. "If there was a fight," he said, "we'd all get into it. An' if nothin' was happenin', we'd just get back in the rig and head for somewheres else where somethin' was. If the car or wagon broke down, hell, we'd shove it in a ditch and move the keg to somebody else's rig. Them feds knew better than to mess with us when our spirits was up like that. If they'd tried anythin', we'd 'uv killed 'em." For a second, Hovit's still-good eye lit up with retrospective menace, even as his rubbery lips curved into a nostalgic smile.

You had only to listen to Hovit for a little while to realize that what made the good old days good was living life on the edge. He had never grown up. Even now, he was still a thrill-seeking youth, trapped in the somewhat wasted body of a middle-aged man. He wasn't into making bootleg whiskey just for the profits, most of which he squandered. What he really relished was the lifelong game of hide-and-seek he played with the Law. The risk and the danger were the turn-ons.

The game never languished for close calls. Once Hovit and a partner named Lester were cornered at one of their outfits in what was now our Brainch. Three federal officers had slipped up to the edge of the Brainch, where they could see Hovit and Lester pretty clearly through the trees. With guns drawn, they warned the two of them not to move. Lester, however, ducked behind the condensing barrel and, using it as a shield, dove into a thicket of catbriers behind him. Hovit was more exposed, so when the feds, furious at Lester's vanishing act, ordered him to put up his hands and stay where he was, he did as he was told. But to reach him, the officers had to cross the Brainch, and, as Hovit grinningly told it, "they was afraid to get their feet wet." The first of them, trying to keep his footing on a rotting log while keeping his eye on Hovit, slipped and fell, momentarily distracting the other two. Hovit seized his chance, dove into the catbriers just as Lester had, and made off up the opposite hillside. "Lester could hear me behind him, y'know, an' he thought I was the feds, so he naturally runned faster an' so did I. Course I couldn't call out, and so we kept goin' an' goin', and all the while them thorns was peelin' the shirt and skin off us like a potato knife. Finally we didn't have a breath left between us, an' Lester just gived up an' fell down, squeakin' 'Don't shoot, oh please sir, don't shoot! I give in!'"

Remembering, Hovit coughed and hooted dimly. "I fell over him an' he squealed like a stuck pig. But we got away. We done reached the road an' got clean away!"

There were times, however, when the game turned deadly. Ten years earlier, there was a particularly relentless federal agent operating in the county — "a terrible man," according to Hovit, by which he meant a man who was admirably fearsome, not afraid of anybody — who was notorious for his success in collaring moonshiners, Hovit himself not excepted. One day he followed a woman he knew to be the lady friend of a local moonshiner, one of Hovit's nephews. He tailed her as she drove along the entrance road of what was now the Place, and then, on foot, descended the very ridge where we sat, heading for the Brainch. "I reckon she was bringin' my nephew some cigarettes or somethin', but anyways, she led that sonuvabitch right down to where the boy was workin' his outfit."

The agent arrested them both and marched them back up the hill to where his car was parked. What he didn't know, however, was that Hovit's nephew had a partner, a man named Horace, who was every bit as terrible a fellow as the agent himself. According to Hovit he had killed a black man and wounded two or three whites without ever going to jail, and had battered and beaten many other men in a long list of fights at roadside joints. This Horace was coming along the entrance road, meaning to relieve Hovit's nephew, at just about the time he and his girl were being arrested by the federal agent. Seeing the agent's car half-hidden among the trees and deducing what was afoot, he stationed himself at the curve where the old widow woman's house had once stood, shotgun at the ready. When the fed's car came into view, with his handcuffed prisoners stashed in the back seat, Horace shot the agent at close range. The car went bumpity bump into a tree, the door sprang open, and the agent fell out, his arm half blown away. Horace and the two prisoners fled, figuring the agent would bleed to death. They were wrong, however. He managed to get a tourniquet around his arm and made it to the county road where someone found him; and so he lived to identify his assailant. "Now that time," Hovit said, "they did give Horace five years, seein' as how he'd shot a fed." But after that experience, the agent was never quite the same terrible man again. "Before long," Hovit said with a sardonic grin, "he gived up that line of work."

Talking about the past had rallied Hovit for a little while, but soon enough he began to wane again, beset by the pangs of alcoholic withdrawal. He put the coffee I'd given him aside. "You wouldn't happen to have a beer, would you, Don?" he asked, knowing full well that I did. I fished a cold can out of the refrig and handed it to him. It was none too soon. Willie had started fixing breakfast, and the smell of frying bacon was turning Hovit's complexion from waxy gray to green. I went out into the morning, meaning to get started on the garden before Hovit did something extreme, like passing out, but when I turned the tractor's ignition key, it wouldn't start.

Hovit chug-a-lugged his beer and tottered over to have a look. He pronounced the battery, which had been giving him trouble for some time, officially dead. "But it don't matter," he said. "I got another one loaned out to a second cousin of mine that lives close by. We'll just get that one."

The second cousin's establishment was located on a hill a couple of miles away, right next to a garbage dump; or more exactly, in it; for there was no clear indication of where the one ended and the other began. It was a surreal and cosmically depressing scene: a bare hill, an unpainted shack, black smoke billowing up from a pile of burning tires, a fleet of dead automobiles, a yard strewn with broken glass and aluminum cans dully glinting in the gray morning light.

Hovit knocked, then banged on the unresponsive plywood door, all the while mumbling that he knew damn well the cousin was inside. Finally the door opened and a young woman, hardly more than a girl really, stepped out on the rickety front step. She was still pretty in a fair, bland way, but her features were already becoming a touch puffy and coarse. She said, "He'll be out in a little." That was it. No greeting, no introductions, not even a questioning look. In fact, she didn't look at us at all. It wasn't shyness; just pure lack of interest. Her face was expressionless except for a hint of vague, undirected anger in the milky blue eyes.

While the three of us stood there mutely, two small boys, perhaps three and five years old, hair blond almost to whiteness, squeezed past the woman and came scooting out the door. Unlike their mother, they stared at us, inarticulate but fascinated. Hovit patted their heads and gave them an exhausted smile. They crowded up to him, but as they did so, a furious frown crossed their mother's face. Her free-floating anger had found a target. "Raybert!" she screamed. "You got on your brother's *shoes.*" It was a fact that the younger boy was wearing shoes that seemed too big for him, whereas his older brother was barefooted; but the mother's fury seemed out of all proportion to the offense, such as it was. "You get inside and take them shoes off this minute or I'll beat the shit outta you!"

Raybert's reaction was to cower behind Hovit's legs; he clutched his worn, baggy overalls so tightly that poor Hovit almost lost his already shaky balance. The boy was trembling. It occurred to me that I had never seen a small child actually trembling with fear before.

"Now, now," Hovit soothed, petting the blond head. "You take off them shoes an' I'll give 'em to your maw." To the young-old girl-woman he said, "He ain't done nothin' all that bad." He gave her the shoes. She gave him a sullen look. At that moment I really loved Hovit. He was so obviously unwell; the beer had only steadied him a little, but he went on standing there, wearily patting the boy's hair, repeating, "Now, now, now," until at last his second cousin appeared and the mother withdrew.

The second cousin was no more disposed to look at us directly than his wife had been. He was in his mid-thirties and had a taut, rather handsome face; but the skin was already beginning to stretch hard across the frame of his skull. In another five or ten years he would look like Hovit.

While he finished scratching himself and buttoning his shirt, Hovit told him about wanting the battery back. For the first time the man seemed aware of me. He gave me a casual, noncommittal glance, nodded, and went to fetch it from a sagging shed behind the house. As soon as he handed it over, we left.

The man never did say a word to either of us. When I looked back as we drove away, he and the little boys had disappeared.

"Now there's a good enough fellah," Hovit said, "but he could live a little better than he do. He just can't stand regular work or a boss, y'know. He runs a little whiskey — but then he drinks half of it hisself. So he just do get by."

When we got back to the Place, Lurlee was waiting there in a blue pickup on whose fenders and doors the mud had splashed a pattern of scalloped red waves. While Willie helped Hovit install the new battery, I invited her to come into the house and sit down. But Lurlee was in no mood for sitting. Her round face was still wearing the furious look I had glimpsed the previous day when Hovit brained himself. Through gritted teeth she said, "I get so damn mad I could tear my hair. The God's truth is, I *do* tear my hair." She looked as if she might demonstrate. "I seen what it did to my paw, my first husband, my uncle — and now him! I *hate* it! Makin' whiskey is one thing, drinkin' it is somethin' else. Jus' lookit him, he can't hardly stand up. And yet, do y'know, it makes him sly. He'll be so drunk he's crawlin' on the ground, but he can always remember where he's hid some whiskey. Out in the corn field, sometimes. Or else he'll steal the car keys whilst my back is turned, and me not knowin' if he's wrecked that good truck or not. The God's truth, I don't know what to do when he gets that way. He don't turn mean and try to beat on me, like some would, but that's the most I can say for him."

She stared grimly at Hovit as he made his shaky way from the tractor to the pickup. When he tried to open the truck door, he almost jerked himself off his feet. "You jus' keep the tractor long as you want, Don," he called, tugging weakly at the handle. When the door still refused to open, he flopped into the back of the pickup, propped himself up against a spare tire, and stared blindly at the sky like someone in a tumbrel on his way to the guillotine.

"Jus' look at him!" Lurlee said as she marched over to the truck and yanked open the door that had defeated Hovit.

Willie and I watched as the truck passed through the gate and disappeared around the curve where the old widow had once lived, and where Horace had shot the federal agent. Then I climbed aboard the tractor and started disking the garden, the putt-putt of the revived engine ricocheting against the low gray sky. What I was listening to, however, was Lurlee's voice saying "I *hate* it!" And what my thoughts kept returning to was that defeated hill and the sight of that little kid cowering behind Hovit's shaky legs.

I felt that I'd had enough of the picturesque subject of moonshining for that particular weekend.

15

The gopher

It was a big help having Hovit's tractor and disk to do the initial groundbreaking for the garden, but after that we bought a secondhand rototiller, relying on it to cultivate the soil, and on hoes and our hands to do everything else. In truth, neither Willie nor I ever would get quite as excited about vegetable life as animal life; but even so, we took great satisfaction in watching the seeds that our own hands planted become the healthy vegetables that our own hands gathered. When, that is, they did become healthy vegetables, which they didn't always. Even when we had nothing to show, however — when the tomatoes were afflicted with blossom-end rot, or drought stunted the sweet corn — we felt so virtuous engaging in what is universally recognized as a wholesome activity that we never considered our gardening efforts wasted. Not only was the physical exercise good for you, but it was a known fact that weeding a few rows of beans or drowning handpicked bugs in kerosene could be as effective as scream therapy for working off stress.

Right off, we subscribed to *Organic Gardening* and read it religiously, enthralled by its paeans to the virtues of mulching, its descriptions of a hundred easy ways to make compost, its heartening assurances that anyone can grow picture-perfect veggies without dosing them and the soil with fertilizers or pesticides. We needed no persuading to eschew pesticides, albeit more out of concern for what they might do to the local bird life than to us. As for composting, we dutifully raked oak leaves and pine needles into hog wire bins, added some cow manure, damped and tamped and aerated just as the organic people advised, and, when the decomposition process was complete, rototilled the rich dark mix into the anemic earth of our garden plot. And it did help, I have no doubt of that. But given the soil we were working with, even the most richly rotted compost couldn't accomplish miracles. After a while I concluded that people who contribute articles to *OG* must be blessed with land vastly more fertile than anything the Place could boast of. Even the Soil Conservation Service people sounded a bit apologetic for not being able to provide a more cheerful analysis of the soil samples we sent them. Our "thin sandy loam," it seemed, was deficient in just about every mineral known to man. Although we didn't apply the huge helpings of lime and commercial fertilizer they recommended, we did decide that if we were going to grow any vegetables at all, we had better use some, and so we did.

The way it worked out, we almost always had the most success with our late winter garden of cold-climate vegetables such as lettuce, cauliflower, cabbage, and broccoli, the reason being that winter temperatures in southern Mississippi, although rarely falling to freezing, stayed chilly enough to keep the bug population down. But even the more vulnerable early summer garden had its qualified successes. The trusty green beans almost always came through for us; and we were usually able to harvest a good many tender baby squash before half the vines withered and died in May of some sort of bacterial wilt. As for the tomato plants, those that managed to survive assorted blights and the ravages of voracious hornworms (which always seemed to attack when we weren't around to pick them off), produced fruit that made their supermarket counterparts look and taste as if they were made of wax.

Even in its best years, the garden never did look like a vegetable wonderland; but once we outgrew our initial cornucopia fantasies we didn't mind that. As a concept, a garden was an important feature in the Master Plan that we were working out; but in practice all we asked of it was enough fresh and frozen produce to supply our own table for much of the year. Which was about what we got by the time droughts, frosts, bugs, and other blights had had their way with it.

Strictly speaking, I suppose the gopher could be numbered among the blights, but that was hardly the way I thought of him. Not even when he moved into the garden for the second time.

Early one morning in April 1972, as the winter garden was finishing up and the summer one was getting under way, I was checking the rows of sprouting greens to see how they were coming along when I was stopped in my tracks by an unexpected yet not altogether unfamiliar sight: The row ahead of me looked as though someone had taken a shovel to it with a vengeance, burying half a dozen plants under a broad apron of raw dirt. But even before I took a closer look, I knew a shovel hadn't done the digging. The dirt had been excavated from a newly dug den, its sizable mouth shaped like a serving bowl turned upside down.

For some time I stood there, staring at that dark hole and the raw dirt fanned out in front of it, shaking my head, smiling and frowning by turns.

I was standing in one garden, but I was seeing another — that first little garden we had attempted during our second spring at the Place, the one that Hovit had rightly called "sorry." Eloise and Cora had helped us plant it, the understanding being that we would all share in its produce. On afternoons when the two women showed up, Willie and I would drop whatever we were doing and join them in working the little patch of ground we had cleared, Willie and me hoeing the thinly chopped soil into rows while Eloise and Cora sprinkled fertilizer and placed the seeds.

Looking back, I could not only see the two women, I could hear them chatting as we worked. Eloise's small talk almost always had to do with domestic themes. Between little gasps and pants from stooping over, she would relate adoring, if not exactly riveting anecdotes about Roddy Ray's accomplishments as husband and father, or, in even more lavish detail, the incredibly cute little sayings and doings of Baby Gladys. At the time I had exchanged more than a few covert eye-rolls with Willie when Eloise got going on some such subject as the precocious way Baby Gladys had taken to potty training, little dreaming that before another spring came around, I would find myself wishing I still had that prattle to listen to and roll my eyeballs at.

Undeniably, however, Cora's commentaries had been a lot more entertaining than poor Eloise's. Cora had both a romantic soul and a robust taste for gossip, and she liked men. She never talked about her own husband, long deceased, but she had much to tell us about the extramarital affairs, drinking habits, and reputed sexual prowess of everyone else's. One of her most moving stories was about the demise of Bubba, the husband of her good friend Lena, some months earlier. It seemed that Bubba had a serious heart condition and the doctors had told him he wasn't supposed to get excited or exert himself. "But one night," said Cora, "the mood was on him real bad, and he kept askin' Lena until she said, 'Awright, Bubba, just go take your bath first.' So he took his bath, and then, sure enough, right whilst they was doin' it, he had his heart attack and died, with Lena pinned down there under him — him bein' a real big man, y'know. And when Lena was wrigglin' out from under him so she could call the doctor, the poor man just rolled right off the bed and landed on the floor! I think that's such a terrible shame, don't you? Lena claims she couldn't help it; but I believe she could'uv been more careful!"

From the way Cora had paused in her seed planting, looking misty-eyed and letting out a sigh, it was obvious that, notwithstanding the rolling-off-the-bed part, the thought of Bubba's
liebestod still had the power to stir her soul.

Cora also filled us in on Hovit's second cousin, the one Hovit
and I had visited in search of a battery: how his first wife had run
off, and how, soon afterwards, the county people had to take his
twelve-year-old daughter away from him because he was "both-
erin'" her. Cora shook her head disapprovingly. "That's why he
took up with that gal he's been livin' with the last five or six years.
Told everybody she was sixteen at the time, when a blind man
could see she weren't a day over twelve herself!"

Another day, Cora confidentially told us what the sheriff had
confidentially told her about what he had told Vera and Wilbur
a little while back: "That if they didn't stop all that shootin' at
each other, keepin' decent folks awake at night, he was goin' to
split 'em up — they're just common-law, y'know — and put one
of 'em in the state asylum and the other in the penitentiary." To
this she added, "I do believe it's done some good. The doctor gave
'em some pills, and I ain't heard a shot out of 'em this past two
weeks."

I agreed, now that she mentioned it, that it had been quiet up
at Vera and Wilbur's house for at least that long.

≠†≠

Since the weather was still cool when we got that first garden
started, Willie and I had decided to try growing winter vegetables
such as broccoli, cauliflower, and two or three varieties of lettuce
along with the usual spring things like sweet corn, green beans,
and squash. Cora and Eloise contributed a good many hills of
cow peas, black-eyed peas, crowder peas, and okra. They said we
could have their share of all that "rabbit food," meaning the
lettuce and broccoli, if the real rabbits didn't get to it first.

As it turned out, the rabbits didn't get it, but something else did. We had just gotten to the point of congratulating ourselves that our rows of lettuce and broccoli were coming up before anything else, as they were supposed to do, when disaster struck. Between one weekend and the next, all but a dozen of the broccoli sprouts had disappeared, and most of the young lettuce plants were missing half their leaves.

Rabbits were by no means abundant at the Place; in fact, weeks would go by sometimes without our seeing one. Still, they seemed the obvious culprits. When Willie pointed to a sizable den hole that had been freshly dug between two of the rows, I shook my head. "We can't blame armadillos. They eat worms and bugs, not vegetables."

The next morning the last of the broccoli had vanished and the lettuce plants were minus most of their remaining leaves. Since I wasn't about to start blowing rabbits away, I resolved to be philosophical about the whole thing and just not worry about it. When Willie started grumbling — he was still in the early stages of becoming a wildlife preservationist — I told him that as soon as we got settled and started a really serious garden, we'd put a rabbit-proof fence around it and that would solve the problem.

There the matter rested until later that day when Roddy Ray came riding up on Joker to have a supervisory look at the garden in which his womenfolk had invested time and effort. "Why shee-it," he exclaimed when he had looked it over and checked out the den in the middle of it. "You got a goddamned gopher eatin' your greens. If you're gonna catch him, you got to come out here after dark and grab him afore he gets to his hole."

I was already learning that Roddy Ray's pronouncements on natural history were not always accurate, but I had assumed that when it came to hunting he knew what he was talking about. Yet here he was, telling me how to catch a gopher — he even remarked that they were "good eatin'" — when I knew for certain that these little ground-dwelling rodents were not native to Mississippi (and even if they had been, a person would have to be awfully hungry to consider eating one of them). It was only because my friendship with Roddy Ray was still in an early stage that I refrained from telling him he was talking through his hat.

That night, however, after Willie had fallen asleep, I kept thinking about what Roddy Ray had said and finally decided I might as well have a look. I armed myself with the flashlight and headed across the ridge, the sleepy dogs trailing at my heels. When I got to the garden I didn't see anything unusual at first, but Sammie did. Keeping a safe distance, he started barking at what, at first glance, appeared to be a huge turtle — except that I was sure it couldn't be that, at least not an aquatic one, not up here on this high, waterless ridge.

Which meant that I had to be looking at a tortoise. A gopher tortoise to be precise — the first of its kind that I had ever seen. I was thrilled that such a remarkable creature should be sharing the Place with me; but also astonished that, large and slow moving as it was, I hadn't been aware of its existence until now. I was glad I had kept my mouth shut when Roddy Ray was holding forth about gophers. He may not have ever heard them called tortoises before, but still, he had been half right, whereas I had been all wrong.

Later I would learn that gopher tortoises are the only one of the three North American members of their genus that live east of the Mississippi, their range limited to the dry sandy hills and flatlands of the Deep South's coastal pine belt. They are prodigious diggers, excavating tunnels up to thirty or forty feet long that end in an enlarged chamber far enough below ground to maintain a relatively stable temperature and humidity all year round. The tortoise is a wonderfully tolerant host, not minding that all sorts of creatures use its burrow as a temporary refuge or permanent home. Some, like the gopher frog, the indigo snake, and many invertebrates, are so dependent on its hospitality that when the tortoise becomes rare, they do too.

In those days, gopher tortoises were not rare in the sandhills but they were both sedentary and secretive, which was why I hadn't realized we had a colony of at least five or six of them in residence on the Place. They spent almost all their daytime hours in their dens (which I had mistaken for armadillo burrows) and came out at night to browse on forbs and grasses. Or tender young lettuce and broccoli if someone was thoughtful enough to plant a garden in a spot to which they could conveniently relocate.

Pleased as I was to add the tortoise to the list of the Place's wild residents, I worried about its making itself at home in the middle of our garden. After all, Roddy Ray and his family had as much claim to its produce as Willie and me. So far, the tortoise had expressed a marked preference for our "rabbit food," but these were about finished off, and I had serious doubts that Roddy Ray would take a tolerant view if it started in on the just-sprouting crowder peas and okra. Besides, he had said that gophers were good eating!

While I was debating what to do, Sammie and, less enthusiastically, a bemused Schaeffer, kept the tortoise barricaded in its heavy dark shell, but now and then it ventured its legs and head out enough to hiss and shift its weight a little closer to the burrow entrance. I had the feeling that if I didn't do something soon, it would make a break for it, dogs or no dogs. So, after a little more dithering, I finally scooped it up — it must have weighed fifteen pounds — and with soothing reassurances and murmured apologies, lugged it over to the index ridge where I knew an abandoned armadillo den was located. When I set it down in front of the cobwebbed entrance, the tortoise made a rush for it, just as I'd hoped. Its carapace was too wide for the hole, but it solved that with a spate of furious digging. Within a couple of minutes it was out of sight.

Evidently the new accommodations proved adequate, for the tortoise never returned to its burrow in the vegetable garden.

Ironically enough, it wouldn't have made much difference to the garden if it had. A week or so later, a drought — the worst in ten years according to Roddy Ray and Hovit — descended on the Place. Willie and I managed to keep our newly planted shrubs and fruit trees watered from drums that we filled at Roddy Ray's pump and hauled to the ridge in the Volksbus, but the garden had to fend for itself. By the time the rains got back on schedule, even a gopher tortoise would have starved on what was left of it.

I don't suppose I had been traveling in time for more than a minute or two, but I came back from that past garden to this present one feeling oddly displaced. Four years and four months had passed since we had first walked the Place with old Mr. Stanton. And only three years since Cora and Eloise had worked — and the venerable tortoise had dug its den — in that pitiful garden of which no trace remained. So much had happened in that time! The first little house. The hurricane. The Place a shambles. Poor Eloise dead. Roddy Ray with a new wife and recently a new baby. And Willie and I, like that tortoise in the garden, obliged to relocate and start all over again.

In retrospect those years seemed to encompass a great span of time, yet they had passed swiftly while we lived them, having been so crowded with beginnings and endings and new beginnings. Except for Eloise's tragic death, there was none of it that I regretted now. Yet still I felt uneasy, troubled by vague presentiments. After all, four years ago there had been no way we could have guessed in our wildest supposings that everything that had happened would happen. It made me wonder what the next four years had in store that I couldn't possibly foresee. Or the next ten. Or twenty. How many more beginnings, how many more endings would we face?

Ever since the day I had shared the spring with the grandfather of all cottonmouths — or maybe even before that — the Place had been making a do-it-yourself animist of me. Not full-time, of course; just every now and again I would see signs and portents in the natural world around me. Which was what I was seeing now as I stared at the shadowy entrance of the gopher's burrow. There was a perfectly good chance that this gopher tortoise was the same one I had lugged away from our first garden three years before. I had moved him from the middle ridge to the index ridge, and a year later we had done the same. He had chosen that first garden as his home, and now he had chosen this one. Moving in with us, you might say, as though his destiny and ours were linked. He, or someone, was trying to tell me something about how some things change and others only seem to.

I wondered briefly if I should come out to the garden when it got dark and intercept the gopher as I had that first time. He must have been busy all the previous night digging himself in; at any rate, there was no sign as yet that he'd been helping himself to the vegetables. We'd begun this garden early in the year, and had long since picked over the broccoli and lettuce; he was welcome to the plants that were left, which were going to seed anyway. Some of the other stuff, the tomatoes and eggplant and corn, was already well advanced in its growing and probably too stalky for his tastes. But the bush beans and kale and . . .

And then I remembered that on that night three years ago, I hadn't been concerned about protecting the garden from the gopher tortoise; I had wanted to protect the tortoise from Roddy Ray.

Some things didn't change. Still staring at that dark hole in the ground, I said, "All right, Brer Gopher; you can stay. You'll be our luck."

16

All livestock
great and small

'm not sure how Willie and I got so deeply involved in raising livestock. I blamed him. He blamed me.

Certainly, Willie's passion for poultry was what started us off. We had agreed from the start that he would have some chickens. And the pair of mallards were a nice ornamental touch for the pond (except when they were in moult and lined it with their feathers). But then he found the Toulouse goslings for sale at a farmers' market — attractive little things, all downy chartreuse — and he just had to have them. A few weeks later, when we were driving up to the Place, he saw a sign outside a trailer advertising guinea keets — baby guinea fowl — for sale, and since they were also irresistibly appealing it followed that he must have them too.

However, I will admit that the cows were my idea.

As for the horses, I blame Roddy Ray for them.

It is a natural, almost instinctive response, once one acquires some land in the country, to start seeing oneself as the farmer in the dell, surrounded by a Norman Rockwell painting's worth of cheerful barnyard animals. I'm not saying that the picture is altogether a false one; Willie and I were vouchsafed much pleasure by our assortment of livestock pets. But there is no denying that tending them can be a pain in the neck, sometimes an expensive one, and the novelty soon pales. On any given day, America is strewn from sea to shining sea with millions of For Sale Cheap chicken coops, hutches, incubators, cages, rolls of wire, and divers feeding contraptions — the reliquaries of countless people's amateur dreams of raising goats, poultry, rabbits, llamas, bees, Shetland ponies, or beagles for fun and profit. My advice, proffered, as usual, from the vantage point of rueful hindsight, is that weekend farmers should forget about the profit angle. The local demand for fresh eggs is practically guaranteed to be out of sync with the number of eggs your chickens can produce; and a side of beef is likely to be cheaper at a meat market than if it comes from a cow you raised yourself. Your best bet is to regard any venture in animal husbandry as a hobby. That way, if you squander a lot of money on fencing or tractors or whatever, you can later convince yourself that the investment was an intentional exercise in therapeutic self-indulgence, worth every penny that you lost.

As for the fun, it depends. Take our chickens, for example. We could excuse them for being unbelievably dumb; but even soft-hearted Willie, after giving them every possible benefit of the doubt, had to admit that they were also mean as hell, pecking on each other every chance they got. Since he could never bring himself to do them in, I was elected executioner whenever a culinary occasion required the sacrifice of one of his charges; but I noticed that, following the success of his first blanquette de poulet, he suffered these occasional decapitations with an equanimity that would have done credit to Madame Defarge.

Both of us much preferred the geese and guinea fowl. Not that they had much going for them upstairs either, but they were nicer to each other and more amusing to observe. The geese were convinced they were the very flower of avian civilization. They were terribly pompous creatures, reminding me of the dignified, corseted dowagers I used to see parading in neighborhood parks when I was a kid, gaggling censoriously among themselves about how the world was going metaphorically to the dogs. But like those stately ladies, our geese were easily discombobulated — especially if our unmetaphorical Sammie and Schaeffer went anywhere near them. When that happened, they would head for the pond in a great fluster, stretching out their wings and necks like bosomy ballerinas, exclaiming the goose equivalent of oh-where-are-the-cops-when-you-need-them? in querulous voices that carried from one end of the Place to the other.

Unlike geese, guineas never become hysterical because they are that way to begin with. Ours had the run of the shaggy lawn, and it was always entertaining to watch them scurrying about among the azaleas and oakleaf hydrangea, their skinny, wrinkled necks and salt-and-pepper feathers vibrating with panicky dismay whenever a blown leaf or the shadow of a blue jay crossed their path. The best show came in the evening as they prepared to go to bed. The birds would mill around frantically for five or ten minutes trying to decide where to roost. Finally one of them would make up its tiny mind and fly to the lowest branch of the nearest available tree. The rest of the flock would follow in fits and spasms. But no sooner were they all huddled together in a row than the birds on the outside, feeling unfairly exposed and insecure, would scramble over the backs of their fellows and squeeze themselves into the middle of the lineup amid outraged screams of protest, much wing flapping, and general consternation. It would take several minutes before the reshuffling was finally accomplished and everybody settled down again. Until, that is, one of the birds that had been rudely shoved to the end of the row would begin looking wistfully at a branch just above the one the flock was roosting on. After a lot of fidgeting, he would flap upstairs and immediately start telling the others how much nicer this new perch was than theirs. Agonies of indecision would afflict the left-behinds. What to do? What to do? they would putt-chuck among themselves. What they would eventually do, of course, was hie themselves, one after another, to the new branch, where they would once again settle down, just long enough for the outside birds to get nervous and want to be inside birds, whereupon the whole scenario would play itself out again. By the time nightfall put an end to the show, the flock would be in total disarray, scattered in disconsolate little bunches of two or three among the uppermost branches of the tree.

They were worth their weight in laughs, both the guineas and the geese, and we enjoyed having them around, so much so that we never exacted an omelette, much less a drumstick, from the lot of them. Like the mallard ducks, they had the great virtue of managing very well for themselves when we were away, as long as some hawk, feral dog, or fox wasn't trying to eat them. But they did have their drawbacks. The geese — there were usually six or seven of them — got along fine with each other, but our human affection for them was not reciprocated. They hissed and honked whenever we got too close, and if we weren't on the lookout, one of the ganders would sometimes rush up from behind and deliver a painful nip. Also on the minus side, geese defecate incessantly — something to do with the inefficient way their bowels work. We found that if we confined ours to a relatively small area they stripped it of every blade of grass and resurfaced it with slimy goose poop in a matter of days. As for guineas, they are the most raucously noisy birds God ever made, an offense to the whole idea of rural peace and quiet. There were moments when I could almost empathize with Hovit, one of the world's many ex–guinea owners, when he told me how, one morning, he took down his shotgun and dispatched half his flock because they wouldn't shut up while he was trying to sleep off a hangover.

The fact is that any type of livestock has its liabilities. Herewith, for what they are worth, are a few first- and secondhand observations concerning some of the pros and cons — mostly cons — of different varieties:

A lot of first-time landowners choose to raise goats because they are such an all-purpose animal, providing meat, milk, cheese, and even, in the case of Angoras, wool to knit sweaters. Personally, however, I have no use for goats. I don't deny that they have personality and intelligence, but the billies tend to be incessantly lecherous and evil smelling, the nannies hard to catch when you want to milk them; and, in most breeds, neither sex is much to look at once it gets past the cute kid stage. What I really have against goats, however, is the fact that this all-purpose animal has an all-purpose appetite for anything green. In historic times it has been largely responsible for turning vast areas of the planet, particularly in Africa and Asia, into deserts, and it will do the same to your Shangri-la if you give it half a chance.

My admittedly biased remarks about goats also apply to sheep, only more so, since sheep don't even have personality or intelligence going for them. Dumb as chickens, they positively invite mauling by the neighbors' dogs, or by coyotes if there are any around. Although their owners are really the ones to blame, sheep are the principal agents in the ongoing defoliation of our own Southwest, as well as many other areas of the globe. The world needs fewer of them, not more.

Rabbits, in ones and twos, are cute and lovable, but when you have cages full of them they become cranky and dull and contract diseases. There is no year-round commercial market for them unless you are prepared to butcher and clean them yourself; if you aren't, you'll end up practically having to pay people to take the young ones off your hands. If you must have rabbits, get a couple of spayed females that will let you pet them.

Of all the animals officially described as livestock, pigs are by far the most appealing. They are cheerful, friendly, intelligent beasts, and very handsome in their stocky way. Contrary to the popular notion, they like being clean and enjoy nothing better than a nice hosing down. The sows, it is true, are apt to absent-mindedly squash their litters from time to time if you don't equip your farrowing pen with a barricade that the piglets can slip under. But the main drawback to owning pigs is that, if you mean to butcher them eventually, you will have to raise more of them than you probably need for your larder. It is a great mistake to own only one or two, since it then becomes impossible to perceive them simply as roasts and pork chops on the hoof. And once you recognize a pig for the charming animal it really is, you will either end up keeping it as a pet for the rest of its natural life, or feeling guilty for the rest of yours because you ate it.

I'm not sure whether bees qualify as livestock or not. In any case, Willie and I eventually kept several hives of them with considerable success. They were a joy to listen to in the spring when they made the blossoming crabapples vibrate with their humming. And we always had a plentiful supply of their honey on the kitchen shelves, with a lot left over to give to friends. We didn't much mind that we were occasionally stung when we pillaged the hives, even when we used a smoker, since neither Willie nor I was allergic to bee venom. Nor did it trouble us that the honey we gathered never paid for the expensive extractor we bought to spin it from the combs. In our case, the only serious drawback to raising bees was *Galleria mellonella,* the wax moth. It insinuates itself into an active hive and lays eggs in combs that the bees are not tending. When its larvae hatch, they devour everything in sight, leaving the interior of the hive a shambles of ravaged combs covered with cloudy webs. If we had been professional beekeepers, or more conscientious amateur ones, we might have nipped these invasions in the bud; but we weren't, and we didn't, so in some years we lost two or three hives to this insidious pest.

Which brings us to cattle and horses.

First, cows. To begin with, I should note that I genuinely respect the vegetarian view that, since ten times as much grain is needed to produce a cholesterol-loaded steak as a wholesome loaf of bread, both we and the planet would be better off if we dispensed with meat-producing livestock altogether. Nevertheless, if, like Willie and me, you are an addicted omnivore, and if you have money to spare, and if your property already has some rangeland on it so you don't have to bulldoze the natural landscape, and if you feel compelled to have some large domestic quadrupeds wandering around, you might want to try keeping a few cows for a while. Dairy cattle, of course, have to be milked every day, so you can forget about them unless you plan to live full-time at your place, vacations included. Beef cattle don't require as much attention, and when they are not being woods cows they are likable beasts, easily made happy if you can afford the fertilizer and equipment for sweet hay and green pastures. Unlike pigs, however, they do not have much character. Willie and I found that the chief satisfaction of owning a small, well-cared-for herd comes simply from looking at them. When they are lolling around under a shade tree, fat and healthy, chewing their cuds, they are so obviously feeling placid and content that you are bound to feel placid and content just contemplating them.

In the spring of 1972 I plunged us into the beef cattle business by buying five Black Angus cows and a square, chunky bull we named Bully. Bully was the very antithesis of Mean Red. Whenever Willie or I entered the pasture, he would come over to us so we could scratch his curly forehead. I chose Angus partly because they are too short in the leg to jump fences; but mostly because they are solid black and thickset, so that when our little herd posed against the dark green backdrop of the Hollow, with a few cattle egrets in the grass around them, I could pretend they were African Cape buffalo lounging at the jungle's edge.

It was the county's recently enacted Fence Law, requiring all livestock to be under fence, that first put it into my head to raise cattle. The new law was a sign that times were changing in the sandhills, and although a lot of people like Hovit cursed and grumbled, it had the effect of making everyone in the county take cattle raising more seriously than they had before. With one side of his forty acres already bounded by my fence, Hovit hired some of his kinfolk to enclose the entire property. Then he brought in a Hereford bull to replace Mean Red, the intent being to upgrade his woodsy-looking herd. Roddy Ray had also gotten the cattle bug. He had bought, cleared, and fenced a half dozen acres around his new ranch home and was in the process of stocking the property — overstocking it, actually — with cows. All around us, other people were doing the same sort of thing: bulldozing pastures out of pinelands, putting up fences, going into debt to buy tractors and cattle and land.

With all that going on, it was bound to occur to me that we had ten acres of suitable open land on the thumb ridge of the Place, and that three sides of it were already enclosed by a sturdy fence that was no longer needed to keep other people's livestock out, but would serve very well to keep ours in.

In fairness (to me) I wasn't just suddenly infected with cattle mania. All along I'd been trying to devise a benign management plan for the Place; now it dawned on me that, with the help of a few cows, I could prove to my own satisfaction, if no one else's, that it was possible to utilize our land in a productive way and still live in harmony with the natural world.

To that end, Willie and I ran a barbed wire fence along the one open side of what was now the Big Pasture, and then bisected it with a cross fence. During the late winter, we rented Hovit's tractor, disk, and fertilizer spreader, and after preparing the ground, sowed it with Bahia grass. We were lucky. There were good rains that spring, and by June of 1972, our newly purchased little herd was standing knee-deep in a fine stand of thick green grass.

Come fall, when the cattle had pretty much grazed both halves of the Big Pasture down, we overseeded the Bahia with winter rye. Meanwhile, we kept the cows on the index ridge, feeding them hay until the rye was ready for them. When it was, we rotated them between the two halves of the pasture, giving one half a chance to grow back while the other was being grazed.

I had it all figured out: Within two or three years the herd would increase to eight adult animals. We would keep it at that number, utilizing less than a fifth of the Place's acreage, selling off, say, three surplus yearlings each fall to pay for fertilizer and supplemental feeding. A fourth animal would be reserved for the secondhand freezer Willie had bought at Goodwill in New Orleans. Ours would hardly be a profit-making enterprise, but it would be self-supporting, and Willie and I would have all the hormone-free beef we could eat at no cost. Most important of all, not a single acre of woodland would have to be cleared, and the local deer and rabbits would thank us for the winter largess of succulent green rye grass.

It really wasn't a bad plan, even though it didn't quite work out. Bully and the cows did their part. Four of the cows were already pregnant when we bought them and dropped healthy calves that first summer. Later on, there would be a couple of stillbirths when we weren't at the Place to act as midwives; but in a mere two years' time we had the requisite eight adults and seven yearlings and calves out there on the Big Pasture's greensward, impersonating a herd of Cape buffalo just as I had hoped. Unfortunately, the Place's soil was so impoverished that phenomenal quantities of fertilizer and lime were required to produce enough grass to support that many cows — plus two horses we had acquired in the meantime; and even then, it wasn't really enough. In order to keep the animals looking placid and content enough to keep us happy looking at them, we had to buy a lot more supplementary hay and food pellets than we had counted on. Meantime, during those inflationary years in the middle and late '70s, the cost of fertilizer and feed was going up like everything else. The price of beef on the hoof was also rising steadily, until we were finally ready to sell our first batch of yearlings, whereupon it took an unexpected nosedive. When the bookkeeper handed us a check for those first three cattle sold at auction, I didn't need a calculator to know we were operating in the red. And that wasn't even counting the work Willie and I had put in, which was considerable. Raising cattle was proving to be a much more labor-intensive and time-consuming avocation than I had anticipated.

But the most serious problem we had to face, now that we had these surplus yearlings to dispose of, was one that had nothing to do with time or money. This was the prospect of having one of the animals butchered for our own consumption. When we sold the first three animals at auction, Willie and I assured each other that the special care we had given them, their sleek lines and gentle demeanors, would guarantee them long happy lives in someone else's pampered breeding herd. However, in the case of the fat, juicy young bull I had selected for our freezer, there was no way to get around the fact that we were sentencing him to death; and so we suffered terrible spasms of guilt. This was not, after all, the same as condemning some malevolent old hen to the stewing pot. Our plump little bull might not have as much personality as a plump little pig, but he was amiable in his bovine way, and very trusting.

Willie did his best to save him. "Why can't we just sell him like the others," he argued, "and then use the money to buy our meat at the supermarket like normal folks do?" But despite the quakings of my own conscience, I held firm. We were cattlemen, I said, and dammit, we had to act like cattlemen. Cattle were what humans had invented to take the place of wild prey, weren't they? so that was how they must be utilized. And besides, I argued, it was hypocritical to prolong the life of our own yearling at the expense of some other yearling that someone else was fattening up somewhere else. But the most telling point, in my own opinion at least, was that I had created a management plan and, by God, I was going to stick to it.

So despite Willie's protests the day arrived when, with the help of Roddy Ray and his rail-sided pickup, the yearling — which we had had the good sense not to name — was carried off to a local slaughterhouse. When I picked him up a week later, all neatly wrapped and labeled, I hoped that the transformation he had undergone would suffice to make Willie forget his qualms. But no; he refused to prepare so much as a hamburger, muttering, whenever I pressed him, vague comments about how trusting the poor animal had been, and what nice soulful eyes it had had. Undeterred, I cooked a nice juicy hamburger for myself; but with Willie looking on as though I were having a snack while snowed-in at Donner Pass, I just couldn't enjoy it as much as I felt I should have.

I don't know how long the impasse would have gone on if we hadn't had a house party scheduled for a few weeks later. After a little persuading, Willie grudgingly conceded that there was no harm in broiling some steaks for our friends, seeing as how they had not been intimately acquainted with our bull and were in no way implicated in his death.

That party occurred in the early autumn of 1974. By then we not only had a whole beef in the freezer, but a spring and summer's worth of fresh and frozen vegetables, so we were able to serve our eight guests a full four course dinner — chicken soup; a salad of baby squash, tomatoes, kale, eggs, and parsley; a main course of corn on the cob, green beans, *and* thick, tender steak; and, for dessert, blueberry pie — all of which, except the flour and some of the condiments, came from our garden, our poultry yard, our pasture — *our Place!*

The full realization that we had produced this bounty ourselves must have hit Willie, as it did me, only when we sat down at opposite ends of the long plywood dining table with our guests around us. When the soup course was over, Willie watched me cut a piece of steak and hold it on my fork for a thoughtful second before popping it into my mouth. He hesitated, then reached for the last steak on the platter, cut off a little piece, and did the same. Chewing slowly, only half-listening to the compliments our friends were showering on us, we exchanged a grin.

After that first bite, Willie went to work on his steak with a will. It wasn't just that these were the most flavorsome steaks he or any of us had ever tasted; he was letting me know that as far as he was concerned the ghost of our delicious young bull was finally laid to rest.

There was at least a sort of logic behind my decision to get involved with cattle. Whereas there is no rational way to explain why I bought Joker and Big Jim — except, as I've said, by blaming Roddy Ray. When he visited us on his own, he always rode Joker; and the sight of him galloping up the drive, looking as dashing and devil-may-care as a Cossack, put it into my mind that I might look that way too if only I owned a horse. I was especially vulnerable at the time because I had been rereading a number of eighteenth- and nineteenth-century English novelists like Austen and Fielding and Trollope and was going through a country squire phase. I figured that now that Willie and I had our own private estate, it was no more than fitting that we should go riding around it like proper gentry. So when Roddy Ray casually remarked that I could have Joker for a very modest sum, I jumped at the chance. And when he mentioned that his uncle also had a horse, a nice quiet one, for sale dirt cheap — just in case I wanted to buy one for Willie — I jumped at that too.

I know more about horses now than I did then. For one thing, I know they eat half again as much as a cow and are generally more expensive to maintain. For another, they tend to fit into one of three categories: They can be high-spirited but tractable, which seems to be the kind most people have; or they can be tractable but somewhat dispirited, which is the kind Willie had; or they can be high-strung, stubborn, man-hating, and hard-mouthed, which is the kind I had.

I was so pleased at the prospect of owning Joker that I didn't ask Roddy Ray about his background until some time later. Then, when it was too late, I learned that he had done time as a bronco on one of those backwoods rodeo circuits — the sort of ramshackle weekend setup where local would-be cowboys win a few dollars if they can just stay in the saddle for a little longer than most of them are able to, and where the broncos buck as they do because they've been jolted by sadistic rednecks armed with electric prods. It seems likely that many of Joker's failings as a mount were attributable to all those traumatizing shocks he had endured. However, that aside, he also had some very fundamental life adjustment problems. Unquestionably, he saw himself as an aggressive, horny stallion — an equine Rambo — yet this macho self-image was starkly contradicted by the fact that he was a gelding. I tried to be understanding, for I genuinely sympathized with the poor brute; but after he had done his best to kill me a few dozen times, I couldn't help but feel like an ACLU lawyer whose clients keep mugging him.

When I test-rode him before I bought him, Joker gave me some warning of what to expect, but not much. True, he was apt to hurl himself into a headlong gallop without any prompting from me. And he did have a hard, bit-chewing mouth. But it wasn't until after he was all mine that he really began living up to his name. As when, without warning, he would veer off course while running at full speed, ignoring the tug of the reins, taking me under a low branch or up against a tree trunk; or as when, seemingly content to move along at a dignified amble, he would suddenly bolt and buck for no perceivable reason; or, most bothersome of all, as when he would unexpectedly swing his rump around while I was saddling him and try for a good swift kick to my ribs. I reminded myself that he couldn't help being like that; as with the scorpion that stung the well-intentioned frog, it was just his nature. But whenever I thought of Black Beauty or Flicka or Smokey, or any of those other nice horses I used to dream of owning when I was a kid, I wondered what I'd done to deserve an animal like this.

In fairness, Joker did have one positive trait. He came when I called him. This was because he had an irresistible passion for Purina dog food, and he knew I always had a handful of it ready to proffer when I wanted to go riding. True, he often tried to take the hand along with the Purina, but I became pretty adept at getting the bit between his teeth while he was baring them.

It was typical of my whole relationship with Joker that I should have discovered his taste for Purina in an unsettling way. Late one night Willie and I were jarred out of a deep sleep by a jolt that would have done credit to a scale 8 earthquake. There was the loud crack of shattering wood. The house shook. Windows rattled. Much shaken and rattled ourselves, we jumped out of bed and peered down from the loft at the living room below. The only illumination was coming through the sliding door from the floodlight on the narrow deck outside. Inside, Sammie and Schaeffer were dark silhouettes jumping up and down, barking like mad. And outside, brilliantly illuminated and completely filling the eight-foot-wide door frame, was Joker. He had jumped over the compound fence, then up onto the deck — breaking the railing in the process — so he could help himself to the contents of the dogs' bag of Purina that we'd left on the porch.

Later that night, after we had chased Joker out of the compound and climbed back into bed, Willie had a bright idea. "We should call the Purina people," he said. "They could come down here and make this TV commercial where Joker is jumpin' the fence and chasin' Schaeffer and Sammie away from their supper, and then gobbling it up himself. It would show how good Purina is." I agreed that the concept was interesting, but neither of us could think of a catchy voice-over to go with the visual. Somehow "Horses will kill for Purina" didn't seem like much of a come-on for a dog food.

Willie's problems with Big Jim, a tall-in-the-withers, slightly swaybacked bay, were of an opposite, less drastic kind. The horse was amiable enough, but to judge from the way he moved you would have thought he'd been on Valium all his life. "I'm not askin' to be the Lone Ranger," Willie would sigh when Big Jim reacted to a heel in the ribs by trotting for three paces and then lapsing into a walk again, "but this is ridiculous."

Nevertheless Willie was fond of Big Jim, and blamed his lethargy on Joker. "That crazy horse of yours is all the time pickin' at him," he complained. "No wonder he's wore out."

We didn't talk about it much, but we could see that there was something a little bit kinky going on between Joker and Big Jim. Joker certainly did bully Big Jim, nipping him on the flanks, yanking his mane, occasionally giving him a playful kick. But when we tried separating the two of them, Big Jim was even more upset than Joker. He would come right up to the fence so Joker could reach over with his big front teeth and give him a reassuring bite or two. After a while, we agreed that the best policy was to be nonjudgmental and just ignore the whole thing.

From all this, one might conclude that Joker and Big Jim were total washouts. But that wasn't quite the case. During those fleeting moments between his attempts to dump me, Joker was an exciting horse to ride, and I did indeed feel, if not look, dashing and cossacky as we flew across the Place's hills and dales at what could be accurately described as breakneck speed. Moreover, because the horses were a familiar, unthreatening presence to the local wildlife, Willie and I were occasionally able to pass quite close to deer, rabbits, even a wild turkey once, without them being aware that we were along for the ride.

One day when we were in the Big Pasture, watching Joker and Big Jim going though their S & M routine, Willie said, "If we could just make one horse out of the two of them, he'd really amount to something." Which pretty much summed it up.

17

A damsel
in distress

One night in January 1971, a little more than a year after we moved into the second house, we had two visitors, one welcome, the other not. It was dark and cold outside. The porch light was on, but other than that, the only light came from the dying fire in the living room, in front of which Willie and I were comfortably settled, a good dinner inside us, cold beers in hand. The dogs were asleep at our feet. Simon and Garfunkel emanated, at a low volume, from the portable phonograph. The sweet, resiny scent of the new cedar plank walls filled the room.

I'm not sure what made me turn my head away from the glow of the fire to glance toward the closed sliding door; but when I did I was thrilled to see that there was a raccoon outside, crouched beside the feeder filled with cracked corn that we had set out for the geese and guineas. He was not, it is true, a very prepossessing representative of his species. His masked face looked pinched, his body was visibly gaunt under the scruffy fur, and he was plainly as fearful as an animal can be. But he was also hungry, and after checking behind the feeder a few times to make sure no horrors were lurking there, he began putting the corn away as fast as he could. Careful not to wake the dogs, I signaled Willie to look. This was the first raccoon we had ever seen at the Place, and for maybe five minutes we watched him alternately feeding his face and rearing up on his hind legs to check things out.

Then, suddenly, the show was over. We hadn't made a sound, the dogs hadn't stirred, but our visitor's nervous vigilance changed in an instant to outright alarm. In an eyeblink, he was gone.

A moment later the reason for the raccoon's flight made itself eerily visible: The beam of a flashlight was boring its way toward us through the dark. At the compound gate it stopped, and the beam played back and forth across the panes of the shut sliding door. Belatedly, the dogs bestirred themselves, Sammie excitedly yammering, Schaeffer woofing worriedly, his thick nails rapping loudly on the bare floor.

During the last several months we had grown unused to lights coming at us in the night. Most people in the area knew by now that we were living back here, and they usually kept away; but even if someone got as far as the gate before turning back, the chances were that we wouldn't notice he'd come and gone since this second house was so much farther removed from the entrance gate than our first little house had been.

What was disturbing about this particular someone's presence was that he hadn't turned back. He was afoot, half a mile from the county road at eleven o'clock on a pitch-black night. He could see our porch lights, he could hear the dogs barking, he must know that this house was on the way to nowhere and that he was trespassing. It couldn't be anyone we knew, and yet he kept on coming. When I asked myself what business he could have with us, none of the answers that ran through my mind were very reassuring.

"Maybe I should turn the dogs loose," I whispered to Willie. "Only I'm afraid whoever it is might shoot them."

"What we need," said Willie, "is a gun."

For a long moment we stood there, invisible behind the shining glare of the porch light, uncertain what to do. Then, above the din the dogs were making, we heard a male voice, unexpectedly plaintive, asking, "Anybody home?"

I pulled the door back a little. "What do you want?" I growled.

Some help, he said. His car was stuck in the mud. He had taken a wrong turn somewhere along the entrance road. From his account I realized that he must have ended up on the old track that led down to the Big Swamp and a washed-out bridge. There had been a heavy rain the preceding day; it would be a quagmire down there.

I told him there was no way I could get him out that night. I'd just get stuck myself.

"I know that," he said. "I was just wantin' you to take us home. I don't live far. I can come get the car tomorrow."

"'Us'?"

"My, uh, girlfriend is with me. I left her in the car."

"Don't go!" Willie whispered. "There's no tellin' who else he's got out there with him."

I wished with all my heart that I could take Willie's advice; but for the life of me, I couldn't think of a decent excuse for refusing to help the disembodied voice. So, telling Willie to lie low till I got back, I pulled on a jacket, collected my keys and a flashlight, and stepped outside.

In a duel of flashlight beams, I sized up the owner of the voice while he did the same with me. He was a lanky fellow in his twenties, with deepset eyes and a thin mouth in a long narrow face. The eyes were gloomily alert, but the jaw was slack and the brows pinched, as with a headache — the look of a man who had been a lot drunker an hour ago than he was now. Without further conversation we got into the van and drove as far along the muddy track as I dared take it.

"You get your girlfriend and I'll wait here," I said, my earlier nervousness having converted, by this time, to irritability.

"Ain't no need to go get her," the young man said with a resigned-sounding sigh. "Here she comes now."

Sure enough, the headlights picked out a figure slogging toward us along the wet, rutted track. Even at a considerable distance it was apparent that my companion's girlfriend was no girl. She must have been at least fifty, almost as wide as she was tall, and wearing an expression on her pudgy face fierce enough to have stopped even Mean Red in his tracks.

"Uh, she ain't exactly my girlfriend," the young man explained as the woman drew close. "I'm, uh, you might say, married. I was out doin' a little drinkin' tonight, y'know, and this ol' gal was at the VFW hall. And, well, you know how it is."

The lamentations of the not-exactly girlfriend loudly preceded her. "This is one fuckin' hell of a way to treat a lady," she bellowed. "Takin' her for a li'l joy ride and landin' her up to her ass in a fuckin' swamp!"

With a smirk, the you-might-say-married young man surrendered the front seat to her. Soon as she had climbed in, she pushed her sagging face close to mine, gave me a long appraising look, then announced, with a smile only half-furnished with teeth, "Now, yo're a *real* genniman, helpin' out a pore gal like this. Not" — she jerked her head toward the back seat — "like that asshole."

"Oh, it's nothing, nothing at all," I said, backing up the van while at the same time trying to escape a near-lethal exhalation of halitosis and stale beer.

The woman lived in one of a small collection of trailers and shacks that were clustered at a junction where the county road met the main highway to the Coast. Willie had christened this untidy enclave Dogpatch, and whenever we passed it en route to or from the Place, we kept our eyes straight ahead, not wanting to stare at its inhabitants staring back at us. Some of these people were kin to Hovit, but so far we had been successful in our efforts not to know them.

So far. Now I had sweaty visions of a cuckolded husband,

shotgun at the ready, peering out from a dark window, hot to find out who was bringing his wandering wife home. Unchivalrously, I suggested that the woman might want to disembark while we were still a small distance from the trailer she identified as home. "For appearances' sake, you know?"

It was the wrong approach. "Fuck appearances!" the lady roared, scorching me again with her dragon's breath. "Ah'm not goin' to *walk!* What you think ah am! Ah thought you was a genniman. You take me to mah do'."

I hastily acquiesced, at which she seemed mollified. "Anyways, you don' have to worry none, honey. My ol' man's out helpin' Hovit at his still."

"I hope!" the young man muttered from behind us.

"*You* hope!" I snapped. "If anyone's watching, it's my van they'll see."

The only effect this observation had on my passengers was to cheer the young man up a bit and make the woman want to comfort me. As she was about to disembark, she suddenly turned, taking me by surprise, and branded me with a kiss. "Yo're cute," she said. Then she waddled up the rickety steps to the trailer, leaving her swain of the evening without so much as a goodnight.

He didn't seem exactly crushed. "Whew!" he said as we pulled away, "I sure gets drunk when I gets drunk. But that's the worst I ever picked up!"

His "I don't live far" turned out to be ten miles. The front light flicked on as we drove up to the inevitable trailer in the inevitable bare dirt yard. When the man got out, giving me a muttered thanks over his shoulder, the aluminum door opened. A slim young woman was standing in the doorway watching him. Even in the harsh glare of the overhead light, I could see that her face was very pretty in a childlike way; but the features were all squeezed up, as though she had been crying or was about to start. She shrank back as her husband lunged up the steps and pushed his way inside. He slammed the door behind him, but even so, I could hear his muffled yelling, "Don't say a goddamned word, you bitch!" as I turned the van around.

Back at the Place, Willie was out on the porch, wrapped in a blanket, waiting to greet me with a relieved bear hug and a lot of questions. He listened to my tale of Prince Worthless, the ogress, the fair maiden in distress with frowning disapproval. When I'd finished, he said, "What we need is for that coon to keep comin' back. He's a better watchdog than Schaeffer and Sammie put together. He'd let us know to lock the doors and pretend nobody's home if people like that come around here again."

I'd forgotten all about the raccoon. It cheered me up to be reminded of his welcome visit. But when I lay in bed that night, it was to the young woman standing in the trailer doorway that my thoughts kept returning. Crazy angry thoughts. Like, if she ever decided to shoot her no-good husband, and I was on the jury, I'd vote to acquit her in a minute flat.

18

Short Tail and Damn Thing

The raccoon did keep coming back, the first of many generations of his kind that would visit our feeders in the years that lay ahead. The Place could offer only temporary sanctuary to wide-ranging wildlife like deer or hawks or foxes; but it was roomy enough for raccoons and other small game to inhabit on a full-time basis and be, if not completely safe, at least safer than anywhere else for miles around.

Since we were gone much of the time, we kept two homemade wooden bins stocked with cracked corn year-round for our free-roaming flocks; which meant that any of the local wildlife with a taste for corn could help themselves whenever they wished. After dark, that could mean rabbits, wood rats, deer mice, or the occasional opossum; but raccoons were the principal freeloaders. At first we were worried that they might lose their natural fear of humans, as they often do in suburbs when people feed them, becoming easy targets for any hunter who invaded the Place when we weren't there. However, they have been oppressed by humans for too long to tame down very much. During warm-weather months they usually preferred to hustle their own grub rather than brave the compound with its reek of man and dog. And when they did come to the feeders regularly, during winter, it was only after they'd done a lot of preliminary peering and sniffing around. To keep them as uncontaminated by the human presence as possible, we positioned the feeders at a considerable distance from the house, rigging the porch floodlights so we could see what was going on without being seen ourselves. Interestingly, music or voices on the radio or TV didn't bother our furry visitors at all; but if they heard a chair scrape or the toilet flush inside the house, they were usually gone in a flash.

Every once in a while, however, a cocky young raccoon or a possum with an IQ that was low even by the undemanding standards of its species did become too bold for its own good, showing up in the compound while it was still daylight. When that happened, I would frighten the too-brazen freeloader off by slamming open the sliding door and rushing out on the porch, waving my hands and jumping up and down, all the while making loud, hostile noises. The first time I did this, I not only startled a diurnal raccoon so badly that it fell into the pond, I also startled Willie, who assumed I was having some sort of seizure and insisted on wrestling me to the ground before I did myself harm. When I somewhat huffily explained what I'd been up to, it only confirmed his first impression of my mental state. "A grown man, acting like that!" he said disbelievingly. "A wonder you didn't give that poor little coon a heart attack like you nearly did me!"

Eventually we came to recognize some of the regulars that visited our feeders. Raccoons' tails are never quite identical. The line of the widow's peak on opossums' foreheads varies considerably. Older animals often have ears that are notched and nicked. And there are variations in size and build. But it isn't just a matter of distinguishing physical features. Individual animals have their own distinctive personalities. There are the dominant types, the nervous wrecks, the smart alecks, the clowns. It takes some practice, but after a while, wild animals of the same species are as easy to tell apart as dogs of the same breed.

In Short Tail's case, however, none of these refinements in the art of wildlife observation were necessary. We named him for the obvious reason. Either his pathetic excuse for a tail was the consequence of a genetic abnormality or, more likely, he had lost most of it in some close encounter of a dangerous kind. At any rate, what was left was so truncated that there was barely room for two black rings to show.

Short Tail turned up at the pond feeder in broad daylight one afternoon in June, less than half-grown and more than half-starved. He looked so much the orphaned waif that on that occasion I exempted him from my policy of terrorizing raccoons that broke the daytime curfew. However, when he showed up again the next day, interrupting the outraged mallards in the middle of their meal, I decided he wasn't going to last long unless he quickly forsook his diurnal way of life. Willie, watching me watch the raccoon through the sliding door, read my mind as usual. "Don't you dare scare him," he said, "leastways not until he's got some more food inside him! The ducks can wait."

"I was going to let him finish," I answered stiffly. And I did wait, along with the ducks, until he seemed to have put away as much as he was going to. Then I threw back the door and started yelling.

The effect on Short Tail was more than I bargained for. Instead of sensibly running away, he scooted up the nearest climbable thing in sight, a young Japanese maple not more than ten feet high, and clung desperately to its slender top branches as they, bending under the weight of his corn-stuffed body, lowered him to within a couple of feet of the ground. There he hung suspended, like a furry beanbag, so woebegone and pitiful to behold that I positively hated myself for having frightened him so badly. Willie didn't say a word; he just stalked outside, closing the sliding door on me and the suddenly interested dogs, and went down the slope to where Short Tail still clung to the deeply bowing maple. Gently, he bent the tree still further, until Short Tail's back touched the ground. At once the little animal let go his grip on the branches and scuttled off into the dogwood grove, as he should have done in the first place.

For all the trauma he had suffered, it was some time before Short Tail realized he was supposed to switch to the night shift. I limited myself to banging on the glass or rattling the screen door by way of frightening him away whenever he showed up during daylight hours, and he did indeed scoot off when I did this; but without a mother to show him the hows and wherefores of being a raccoon, he proved a slow learner. Once he got the idea, however, he did finally become nocturnal, literally overnight.

He still gave us plenty to worry about. During that summer and fall he kept returning regularly to the feeders, and we wondered how he was ever going to make it on his own if he kept gorging himself on corn. I revived the window-rattling treatment, but he would simply hide out for an hour or two before trying again.

Then, in December, just when our other regulars were beginning to show up at the corn bins, Short Tail stopped coming. He simply vanished at the very time of year when natural food supplies were getting scarce. I felt sick at heart, certain that he had become too dependent on human handouts and had ended up dead in some neighbor's yard. But Willie would have none of that. "You'll see," he said. "He's just a little shy of them other coons. Not having a mama, he don't know how to act." Sure enough, late in January, Short Tail reappeared at the feeders, noticeably thinner than when we had last seen him. As Willie had theorized, he did seem leery of his own species at first, as though he weren't sure whether he was a raccoon or not. But after a couple of weeks he began to get things straightened out. He learned what there was to learn of raccoon etiquette, sharing the feeders with some of the younger set, quarreling with others, and always keeping a polite distance between himself and the grouchy old boars and bossy matriarchs. When spring came around, he was the last to forgo cracked corn in favor of more natural fare, but eventually he did give it up. Three or four times that summer we saw him late at night helping himself to a little snack; but by

September even these infrequent visits ceased. Certainly I wanted him to be self-sufficient, but I couldn't help but wish we might still have a glimpse of him once in a while, just to be sure he was all right. When, in midwinter, he finally did return to the feeders, looking as runty and short-tailed as ever but evidently in good shape, I welcomed him with a sigh of relief. Willie, of course, had never doubted that he would eventually turn up again.

Raccoons were often more tolerant of opossums at the feeders than of other raccoons, possibly because they felt it was unsporting to pick on a creature that was so obviously mentally challenged. At any rate, it was not unusual to see the two species grubbing around within inches of each other, looking for sunflower seeds under the bird feeders or even dining side by side at the corn bins. Not that the opossums ate much corn; it seemed to be a food of last resort for them. This surprised us, considering the stories Hovit and Roddy Ray had told us about their unfussy eating habits: how they liked to settle down in a bloated cow carcass and feast for days from the inside out; and how you could bait them anytime you wished if you used really rotted meat. We didn't try the rotted meat, but if birds and squirrels had left a lot of sunflower seeds scattered on the ground or if we put out some dry dog chow as a special treat, we could count on seeing possums; otherwise, they were only occasional visitors at the feeders, and then only if the weather wasn't cold. Even in our subtropical latitude, where it was sometimes possible to get through an entire winter without a freeze, they apparently spent much of the season holed up in semihibernation.

Which, for their own sakes, was just as well. In the sandhills there is no other animal, with the possible exception of the armadillo, that is so unwary. Many is the time that, taking a stroll on a summer night, I have walked right up to an opossum before it was aware of me — so close I could have bopped it on the head with my flashlight. When it finally did react — much too late, had I meant it harm — it would sometimes scuttle off or scramble up a tree, but it was just as likely to sit back on its haunches in a transport of fear, jaws wide open, drooling all over its furry chest. If I happened to have the dogs along, it would skip the drooling part and faint straightaway — that famous ploy of playing possum, which isn't a ploy at all but an actual swoon. The unwitting tactic always worked with Sammie and Schaeffer; they were content to give the comatose creature a sniff or two and then move on; but I doubted that it was as successful with the abandoned, half-starved dogs that sometimes roamed the area.

Among all our possum encounters, one in particular stands out. Willie and I had just arrived at the Place one evening at dusk and were busy unloading the van when we noticed that the dogs were paying a lot of attention to an empty oil drum standing beside the shed. Approaching it, we heard agitated scrapes and thumps issuing from its interior. When we peered inside, from its dim depths a possum was peering back at us. It took a long aghast look at us, hissed a bit, and went into the usual drool routine. To our surprise, though, it chose not to pass out.

In a situation like this, Willie's reaction was easy to predict, so before he could even open his mouth I reminded him that it was against house rules to make a pet of a wild animal. However, Willie already had his arguments neatly lined up: If we only kept the opossum for a week or two, we wouldn't be making a pet of him, would we? And seeing as how it was our barrel that the poor thing had been trapped in without food or water, we were obligated to put some weight back on him before we turned him loose, weren't we? And since it so happened that the cage in which we kept our guinea keets and other young poultry was unoccupied at the moment, we had a nice, comfortable place all ready for him, didn't we? So what was the harm?

My own reaction was as predictable as Willie's. After having said absolutely no to his arguments several times over, I helped him pour the possum from the drum into a burlap sack, and from the sack into the nice, comfortable cage. There we left him to settle down for the night, amply supplied with water and dog food, while we went back to the unfinished business of unloading the van.

"We'll call him Pogo," Willie said as we lugged sacks of cracked corn, cattle pellets, and fertilizer to the shed.

"Not very original," I replied, "but since he'll be gone in a few days it doesn't matter. Meantime, just remember, you clean the cage."

That was that, as far as I was concerned.

Only it wasn't. Early the next morning, while I was in the middle of a pleasant dream that had me sailing through the skies on the back of an eagle, I felt Willie's hand on my shoulder, shaking me awake. "Come look! Come look!" he was saying in a horrified voice. "Poor Pogo is all tore up!"

Grumbling, "I told you we should have let the damn thing go," I followed him downstairs and out onto the front deck where the cage reposed. I hadn't known quite what to expect, but Willie was certainly right. The opossum was horribly mutilated. It had been too dark to see him clearly the night before, so there was no way of knowing whether he had injured himself before or after we put him in the cage; but injured he surely was. He was half lying, half sitting, slumped against the cage's wire mesh, hissing at us with an outrage that, in an opossum, seemed unnaturally aggressive. With his black, gimpy-looking paws he was trying to cover his protuberant belly. And no wonder! There was a ghastly wound across his middle, from which his entrails looked about ready to spill out if he moved around the least little bit. I squinted my eyes until the gash was a red blur.

"I'll call the vet," I said.

Ol' Doc Haley, our local veterinarian, lived fifteen miles away. He was scrawny and cranky and toothless; and because he disdained false teeth, he looked as though he was trying to swallow his chin whenever he shut his mouth, which he seldom did. He would go into tirades about city veterinarians who were afraid of "real animals" like horses and cows, and who pandered to "rich ol' ladies and their gawdamned lap dawgs." He was also outraged by — and envious of — the fees they charged. Since we were raising cattle at the time, and obviously did a lot of brute labor around the Place, we were not quite consigned to the rich old lady category, but the good doctor could hardly be blamed for regarding us with a critical eye. We were outsiders, and I talked funny, and Willie and I lived under the same roof. Still more outlandish, our pampered and useless dogs did, too.

Yet with all his quirks and prejudices, I liked Ol' Doc Haley. Though in his seventies, he was full of ornery life; and he was a capable and honest vet. He had shown us how to deliver a breech-birth calf so we could do it without his help the next time; and when Schaeffer was kicked by Mean Red, he had charged us only a couple of dollars for draining the resulting swelling, saying with his usual tact, "I can't take advantage of somebody dumb enough to bring a dawg way up here just for a li'l hematoma when any fool could'uv seen it would'uv cured itself."

Now I braced myself as I dialed his number, anticipating how he would react when I told him what the problem was this time. He didn't fail me: "A possum! You mean to say yo're worried about a gawddamned egg-stealin' *possum!* Hell, boy, just knock it in the head with a stick. That'll cure whatever ails it."

I told the Doc that the animal was, uh, well, sort of a pet.

"Hope you ain't keepin' him in the house with them dawgs," said Ol' Doc caustically. "Possum'll shit all over everything." There was a pause during which I could hear him exhaling loud sighs of martyred exasperation. Finally he said, "Well, it's yore money. Bring the damn thing in and I'll see what I can do."

"I can't," I said, voice full of woe. "I'm afraid if I try to get him out of his cage, his insides will fall out."

To my surprise, instead of launching into a string of invectives at this news, Ol' Doc sounded, for the first time during our conversation, more interested than annoyed. He asked me to describe exactly what Pogo's injury looked like. I was tempted to run out to the cage and take another look, this time with my eyes unsquinted; but, fearful of keeping the old man waiting, I decided to go for an impressionistic description instead. When I was finished, a brief silence at the other end of the line was followed by an unpleasant uh-uh-uh sound which went on for some time. Finally I realized what it was: Ol' Doc Haley was laughing! Something I hadn't thought he knew how to do.

By now my reader, if he or she knows anything at all about opossums, may have guessed at the revelation that was beginning to seep into my consciousness even before Doc Haley, between uh-uhs, mockingly spelled it out. I had known all along that the opossum's main claim to fame is that it is our only native marsupial. Which is to say, it belongs to an order of mammals, the females of which, for want of a placenta, must rear their embryonic young externally, usually with the aid of an abdominal pouch. But that knowledge had remained an abstract, if interesting, bit of nature lore tucked away in an attic corner of my mind — until now, that is. Now I realized that the ghastly gash that had shocked Willie and me was in fact this half-open, bright pink *marsupium* seething with tiny, hairless, red baby opossums, each latched on, full-time, to a maternal nipple.

As I hung up the phone, Ol' Doc Haley was loudly announcing to whoever was in his office, "Wait 'til you here what this fellah done called me about! Uh-uh-uh. You ain't never goin' to believe it! Uh-uh-uh." To Willie I said, somewhat coolly, "Guess what? You're going to have to give Pogo — *your* Pogo — a new name. The damn thing's a mother!"

But even though Damn Thing (as I persisted in calling her) had made a fool of me, I couldn't help but share Willie's interest in her and her gruesomely underdeveloped brood. Willie was fascinated by the whole idea of possum pregnancy — "Like having a live human baby eight and a half months before it's due!" — and I was curious to see how quickly the young would develop.

So I was easily persuaded to keep Damn Thing and her family longer than the agreed-upon week. The only problem was that Damn Thing had other ideas. Seized by some dim awareness of her maternal function, she refused to calm down. Even when we provided her with a box full of leaves to nest in, she would poke her head out and throw a temper tantrum every time we passed by. She hissed and drooled, but there was no question of her fainting, not that we wanted her to. When, after several days, she still showed no sign of becoming used to us, even Willie reluctantly agreed that her agitation could hardly be doing her or her babies any good. "Might sour her milk," he sighed. So late that evening, our feelings rather hurt at being so utterly rejected, we lugged the cage over to the Hollow and left it there, door open. When we collected it in the morning, Damn Thing & Company were long gone.

19

The cogitating deer

During the late '60s and early '70s, a good many of my students were among the legions of mostly young Americans who were "into" spiritual self-discovery — a quest they pursued with the help of drugs, transcendental meditation, vegetarian diets, psychedelic music, and (very important) communion with the natural world. At the end of every spring semester at least two or three of them would drop by the office, decked out in brand-new backpacks and hiking boots, to tell me that they were off to some Rocky Mountain wilderness where they could get in touch with themselves amid the glories of Nature.

Naturally I wished them luck, but I couldn't help being skeptical about their prospects. In my experience, what you get in touch with amid the glories of nature are the glories of nature, period. The self isn't what you find; it's what, with any luck, you are sometimes temporarily able to lose.

I'm not talking here about losing one's Selfhood in Oneness with God or the Universe or anything seriously mystical like that. I just find that sitting down by a tree or a rock and contemplating the natural scene, any natural scene, in an appreciative, quietly passive way can distract one for a while from the tiresome subject of one's own affairs. Not that this is something I do all that often. My interest in the natural world has always tended to be too involved, too protective and meddlesome, to allow much time for just sitting around *looking* at things. But whenever I have managed it, I've come back to myself afterwards feeling more calm and clear-headed, more capable of dealing with the way of the world than when I left.

Almost any spot on the Place was suitable for that sort of communing, as long as there was a stump to sit on or a tree to lean against, but the Hollow was where I usually planted myself. In the near and middle ground — there were no really long views at the Place — it offered the greatest variety of things to keep the eye engaged. In the piney woods or at the edge of the pitcher plant bogs the close-up views were variegated enough — sometimes, for example, a dozen grasses and sedges in bloom at the same time — but at a little distance the prospect tended to be somewhat uniform. In the Hollow, on the other hand, every perspective, every tenth of a perspective, was different in terms of texture, color, pattern. On a day in October, for example: A single mushroom gleaming whitely on the forest floor a few yards to my right; below, a lurid green cluster of royal ferns growing in an islanded spot where the ground is just right for their specialized needs, not too damp, not too dry; overhead, a large green Nephila spider, with hairy tufts on the double knees of her long legs, at rest in the off-center center of a web so enormous — and so strong! — that walking into it can give you a fleeting case of the sci-fi horrors; nearby, to the lower left, the magenta berry clusters of a French mulberry poking — with no regard for color coordination — through a screen of red-berried yaupon; and farther off, a large holly, its trunk stained by the lash-like stripes of a red lichen that seems to attach itself only to this one tree species.

Of course, Camille had had a lot to do with shaping the Hollow's visual diversity. The hurricane had itself been a natural occurrence; but it had unnaturally disrupted the successional stages that the Hollow's vegetation would have otherwise adhered to. When it struck, the canopy of the maturing hardwoods was just becoming sufficiently dense to prevent all but a sprinkling of sunlight from reaching the forest floor, thereby suppressing the growth of all but the most shade-tolerant plants and saplings. The storm had torn that canopy apart and let the sunlight back in. Not evenly, however. When I first viewed the Hollow after the storm, it had appeared to be as utterly demolished as our first little house; nothing left but bits and pieces. Yet it had rebuilt itself so swiftly that within three years the outline of its pre-Camille aspect was becoming recognizable again. Trees that had been half-uprooted stubbornly refused to die. Hundreds of others were feverishly replacing their amputated limbs and sheared-off crowns. Those that had merely been defoliated were taking advantage of the gaps around them to extend their canopies as swiftly as they could. The openings below were choked with young saplings, each desperately trying to outrace the others in its climb toward the closing gaps in the Hollow's broken roof. Meantime, with the same impartial energy, the forces of decay were also at work. The splintered surfaces of dead tupelos, bays, and maples were covered by oysterlike fungi and small ferns, while under the rotted bark legions of termites and borers reduced the heartwood cores to humus. All around on the forest floor this silent work went on, the boles of once tall trees melting almost visibly into the damp loamy earth.

Well then, whenever I managed to lose myself among these changeful wonders of the Hollow, I was very glad I did; but the spell of self-absence would last only as long as I was able to experience the Hollow's subtle cycles and transformations, its delicate patterns and fretwork as pure sensation, without consciously thinking about what they meant — to the Hollow itself, to the Place's ecology, to the local wildlife, to me.

Sooner or later, of course, I would start thinking about all that. Something interesting would happen and the entranced onlooker in me would convert to the involved participant. A moth would fly into the Nephila's web, the spider would begin the grisly business of wrapping it in a silken shroud, and I would shudder with vicarious sympathy. A gray squirrel, reassured by my stillness, would descend from its hiding place in a snag and start munching on that white mushroom to my right, and I would want to know how it knew the mushroom wasn't poisonous when I, a certified intellectual with a Ph.D. and a book on mushrooms back at the house, knew no such thing. Then I'd start wondering whether the squirrel was eating the mushroom because it was a preferred food or because the Hollow's altered ecology had reduced its regular food supply. And so on.

Or I would see what Willie called a Mystery Bird — a genus that was still distressingly common at the Place. Willie and I — especially Willie — had the best intentions when it came to birding, and we loved seeing and identifying new species. But we lacked the collector's instinct that impels a true birder to travel hundreds of miles just to add a bluefaced booby to his life list. Even on our own turf, we didn't measure up, being handicapped by lack of patience, a tin ear for bird music, and a tendency to forget to bring along the binocs when we went for walks.

In spite of these shortcomings, we managed between us to identify more than eighty bird species on the Place over the years, including such rarities as swallow-tailed kites, a peregrine falcon, an osprey, and those seven famous wood storks. But that still left a lot of Mystery Birds, mostly migrants, that we'd see but couldn't put a name to.

Warblers were the worst. We managed to identify the ones that stuck around in spring and summer — the black-and-white, the lovely prothonotary, the pine, the hooded, the endearing little parula — even though there wasn't one of them that would hold still for three seconds in a row. But the fall migrants were something else. According to the guidebooks, there could be a dozen species taking a rest break at the Place while en route to warmer climes. However, you'd never guess that to look at them. Most were immatures wearing the same dull greenish brown on their backs and the same more or less dull yellows on their breasts; as alike, at a little distance, as olives in a jar.

So there I'd be, sitting in the Hollow, contemplating autumn in the subtropics (where the yellow poplars turn yellow and the swamp maples turn red, and that's about it), with my self-centered Self on hold for a while, when into view would flit a little warbler. This time I would have my binoculars with me, and while he paused briefly between flits, I would see that this little warbler had a greenish-yellow breast and *no wing bars,* which narrowed the possibilities down quite a bit. Now all I had to do was see if he had the thin eye *ring* of a Nashville warbler, the thin eye *band* of a Tennessee, or the faint eye ring *and* eye band of the orange-crowned (which, needless to say, rarely reveals its orange crown), these being the only perceivable distinctions between the three species. Only somehow these markings seemed never to be as perceivable in the gladey light and shadow of the Hollow, even assuming that I got the bird's tiny head focused in my glasses, as they were in the pages of *North American Birds.* The warbler would pose patiently for all of one and a half seconds and then fly away for good, leaving me with nothing but a case of eye strain and a Self no longer lost.

Even after all these years, I'm still a washout when it comes to identifying migrant fall warblers; and I'm only marginally better at recognizing them when they show up in spring wearing adult plumage. Which is too bad, because now more than ever I want to know more about them. According to all the authorities, their numbers have been steadily decreasing for the past two decades, some species more than others, and there is a growing body of evidence indicating that the destruction of their habitats here in the States is at least as responsible for the declines as the ravaging of Central and South American rain forests. So it might be a useful thing to keep track of their numbers from year to year. With that worthy aim in mind, I still keep trying to sort out all the look-alikes, hoping that someday there will come a breakthrough and my identification skills will miraculously improve. Meanwhile, there are two things I know for certain. One is that many of these migrant Mystery Birds prefer the upland hardwoods of the Hollow as a rest stop to any other area on the Place. The other is that developers and timber companies have almost totally wiped out this type of forest habitat in the sandhills during the last twenty years.

Of all the interesting occasions when I was distracted from contemplating the Hollow by something that was going on in it, I suppose the most memorable was my encounter, if you could call it that, with the Cogitating Deer. It was a murderously hot day in June. I had taken up a comfortable position against my favorite oak tree when I heard hounds coming in my direction, excitedly baying a hot trail. When I turned my head toward the sound, I realized that I was not the only one tuned in to them. A doe was standing not a dozen yards away, faced in their direction, her attention so focused on their approach that she hadn't noticed me.

In much of the Deep South it is perfectly legal to drive deer with dogs. A half-century ago, when there were still large roadless tracts in the region and hunters were positioned in widely spaced "stands" deep in the woods, there was some justification for the practice since the odds favored the deer. Now, however, this sort of hunting too often resembles a one-sided war. Walkie-talkies are used to follow the course of a drive, and hunters by the score line up like firing squads beside the roads that crisscross almost every woodland. Public roads are supposedly off limits, but on our way to the Place, Willie and I would often see long lines of hunters strung out along the shoulders of the highways, waiting for the dogs to drive some hapless deer into view. Even when the hunting season is over, although the guns may be put away, the hounds are not. To keep them trained to the chase, many of their owners allow them to run deer all year round.

Which explained why hounds were pursuing the Cogitating Deer across the Place on this hot summer day. To judge from her girth, she was heavily pregnant; and it was evident that the dogs had been running her for some time. She was badly winded, sides heaving, tongue protruding from her open, panting mouth. But she hadn't just stopped to take a breather. It was plain as could be that she was weighing her options, considering what to do next.

Although their attitudes have been changing a bit of late, most animal behaviorists still try to tell us that animals don't really *think,* even though those of us who own dogs or cats often see them solving problems in situations where instinct cannot guide them. Well, my deer was in a situation now, a bad one, and she was unmistakably giving it some serious thought. As I watched, she turned her head to the left, then to the right (staring past my motionless figure), then toward the dogs, clearly measuring their advance, then behind her. She repeated this sequence several times, each time staring longer and longer to her left. Finally, her mind made up, she stood there quietly, facing the hounds, waiting until they were actually in sight. Which they soon were, three of them, noses to the ground, yodeling excitedly at the freshness of their quarry's trail. Yet even when they were almost on top of her, they never saw my cogitating doe. At the last moment, she leaped to the left, clearing a thicket of yaupon, and disappeared.

The minute she was gone, I pounced on the dogs and hustled them to the gate — wishing it was their owner I had by the collar instead of them. But still, I couldn't be sorry the incident had occurred. I had had the rare opportunity of watching a wild animal while it was methodically thinking things out and making a conscious choice.

20

Putting things back

Not just the Hollow but every nook and corner of the Place was energetically transforming itself during the years following Camille. Slopes where an older generation of pines had been devastated by the storm were bristling with loblollies, slash, and glistening longleafs that shot up three feet or more in every growing season. By the mid '70s, many of the trees in our slash pine plantation were twenty feet tall. Except for the Big Pasture and a couple of clearings we kept open on the middle and index ridges, meadows were converting to brushland, brushland to thickets, thickets to young woodlands.

In this ongoing metamorphosis Willie and I had no small part to play. The fence had given the Place's vegetation a three-year head start on the Fence Law in eliminating the depredations of free-roaming livestock; but even more important, throughout the first dozen years of our tenure we were more or less successful in our efforts to banish woods fires from the property. The locals still often set them along the county roads, even though the burnings no longer served the purpose of improving woodland grazing. The rationale, to the extent that there was one, was to keep the woods open so that deer, when they were flushed during game drives, would have less cover in which to hide. But I suspect the real motivation had more to do with youthful devilment and simple pyromania, fueled by booze.

These fires were always set at night, and almost always in March when the woods were dry and the winds pretty strong. During the early and mid '70s, we could count on at least one or two of them a year coming at us from the edge of the nearby county road. If Willie and I were at the Place, we hopped out of bed at the first whiff of smoke, jumped into heavy jeans and long-sleeved shirts, grabbed leaf rakes from the shed, and drove as close as we could to the advancing blaze. En route we bitched and griped and cursed the arsonists, but in a weird sort of way, we rather enjoyed playing Smokey the Bear. Woods fires in the Southern pinelands are not in the same class as the holocausts that sometimes incinerate subdivisions in California or fire-fighters in the Rockies. At times they can get hot and lively enough, the flames soaring twenty feet high when they hit a thicket of yaupon festooned with dead pine needles; but for the most part these piney woods fires stay fairly close to the ground, especially in woods that have been burned pretty regularly. If the wind isn't too strong, and the fire doesn't extend along too wide a front, two able-bodied men have a good chance of putting it down using nothing more than the aforementioned leaf rakes. The trick is to work steadily along the advancing edge of flames from one end to the other, raking the fire back into itself while trying as best you can not to suffocate from the smoke. It is lung-choking, strenuous work, requiring occasional broad jumps when a variable wind throws a wave of scorching heat in your face; but it can be exhilarating, too. Although the blackened after-math was pretty dismal looking, the fire itself, moving through the silhouetted columns of pines, was a beautiful sight in its *Walpurgisnacht* way. And for us it was also almost fun, certainly a challenge, to dance like warlocks with the flames. In every man there is a small boy that never grows up — and in that small boy there is a would-be incendiary. Willie and I, while innocent of starting these fires, could enjoy watching them burn even as we strove to put them out.

We had an important ally in Roddy Ray's mother, Cora. She had a keen nose for smoke; but even more important, she maintained an amiably flirtatious relationship with the forester who manned the fire tower ten miles down the road. It was a comfort to know that if someone set the woods afire when we weren't around, the forester was sure to send a crew to the rescue the minute Cora rang him up.

Even back in the early days I knew that fire was not necessarily an enemy to forests in the South or anywhere else; that it was in fact vital to the ecology of Southern pines, which tend to be more fire resistant than the hardwoods that would otherwise displace them. But everywhere around us in the sandhills, hardwood forests were being obliterated to make way for pine plantations, so it seemed to make ecological sense to keep fire off the property for a good long while and give the hardwoods the edge. I wanted the Hollow, the Oak Grove, the cypress and tupelo woodlands of the Brainch and its tributary ravines to expand their borders somewhat, thereby creating the maximum variety of habitats that the Place was potentially capable of supporting. I figured that, with or without fire, the pines would take care of themselves. In principle it was a perfectly good management policy. The problem was that, in this as in so much else, it was important to know when enough of a good thing was enough.

One day soon after we bought the Place, when Willie and I were exploring the damp, tangled area where the Hollow merged with the Brainch, we discovered a clump of southern magnolia sprouts growing from the stump of a parent tree that had been killed by fire. During the next few months we found two more such clumps. At the time I was simply pleased that we could list the species, no matter how pitifully represented, among the Place's flora. But before long the real implication of those discoveries began to sink in: Magnolias were one of many trees that were very intolerant of fire, yet they were native to our Hollow for the good reason that, under natural conditions, fire would not have been able to reach them in its damp, not very combustible depths. Yet, in the recent past, it had. The apparent explanation was that the Hollow itself had been so altered and diminished by timber cutting and the encroachment of livestock that, during times of drought, it could no longer protect its more vulnerable tree species against a fire's advance. Which helped to convince me that, in banning woods fires, I would indeed be helping to restore the Place to a more natural state.

A botanist I am not. I could recognize a magnolia when I saw one, but what about other trees and plants native to the Place that I knew nothing about and that might now be in the same fix as those forlorn magnolia sprouts, assuming they still survived at all? The more I thought about it, the keener I became to find out what I could about the Place's original flora, and to supplement or reintroduce species that were in trouble or were already gone. Luckily for us, Willie and I had a couple of naturalist-gardeners among our friends who were glad to help us out. They spent a day crisscrossing the Place with us, identifying a lone parsley hawthorn — burned back and resprouting like the magnolias — on the slope above one of the pitcher plant bogs; a couple of fringetrees, otherwise known as Grancy-graybeards for their wispy white clusters of blossoms, at the back of the Oak Grove; a cluster of Chickasaw plums near the widow woman's homesite; a pair of sourwood trees and several burned and resprouting black cherries at the Hollow's edge. On our own we found a few young sweet gum and a single clump of palmetto in the Brainch below the Big Pasture, and an isolated colony of yucca growing just beyond the property's western boundary.

We learned that there were many other trees and shrubs, most fairly common in their overall range, that might once have been native to the Place but weren't present now. Among them: redbud, river birch, oakleaf hydrangea, star anise, Southern crabapple, bigleaf magnolia. Almost all of these species had in common an intolerance of fire and a concomitant preference for damp hardwood hollows and brainches where they could be relatively safe from it — in short, the very sort of habitat I was doing my best to augment at the Place. We decided we would try our luck with as many of them as we could find.

What we had in mind was to create a small-scale arboretum, mostly within the compound surrounding the second house. This we did over the course of three or four years, collecting and planting virtually all the species I've just mentioned. It wasn't an entirely "natural" set-up, of course. We could plant a good many native trees and shrubs in a two-and-a-half-acre enclosure, but there was no way we could create an accurate facsimile of all the different microhabitats in which they would have grown under totally natural conditions. But even if that had been possible, Willie and I didn't aim to be purists in our approach to landscaping. We saw no reason why the compound couldn't be an ark for rare or extirpated native vegetation and still support a lot of other things as well. As far as we were concerned, the camellias, gardenias, and several varieties of azalea we planted were so much a part of any traditional Southern garden that they might as well have been native. Camellias were a special favorite of Willie's because they bloomed in the gray heart of the subtropical winter, so it was a point of rather smug satisfaction with him — me, too, for that matter — that these magnificent shrubs, as well as the azaleas, flourished much more happily in the poor but acid soils of the Place than in the pampered gardens of our city friends. As for the Japanese maples, they were beautiful, and that was enough, although it gladdened us to learn that squirrels found their winged seeds as appetizing as those of the native red variety.

We also planted a lot of wildlife foods, some indigenous, some not: pyracantha, bush lespedeza (mostly for the quail), blackberry, Cherokee rose, black cherry and cherry laurel along the compound fence; and domesticated blueberries, figs, and grapes (which we and the birds shared) near the vegetable garden.

Around the house we sowed winter clover to feed the rabbits as well as to give the native grasses a nitrogen boost.

It wasn't necessary to plant pines, live oaks, red maples, or dogwood in the compound because the squirrels and birds had already done that for us; although when we chose the index ridge for the site of our second house it had required some imagination to see those wind-blasted, scrawny-looking saplings as the tall, wind-catching trees they have since become. For all our successful introductions, their presences dominate the compound as they do the surrounding woods. There are photos of the house taken soon after it was finished in which the red oak at the corner of the front deck and the live oak at the rear are hardly noticeable. Now their branches reach across the roof and touch.

It still takes me pleasantly by surprise to see what the fullness of time has made of our landscaping efforts. The sweet gum we planted twenty-three years ago towers forty feet above the pond. A magnolia at the compound gate — a little potted thing when we bought it — is almost as tall. The spindly stick of a Southern crabapple that I set out halfway down the slope is now, at the onset of spring, a sprawling cloud of sweet-scented blossoms vibrating with the hum of bees. Throughout the compound and along the entrance drive there are banks of azaleas, some ten feet high, that we acquired as Wal-Mart bargains or cuttings donated by city neighbors. Growing through a hole in the expanded deck at the side of the house is a parsley hawthorn, hardly more than a foot high when I planted it there, that is almost as large as those lovely shrub trees ever get.

In the fullness of time. I always loved that phrase; but only now, when I see the passage of half my life made visible in the green growing things around me rather than measured by calendars and the tick-tock of clocks, do I begin to understand what those words mean to me. Not the same meaning they must have for parents who watch their children grow up, get married, have children of their own — that tangled awareness of generational change, genetic immortality, lost innocence, growing old. It comes closer to the less-complicated wonder that Willie and I sometimes felt at odd moments, years after the house was finished, when one or the other of us, looking up at the cedar paneling or the heavy exposed beams of the roof and remembering all those bent nails, mashed thumbs, mismeasurements, would exclaim out loud, "Did *we* really build this?"

The feeling I get looking out across the compound these days is similar to that, but not the same. The same wonder, the same sense of accomplishment. But a tree is not a house. It builds itself. Maybe what it comes down to is a consoling consciousness that my life, and Willie's, are linked in some fundamental, organic way with the lives of all these verdant trees and shrubs we planted years ago. Not unlike, perhaps, the symbiotic link between an oak and the squirrel that buried an acorn and forgot to retrieve it. I look at — I *behold* — that excellent sweet gum, its starry leaves throwing their shadows on the quiet pond; and because, unlike a squirrel, I remember that I planted it, I feel, in a nice quiet way, almost as old and as impressed with my work as God.

If the harsh, infertile soils of the Place can produce such a garden grove, then other hardscrabble places anywhere in the country can be made to do the same. But I'm bound to add a cautionary note: In landscaping, as in anything else, it's possible to have too much success. Here at the Place our efforts sometimes panned out not only better than we hoped but better than we wished. When we first set out the young magnolias and crabapples and bigleaf magnolias, for example, their little sticklike shapes looked pathetically lost in the wide open spaces of the compound slope. Yet ten years later we were cutting down half of the sizable trees they had become just to keep the rest, as well as our small patch of wild grass lawn, from being shaded out. It's a hard thing, I can tell you, taking the axe to a tree one has planted oneself just when it is becoming something to look at; but it's the only remedy if proper spacing is ignored.

Still, a few clean chops and that problem was solved. Whereas there was no such neat, if drastic, solution to our two other big mistakes in landscape planning: transplanting native bamboo cane from the Hollow, where it grew rather thinly, to stretches of the compound fence, where it was supposed to act as a feathery, see-through screen; and introducing wisteria to the Place for the sake of its lovely April blooming. In a matter of two or three years, we were gratified to see that both introductions had lived up to our expectations. Unfortunately the bamboo and the wisteria had their own agendas and couldn't have cared less whether we were gratified or not. Within another year or two they were sending out runners and deep roots in all directions, hell-bent on taking over the whole compound. Once they started doing that, there was never a question of getting rid of them altogether; it was all we could do to keep them under control. Willie and I didn't mind the ordinary chores that having a lot of vegetation around the house entailed — raking, trimming, mulching, even cleaning out rain gutters; but after a while we *really* hated having to amputate wisteria vines and dig up the tentacle roots of that irrepressible bamboo every other month or so. I will admit that when I'm not actually engaged in that thankless labor, and the wisteria is in bloom and the bamboo is temporarily backed up against the fence where it belongs, they and I are briefly reconciled. But if it was to do again . . .

The obvious moral here is that, when planting oases, arboretums, rustic groves, or, where appropriate, prairie meadows and cacti gardens, you would do well to plan the big picture, think long-term, and then think twice, before you start sticking all those innocent little green shoots and sprigs you've collected into the ground.

21

Fafnir

In September of 1976, when two of my nephews came South for a weeklong visit, Willie and I took them canoeing one day in the Honey Island Swamp, which lies along the Louisiana-Mississippi border midway between New Orleans and the Place. It was a very pleasant outing, so much so that we were all, I think, a little sorry to see ahead of us the bridge where we were to take out and head back to the city. We stopped paddling as we approached it, and the two canoes, with one of my nephews in the prow of each, came abreast of each other in the narrow stream. We fell silent, taking in our last few moments of swampy solitude before the world of highways and traffic overtook us.

Notwithstanding the obtrusive presence of the bridge a hundred yards downstream, the scene could hardly have been more peaceful. Which left us wholly unprepared when, in the midst of that stillness, the quiet surface of the water suddenly erupted not more than two or three feet in front of the canoes, long enough to expose in swift succession a grinning toothy mouth, a corrugated streaming back, and the ridge of a formidable tail.

"An alligator!" the nephews whooped delightedly. "A *big* one! It must have been eight feet long!"

Willie and I sat in the rocking canoes, not saying anything.

There was no need to. We both knew that the alligator could only be Fafnir.

Fafnir was not quite a foot long when I first laid eyes on him in 1967, about a year before Willie and I bought the Place. I had arrived at a friend's house for dinner one evening to find the maid, with whom I'd always thought I was on friendly terms, leaning out of a front window, waving a large linen napkin in my direction, exclaiming "Shoo, shoo! Go 'way!" I was just about to get my feelings hurt when I realized that her eyes were fixed not on me, but on the pathway in front of me. When I looked down, there was Fafnir, his small jaws wide open, trying to hold at bay the whole hostile world.

While the maid went in search of a cardboard box that I could stow him in, my hostess explained that some neighborhood kids had tossed the little reptile into her swimming pool earlier that evening and he'd been lurching around the lawn, probably half blinded by chlorine, ever since. She had been just about to call the SPCA when I showed up and decided to adopt him.

Willie and I became very attached to Fafnir. When he was small, he lived happily in the fish pool in the walled garden of the city house; and he quickly learned to come for his horsemeat dinner whenever we rang a bell. He grew quickly, however, almost a foot a year, and when he was old enough to climb the back stairs, he got into the bothersome habit of inviting himself into the house whenever one of us forgot to close the porch door. Usually these incursions occurred at night, and once he was inside he invariably headed for the bathroom, apparently because it was the dampest place he could find. The first several times he did this, the dogs and our tabby cat, Reprieve, gave the alarm. We would awaken to what sounded like a tap dance being performed on the hardwood floors, and when we switched the hallway light on, there would be Fafnir plodding determinedly toward the bathroom door, utterly indifferent to huge Schaeffer, squat Sammie, and bristling Reprieve, all of them terrifically agitated, jumping up and down around him as though they were on pogo sticks.

Eventually, though, first Sammie, then the cat, then even faithful Schaeffer became fed up with us forgetting to close the porch door, and began to ignore Fafnir just as he had always ignored them. Which left Willie and me to discover Fafnir's bathroom visits for ourselves. In the small hours, it could be an unsettling experience, I can tell you, stumbling barefooted into the dark bathroom to take a leak and stepping on the tail of a four-foot alligator while groping for the light switch.

Fafnir never bit us when this happened, but he complained in a horrible hissing voice. After Willie and I had stepped on him two times apiece, and then argued with each other about who had forgotten to close the porch door, we decided we had to put an end to the alligator's fixation about becoming a house pet. At the time, in the early '70s, turning him loose in some nice swamp was not an option. Alligators were still being poached for their hides throughout the Deep South, and we were much too fond of Fafnir to think of him in terms of ladies' accessories. So we carried him up to the Place and installed him in a comfortable pen, furnished with an old bathtub, below the dam of our newly completed house pond.

For several years Fafnir seemed well pleased with the new accommodations, even digging himself a spacious den in which to sleep away the winter months. But his stay at the Place was indirectly responsible for causing Willie some — in my view — unwarranted discomfiture. It was during this same period that we were raising Griswold the barn owl, and I suppose the little flap we had had — also, in my view, unwarranted — about my storing rat parts in the freezer could have made him overly sensitive about the new feeding program I had devised for Fafnir. At the time, both Fafnir's appetite and the price of horsemeat were increasing at a wildly inflationary rate; and since we had invested every spare dime in building the second house, I was looking for ways to cut household expenses. One day while we were driving up to the Place I hit on an ingenious solution to the problem of the horsemeat bill. Was not Fafnir a creature that, in its natural haunts, would relish a meal of opossum or raccoon, all the more tasty for being a little overripe? And was not the highway all too often sadly littered with the corpses of those very animals? And did it not follow that I would be putting those pathetic little carcasses to a useful purpose by feeding them to Fafnir while at the same time saving myself several bucks a week? The answer to these questions was, of course: Of course.

It was that rare thing: a perfect solution. Unfortunately, Willie stubbornly refused to see the beauty of it. Whenever I spotted a reasonably fresh-looking, more or less intact road kill and pulled over to the shoulder of the busy highway to collect it, he would give a wild-eyed look out the back window at approaching cars, then stick his head under the dashboard, groaning, "Oh Lord, people gonna think we're fixing to eat that thing ourselves!"

Schaeffer shared Willie's embarrassment, but Sammie welcomed these unscheduled additions to our cargo, sniffing them with gusto and rolling on them if he got the chance. As for Fafnir, just as I had thought, he was delighted by the change in his diet.

We kept Fafnir until he was eight years old and seven feet long. By then two things had happened that made us resolve to give him his freedom. One was that alligators had been put on the federal Endangered Species List so there was no longer a legal market for their hides. The other was that Fafnir turned out to be a she rather than a he, a fact that she made clear to us by undergoing a false pregnancy and then guarding the mud nest she had built with a touching but fierce display of maternal solicitude. After that there was nothing for it but to fatten her up with as many road kills as we could find before roping her and carting her off to a wildlife management area in the Honey Island Swamp. There we pulled off the highway beside a bridge, cut her loose, and, with genuine emotion, wished her well as she slipped into the dark waters of a swampy creek.

Now, a year later, at that same bridge on that same creek, Fafnir had come as to a rendezvous to bid us, for old time's sake, a friendly hello and final goodbye.

22

Coexisting

Whatever the season, Hovit always carried a pistol or a shotgun with him when he went out in the woods. For a man with only one eye, he was a pretty fair shot; anything that flew, ran, crawled, or hopped (frogs were not exempt) was an excuse for target practice. Roddy Ray, himself a relentless hunter, complained that before we bought the Place, Hovit used to shoot squirrels in the Hollow even in summer "when they don't hardly have no fat on them yet." I could well believe this, having once seen him coming back from his pasture pond carrying half a dozen blue-winged teal he had blasted out of the water. Since it was early spring, they couldn't have had much fat on them either.

Nevertheless, knowing of our enthusiasm for wildlife — live wildlife — Hovit was tactful enough to soft-pedal his penchant for killing things whenever he came by to see what Willie and I were up to, which he often did when he'd been on a binge and Lurlee was making life miserable for him at home. At such times he was glad to share with us the nuggets of nature lore he had picked up in a lifetime spent making moonshine in the great outdoors. Right here on the Place, he assured us, he had seen milk snakes sucking milk from his woods cows' teats, and hoop snakes that rolled downhill with their tails in their mouths. On one occasion he had had to run for his life from a whip snake — a folkloric relative of the slender and quite harmless coachwhip snake — that was hell-bent on skinning him alive with its lashing tail. And lately he had been seeing "these real big deer, almost twice as big as the regular kind" in the neighborhood. "The Government's been turnin' 'em loose," he confided, "only they don't want us to know nothin' about it."

This was pretty tame stuff, however, compared to Hovit's encounters with wildlife in the Big Swamp, where he sometimes set up a still when the revenuers made things hot for him closer to home. The Big Swamp, located about a quarter-mile beyond the northwest corner of the Place, was a boggy, heavily wooded slough into which our brainch and two others drained. It wasn't really all that big except by sandhill standards; but like all swamps it closed in on itself, creating, like a well, a perception of depth out of all proportion to the surface space it had to work with. The creek that sidled through it was wide and deep enough so that even during droughty summer months you couldn't jump across. And in some places you had to do a balancing act on a network of tree roots to get around the swamp at all. During one of my exploratory forays, a misstep landed me up to my knees in gluey mud that sucked the loafers off my feet when I pulled myself free. After that, I could easily believe Hovit when he said that back in no-fence days the Big Swamp had proved a deathtrap for a good many of his cows.

I also wanted to believe him when he spoke of bobcats inhabiting the Big Swamp, even though his account of them would give a naturalist pause. He explained to me that they came in two varieties. One was the familiar bobtailed kind, but the other, which he also saw frequently, was "sort'uv bushy-tailed" — the consequence, he speculated, of their fooling around with the local tomcats. However that might be, a discussion of bobcats, both standard and bushy-tailed, was just Hovit's way of warming up. In a spirit of kindly, if bleary, sharing, he would soon move on to the subject of bears and black panthers. "Now a lotta folks don't know this, Don," he would say, "but there is two kinds of bears we got around here. There is your regular big bears which ain't too common anymore, and then there is these little bears, what we call hog bears because they're 'bout the size of a good-size hog. I see 'em all the time when I go messin' around in the Big Swamp. Why, hell, I've seen 'em right up by the house a bunch of times. They're little, but they're mean and sly, y'know. I've had to shoot at two or three of 'em that was sneakin' up on me."

Hovit had also seen panthers a bunch of times, and he's not the only one. Sometimes it seems that everybody in rural Mississippi has had an encounter with these fabulous creatures at one time or another. Unlike bobcats and bears, they come in only one variety: large, long-tailed, and invariably as black as ink. Even Roddy Ray, who is not a heavy drinker, has observed black panthers "playin' like kittens, chasin' each other up and down a tree," right alongside the county road. Such sightings are always accepted as gospel truth. One of Lurlee's grandsons came barreling up to the house one day in his pickup, all excited, brandishing his shotgun, wanting to know if I had seen the black panther that a couple of young girls had spotted crossing the road, heading straight for the Place. When I told him I hadn't seen any panthers but I *had* seen a stray black mutt on the entrance drive, he blinked, registering the possibility that he might be dealing with a case of mistaken identity. But then he said, "Naw, it couldn't 'uv been a dog. The girls said that panther was *big*." He was convinced he had come within a hair of seeing it himself, and was terribly downcast that he had missed the chance to kill it.

I knew better than to try to convince him that his black panther did not exist. The real panther, or "painter," that once roamed the Southern wilderness was a subspecies of mountain lion, practically identical in all respects, including its tan color, to its Western counterpart. A relict population of this Southern race hangs on, just barely, in south Florida, but it has been extinct in the rest of the South, including Mississippi, since early in this century. Having only the name and the memory to work with, an older generation of Southerners, growing up on Frank Buck's *Bring 'Em Back Alive* and Johnny Weissmuller's *Tarzan* flicks, imaginatively transferred the blackness of Asian and African panthers (a melanistic phase of the leopard) to the tawny animal their grandfathers had wiped out way back when.

As for the Mississippi black bear — that embodiment of wilderness that Faulkner wrote so eloquently about — there are maybe twenty or thirty of them left in the state, holed up in a couple of bottomland tracts that are nowhere near the Place. Hovit had no doubt inherited the term "hog bears" from a time when the animals were more numerous and occasionally raided someone's pigsty.

What fascinated me was the tenacity with which not just Hovit but so many of my neighbors clung to the conviction that their pillaged backwoods could still support panthers, black or otherwise, and bears, hog-size or regular, not to mention super deer or Zorro-like whip snakes. Maybe the cultivation of such bestiaries has something to do with the need of many country people to invest Nature with the sort of mystery and excitement they feel it ought to possess, the same need that populates abandoned houses with wailing ghosts. More likely, however, it is a nostalgia for a less-tamed world, one that they miss if only because, like Lurlee's grandson, they want the fun of destroying it all over again. I dunno; I think that misplaced faith and longing is sort of sad. So much of the real mystery and excitement of the natural world is still there, all around them; yet they don't seem interested in hearing about that, or discovering it for themselves.

Myself, I am endlessly surprised by the fact that the glass is still half full. Although top-of-the-line creatures like panthers, black bears, red wolves, eagles, and ivory-billed woodpeckers may be long gone from the sandhills, along with the unbroken forests that once sheltered them, most of the wildlife species that lived here one hundred years ago are still present, although some are barely hanging on. For me, seeing them, learning about them is

an enthusiasm I wish were more communicable, sort of like the
flu. I would love nothing better than to infect people like Hovit
and Roddy Ray. But not *just* people like them. Even card-carrying
Audubon types too often change their ecological tune in a hurry
when they feel threatened by Lyme disease or woodchucks in
their flower beds or even the squirrels that raid their bird feeders.
My own feeling is that when people come into conflict with
wildlife — and the odds are that this will happen occasionally to
anyone who owns land in the country — the interests of the
wildlife should come first. Which, however, doesn't mean you
have to passively accept any damage that might befall.

Since Willie and I were not living at the Place full time, we
couldn't always react quickly when a conflict of interests did crop
up. Given that circumstance, the amazing thing was how rarely
problems occurred. We did keep the chickens penned up while
we were gone, and the ducks usually stuck pretty close to the
precarious refuge of the pond; but the geese, and especially the
guineas, roamed in and out of the compound at will, noisily
advertising their availability as a free lunch for any fox or hawk
that happened to be passing by. Yet more often than not the local
predators ignored what amounted to an invitation to entrap-
ment. Months would often go by without a single casualty.

In the case of our resident red-shouldered hawks, the explanation was both simple and instructive: they might help themselves
to bite-size baby ducks, but they weren't really programmed to
attack adult poultry. On several occasions I observed one of the
pair perched in a pine at the edge of the pond — a favorite
observation post when they thought we weren't around — while
directly below the guineas screamed their silly heads off and the
ducks swam around in anxious circles, gabbling in alarm. The
hawk would act as though they weren't there, its attention fixed
on the pond's iris-crowded edge. Then suddenly it would swoop
down and fly off with a crawfish in its talons!

For a couple of years, the broad-winged, red-tailed, and Cooper's hawks that sometimes frequented the Place seemed equally uninterested in tackling a full-grown duck or guinea, much less a bellicose goose. But one autumn evening in the early '70s, Willie and I arrived at the Place to find a recently slain mallard drake lying in the grass near the edge of the pond. The breast feathers had been neatly plucked and most of the flesh removed with almost surgical skill, clear evidence that the assailant had been a bird of prey.

"Just when I was getting to really like those hawks," Willie sighed, "they go and do something like this." I agreed that our resident red-shoulders seemed the likely suspects, notwithstanding their previous restraint. But I proposed that we leave the duck where it was. Then, if they came back for seconds, we'd know for sure.

Next morning we were awakened by a louder than usual chorus of duck and guinea voices. When I got up and looked through the upstairs sliding doors, there was a large, fierce-eyed hawk on the lawn below making a hearty breakfast of yesterday's dead duck. Now and then he raised his head to look everywhere but up at me looking down at him.

Willie had come up behind me. "Well, leastways he's not one of ours," he whispered, sounding relieved.

The hawk was a red-tail, the one species of raptor, in the East at least, that sometimes deserves the name "chicken hawk," although the ones we occasionally sighted had never caused us any problems before. Even now I was impressed that this fellow, instead of helping himself to a nice fresh duck or guinea, which he could easily have done, was content to dine on leftovers.

Still, having set him up with a poultry smorgasbord, it seemed all too likely that he might keep coming back for more. So, not knowing what else to do, I opted for the terrorize-the-coon routine, this time with Willie joining in. We yanked open the sliding doors and began hopping up and down and whooping and hollering like drunken Mardi Gras tourists on a Bourbon Street balcony. Downstairs, Schaeffer and Sammie, uncertain about what was going on but eager to help, added their voices to the din. The tactic worked. The scandalized hawk, a gobbet of duck still dangling from his beak, heaved himself into the air and sailed away among the pines, never to return — at least not for another meal of duck.

With the fox, we were not so lucky. Foxes are often thought of as rather furtive animals; but in fact they can be quite bold, even cocky, in their dealings with humans. They can also be very single-minded about getting what they want, as our guineas would learn to their sorrow.

Both red and gray foxes hunted the Place. The red is said to be the more clever species of the two, but the gray has the ability, almost unique among canids, to climb trees when hounds pursue it, which may explain why it is still fairly common in the sandhills and the red is not.

During the years that followed my confrontation with the angry old fox hunter, we were awakened less and less frequently by the racket of fox hounds echoing across our land. I wanted to believe that Schaeffer's gallant charges, my angry imprecations, and the impeding fence all helped to account for this welcome change. But the main reason, I suspect, was simply that the old fox hunters were dying off and they had few replacements. Running foxes, after all, was not the same as running deer, since one didn't have the satisfaction of killing the quarry oneself. And now that every little trailer and ranch house in the sandhills was furnished with a TV set, the younger generation found it more entertaining to drink beer at home than to sit in a pickup listening to the music of the hounds. Which, now that I think of it, just may be the only constructive social change that television has ever brought about.

None of that had anything to do with the behavior of our fox, however. What did was his mate's decision in the mid '70s to raise a couple of kits in a secret corner of the Place. With a family to feed, he could hardly have been expected to be as considerate of our interests as we had always been of his.

He had his modus operandi pretty well worked out. Every other day or so when we and the dogs weren't around, he arrived at the compound while it was still dark and concealed himself near the tree where the guineas were roosting. Then, when they flew down at crack of dawn, he would grab whichever one landed nearest him and carry it off. So much for the proverbial good fortune of early birds.

At first we weren't even sure we were dealing with a fox. Sammie knew, of course. After excitedly sniffing the clues — there was always a scattering of feathers, as well as a trail of down leading off toward the compound fence — he would rush up to us, tail wagging cheerfully, to report that the mystery was solved. But all we knew was that our predator was not a hawk; it could have been an abandoned, starving dog — by no means a rarity in the neighborhood — or even an unusually enterprising raccoon or possum. However, the week after the losses began, it rained, so when we arrived the following weekend I was able to discover a neat little footprint in a muddy spot near the pond. It was hardly larger than a large cat's, but the marks of the toenails were clearly visible, which wouldn't have been the case if a cat had made it. That, plus the efficient strategy of the attacks, plus the fact that we could discover no bones or other carcass remnants, convinced us that our freeloader was indeed Brer Fox.

By the end of the fourth week, I had decided what had to be done to save not only our remaining guineas but also the ducks; for by now the fox was varying his menu by helping himself to some of them as well. However, I had a curious presentiment that something should happen before we undertook this rescue mission — that something *would* happen, if we arrived at the Place so quietly and unobtrusively that the fox would not realize we were there.

This we did. After checking out the feathery remains of two

more guineas, we and the dogs kept to the house that evening —
a real penance because spring was well launched at the time, and
the compound was aglow with blooming azaleas, dogwood, and
sweet-scented crabapple inviting us to come outside.

At first light the next morning I awoke to the lamentations of
our surviving guineas and ducks. The dogs, sprawled on the
living room floor, ignored the racket. Willie slept on. I pulled on a
pair of jeans and, barefooted, slipped out of the house.

The casualty this time was the next-to-last of our mallard
drakes. I followed the usual trail of feathery down until it faded
out; then I climbed the compound fence and took off in the
direction that the trail had been headed. I crossed the middle
ridge near the spot where the first house had stood and went
down the opposite slope to the still raw edge of the dysfunctional
Big Pond. There in the wet clay was the neat little track of our
duck thief, pointed toward the narrow brainch below the dam.
The quill of a single iridescent feather, lying in the nearby grass,
was aimed in the same direction.

I descended into the brainch and made my way slowly along
gray aisles of lichen-mottled sweet bays and tupelo. The spongy
wet sphagnum allowed easy and silent going for my bare feet.
A thin blue mist hung in the damp air like cigarette smoke.
Branches overhead dripped a cold heavy dew. The rising sun was
just beginning to assert its oblique presence among the trees. The
atmosphere, instead of being a transparency through which light
passed, had become itself a kind of light. Bronze air. In that light
every dew-soaked leaf and twig was incandescently beaded like
the jeweled trees in an Irish fairy tale.

The world was absolutely quiet. In that stillness I concentrated
my whole being on the quarry that, until now, I hadn't quite
realized I was hunting. And, as though I had summoned him, the
fox — a red fox — leaped up onto a fallen log just a few yards
away and for a moment posed there. He was a beautiful creature,
sleek and healthy — as well he might be, given his current diet.

His orange coat, set off by jet-black leggings and a dashing white ruff, glowed against the gray-green backdrop of the brainch.

I didn't move, didn't breathe. He stared at me, his eyes intelligent and curious; but he hadn't caught my scent and he hadn't heard me approach; I was to him no more than an unusually ugly and misshapen tree. I had the peculiar sensation that I had passed through some invisible barrier; that I had left the human world behind and become part of the otherness of this animal's "other kingdom," where what mattered were those things that are important to foxes.

What was mattering to the fox, at the moment, was a flea. He balanced himself on three legs and gave his right ear a vigorous scratching with his right hind foot. That done, he took one last, rather self-satisfied look around him, hopped off the log, and trotted off with the purposeful air of someone who has important business elsewhere.

I remained there for some time, the way one does in a theatre after seeing a memorable performance, feeling unready to go back to the world of everyday. And for weeks and months afterwards, when my wanderings took me along the edge of that small brainch, I would think, "That is where I saw the fox," and my spirits would do a little jig. There is no accounting for it, this special delight in seeing an elusive wild creature in its native habitat, especially when the habitat happens to be one's own as well. As far as I was concerned, it was compensation enough for the loss of a few ducks and guineas.

Well, more than just a few, actually. At this point, the body count had become pretty grim. So Willie and I went to work that morning building three covered, eight-by-eight, wire mesh pens, about thirty inches high, and equipped them with the same sort of dispensers and feeders that kept our chickens fed and watered when we were not around. Into these "safe houses" we lured the ducks, guineas, and geese with helpings of corn, and there we left them when we took off for the city that Sunday night. The next weekend we turned them loose while we were there, dragged the pens to clean patches of grass, and again confined them when we left.

We could have kept that up indefinitely, I suppose, but it was spring, and in such unprivate living quarters the birds refused to nest. So, at the end of the third week, we crossed our fingers and let the whole lot of them go back to their rambling ways. To our relief, when we returned to the Place the following weekend, we found that the strategy had worked. The fox and his vixen, no doubt miffed at finding their food supply cut off, had evidently moved their kits to a den somewhere else — something foxes tend to do anyway — and had gone back to their usual eclectic diet of rats, mice, blackberries, carrion, and the occasional grass-hopper.

The fox was the single most relentless nemesis that our adult fowl had to deal with. But Willie, who liked to count his chickens before they hatched, insisted that a wild animal that devoured eggs was just as much a predator as one that devoured the birds that laid them. If one goes along with that view, I guess it could be said that egg predation was an even more intractable and persist-ent problem.

Actually, it was a problem we didn't even know we had for a long time — months, maybe even a year. We just thought we had lazy chickens. Whenever we arrived at the Place, the first thing Willie did was head for their pen, gather the few eggs he found in the nest boxes, and then berate the hens for their poor showing. It wasn't that he cared all that much about the paltry number of eggs collected; we didn't eat that many of them anyway. But he was a staunch believer in the work ethic, and it aggravated him that "those no-account chickens been sitting on their lazy tails all week with nothing to show!" Nervously clucking, the hens would try to explain that the fault was not theirs, but to no avail.

Not, at least, until one morning when Willie came stomping into the house and told me to put some clothes on and come with him. When I asked him what was up, all he said was, "You'll see," in an aggrieved voice. I dutifully got dressed and followed him to the wire coop at the edge of the compound. From outside the enclosure, I couldn't see anything unusual about the way the little flock was behaving. Not that that proved anything; chickens have so little emotional range that it is difficult to interpret any but their most extreme reactions, as when, for example, one of them suddenly realizes its head has been lopped off. Once we stepped through the gate, however, I did notice that one hen seemed a little agitated. She was clucking rapidly and craning her neck toward one of the nest boxes, at which Willie was also pointing an accusing finger. When I peered into it, a snake was peering lidlessly back at me — while trying frantically to unhinge his jaws from an egg he had been attempting to swallow whole. He had been caught *in flagrante delicto,* and he knew it.

It was a young gray rat snake, less than two feet long. Willie and I frequently saw these demurely patterned gray and brown snakes in the compound, but it had never occurred to us to link their relative abundance with our chronic egg shortage. I knew snakes could unhinge their jaws to gulp down outsized prey; I had seen them do it many times in sex-'n'-violence nature films, but I hadn't realized that some of them had a taste for eggs. In fact, from what I'd read, both their nearsighted eyes and their bodies (which pick up delicate vibrations in the ground) were specifically designed for the purpose of capturing moving prey. And yet here was this smallish snake engulfing something that was about as mobile and warm-blooded as a large, smooth rock. So much for my qualifications as a herpetologist.

Aside from stealing eggs (and baby chickens if they got the chance), our rat snakes were inoffensive, even helpful neighbors, patrolling around the house's supporting piers so efficiently that we almost never saw a mouse inside the house itself.

However, there was an occasion when one of them precipitated a scene so embarrassing that I still cringe every time I think about it. Adelaide Dartwood, a middle-aged uptown dowager of whom we were very fond, had come to visit us in Mississippi for the first time. She was kindhearted and sentimental, and she loved small animals; but she would have been the first to admit that she was not much into nature worship. Her idea of someone having a really nice time in the out-of-doors was Marie Antoinette playing shepherdess at le Petit Trianon. She tried. She made polite little remarks about the Place, the fresh air, the sweet little birds flying around; but you could tell she found the whole scene pretty primitive. After sitting on the deck behind her sunglasses for a while and having two or three glasses of chilled wine, she felt the call of nature and retired to the bathroom.

She couldn't have been in there for more than a minute when the air for a mile around was sundered by her screams. Willie and I, along with Schaeffer and Sammie, rushed to the rescue, all of us trying to squeeze through the narrow door at the same time. We found poor Adelaide in a terrible state of disarray, no longer screaming, but wordlessly pointing at the corner of the bathtub nearest the toilet, where she was still enthroned. There, curled around the old-fashioned bathtub's leg — a cast iron ball gripped by a dragon's claw — was one of the younger members of our rat snake colony, a slender thing not more than eighteen inches long, trying his best to look as though he, the ball, and the dragon's claw were all part of the same ensemble. I made a grab for him, but he quickly slithered into the dark recesses under the tub — which understandably set our friend to screaming again. It was a pretty hectic scene for a while there — getting Adelaide out of the

john, scrambling around on hands and knees searching unsuccessfully for the snake, and finally stuffing a towel under the shut
bathroom door to make sure he stayed out of sight.

While wondering if our insurance covered snake fright, we did
our groveling best to soothe our stricken guest. Even Schaeffer,
who rarely deigned to notice anyone except Willie and me, felt
implicated enough in the debacle to give her trembling hand an
apologetic lick. Happily, when she finally calmed down, Adelaide
was very gracious and forgiving. In time, she would even trans-
form the episode into a humorous anecdote to be told at dinner
parties in the city. But she never did visit the Place again.

As for the snake, it simply vanished, apparently exiting the
house the way it must have entered, via the hole in the floor that
accommodated the bathtub drainpipe. Needless to say, when we
were next in town, the first thing we did was buy some pipe hole
covers at the hardware store.

Keeping rat snakes out of the bathroom was one thing; keeping them out of the chicken coop now that we knew they were
confirmed egg eaters was something else again. The enclosure
was too large to be made effectively snakeproof. So what to do?
The answer we eventually came up with was: not much. The gray
rat snakes went their way and we went ours. Egg production
continued to be low, but since there were always enough eggs for
us, and since Willie was not keen on surprising the snakes after
dark, when they usually did their poaching, we tacitly agreed to
leave well enough alone.

Over the years we occasionally had other problems with predators. Every now and then during fall or winter, migrant hawks,
presumably red tails, would leave another picked-clean cadaver
of a guinea or a duck on the lawn. Once a pack of half-starved
stray dogs killed two geese in a single day. Come spring, raccoons
or possums sometimes discovered the hidden nest of a guinea
hen or a mallard. And occasionally a bird simply vanished without a trace.

In the final analysis, our best defense against predators was the attitude we adopted: our flocks of domestic fowl were an indulgence, nice to have around, but they were expendable; the Place's wildlife, including its hawks, foxes, raccoons, and snakes, was not. Sometimes, as with the fox, we were able to cut the losses by temporarily confining our free-roaming birds in portable cages. But an even more effective measure was our practice of kidnapping newly hatched broods and raising them ourselves, thereby ensuring a supply of replacements when their elders met untimely ends.

Our guineas, geese, and ducks continued to meet such ends from time to time because we chose to allow them the run of the Place. But if such losses seem as unacceptable to other owners as they no doubt did to our guineas, geese, and ducks, the solution is simple enough: a well-made enclosure, such as we built for our chickens, faced — and roofed — with a high quality two-by-four-inch mesh, will keep any poultry safe from any predator — with the exception of an egg-filching snake.

Indeed, wire mesh is the answer to a long list of wildlife problems. Many is the time that, leafing through the relevant pages of the late, lamented Sears, Roebuck catalog, I wished I had the talent to write a poem dedicated to the many wonderful varieties of wire mesh: to the hog wire mesh fencing (topped by barbed wire) that wildlife can jump over or slip through, but which hounds must climb; to the wire mesh poultry fencing that keeps the fox and the hawk (and in some areas the coyote and weasel and skunk) from being led into temptation; to the rat- and snake-proof wire mesh screening on cages in which ducklings, keets, and goslings are reared; to the bordering of foot-high wire mesh that discourages armadillos from digging up flower beds and young azaleas (although not, alas, lawns); and to the wire mesh cylinders that prevent cattle (and deer, in areas where they are numerous enough to be a problem) from molesting young fruit trees.

If I did write such a poem, its theme would be the same as this chapter's: Anyone who buys land in order to live close to nature has the duty to either grin and bear it when conflicts with wildlife occur, or else invest the labor and money necessary to prevent those conflicts from happening. To reach for a gun when some rolls of wire mesh would solve the problem is inexcusable.

23

Schaeffer's Hill

During the spring of 1975, Schaeffer began to have trouble getting around, walking as though he had invisible hobbles on his hind feet. Both Ol' Doc Haley and our New Orleans vet, having ruled out hip dysplasia, proposed arthritis as a tentative diagnosis. But when the dog's condition worsened, I took him to a different veterinarian in the city and this man advised us that Schaeffer was suffering from fibrocartilaginous emboly, an incurable spinal condition that would eventually paralyze him.

"Eventually" came closer with every passing week. The one thing we could be grateful for was that the dog didn't seem to be in any serious pain. He had a healthy appetite, and his dignified but loving nature was as much in evidence as ever. But he was terribly frustrated by the failure of his hind legs to obey him. When he tried to keep up with Sammie during their morning runs, he sometimes looked as if he was on an exercise machine, pedaling hard and going nowhere. Within two months he could no longer climb steps or get in and out of the van without help, and soon after that he began to lose control of his bowels. He had always been, as Willie said, such a proper-acting dog, that now, although we didn't mind cleaning up after him, it broke our hearts to meet the look of bafflement and agonized apology with which he greeted us when we came downstairs in the mornings to find that he had messed his pallet.

Schaeffer had never lacked for affection during his nine years with Willie and me. But now, I think, he sensed a difference in the way we spoiled and petted him. Although the concept of death might have been beyond him, our solicitude, perhaps even more than his worsening condition, made him aware that we felt powerless to help him, and that there was no going back to the way things had been before. Often in the evenings, we took turns sitting on the floor beside him. He would rest his huge head in Willie's lap or mine, sometimes for an hour at a time, his expressive eyes staring broodingly into our faces as though memorizing them, the way someone going blind might try to memorize the quality of light.

Twice I took him to Doc Haley, meaning to have him put down; and twice I turned the van around outside the office and headed back to the Place. Each time Willie was standing on the porch when I arrived, his lower lip trembling as it always did when he was feeling emotional and upset. Each time his face broke into a beaming smile when I lifted Schaeffer from the van.

Yet he knew as well as I did that we were just postponing the inevitable. Hugging the Great Dane's neck, he bitterly complained, "If those vets are so smart, why don't they invent a wheelchair for dogs! And some dog diapers! Then we could keep him alive for years yet."

But they hadn't and we couldn't. The third time there was no turning back. Ol' Doc Haley, although embarrassed to see a grown man shedding tears, made no objection when I asked him to bring himself and his syringe out to the van. There the deed was swiftly done. Before Schaeffer could know what was happening it was over, and his beautiful head lay still and heavy in my lap.

That afternoon Willie and I buried him under a little grove of three oaks that stood apart on the middle ridge. It wasn't something we consciously decided, but from that day on, the ridge took the name of Schaeffer's Hill.

Sammie had been devoted to Schaeffer in his Sancho Panza way, so it wasn't surprising that during the rest of that unhappy weekend, and the following week in the city, he was agitated and restless. Yet he seemed more expectant than distressed, no doubt supposing that sooner or later his huge buddy would be coming back home. Given Sammie's usual short attention span, Willie and I assumed that in a few more days he would forget what it was he was supposed to be expecting and return to being his normal daffy, exuberant self. But it didn't happen that way. The next Friday evening, after arriving at the Place at the usual hour, Willie and I were carrying groceries and other gear into the house when a spiraling, unearthly yodeling, coming from the deck outside, stopped us in our tracks.

It was Sammie, sitting on his fat backside, his nose pointed skyward, howling his heart out. Somehow, suddenly, it had dawned on him that Schaeffer would never come home again.

Eight months later, we would bury Sammie on Schaeffer's Hill beside his friend. He had been several years the Great Dane's senior, and it was age, not grief, that did him in. He was a pragmatic little dog, after all, and although he went on missing Schaeffer for some time, he seemed to enjoy the fact that during that last phase of his life our attentions were lavished solely on him. Since he had lived the canine version of a long life, and suffered no lingering illness at the end, his death was a little easier for Willie and me to handle than Schaeffer's had been. Nevertheless, I felt that I had had enough of such losses. I just didn't want any more dogs around for a while. I failed to communicate this attitude to Willie, however, and two months later he came home from a visit with his mother carrying a small brown ragamuffin of a puppy that he had found abandoned in the street outside her house. Willie assured me that the foundling was a German shepherd — the same claim he had made for beagle-eared Sammie when he had come to his rescue more than a decade earlier — and proposed that we name him Teddy. The puppy, ecstatic and overexcited at the prospect of having found a home, wagged his stumpy tail, licked Willie's face, and peed on the rug as soon as Willie set him down.

Teddy was a rollickingly good-natured little animal, and as time went by I became increasingly fond of him. But from the start he was Willie's dog, which suited me just fine.

Unfortunately, it didn't suit Willie. About three months after Teddy joined the household, Willie presented me with a six-month-old black Great Dane. It was such a well-intended and costly gift that I had to seem pleased. Inwardly, however, my heart sank. The last thing I wanted was another dog, but if Willie had to give me one, I wished he had chosen another runty mutt like Teddy. Inevitably this Dane pup would remind me of Schaeffer, yet he would never *be* Schaeffer. There was no way I could ever learn to care about him.

I had to name him, so I named him Luke. I wasn't mean to him. I patted him, defleaed him, threw him his rubber bone to catch. But all the while I was thinking, *My God, this dog is a klutz!*

Luke was as clumsy as Schaeffer had been poised, knocking carvings off the coffee table with a wag of his tail, or stepping in his water bowl and spilling it, then standing around looking anxious and confused. Like all puppies he was playfully destructive, but unlike most, he was big enough to do serious damage, chewing up books, potted plants, the legs of chairs. He drooled. He was hard to toilet train. He allowed Teddy, at one-fourth his size, to bully him. In the city he tugged at his leash instead of walking along at a measured pace as Schaeffer had; at the Place he would gambol about the compound driving the geese and guineas crazy. The worst of it, though, was that he wouldn't leave me alone. He loved me! When I arrived home, he would jump up to give my face a huge slurp, nearly knocking me off my feet. He would follow me from room to room; and as soon as I sat down, huge as he already was, he would throw his ninety-plus gangly pounds into my lap, and then looked crushed when I pushed him off.

Despite my frail dissembling, Willie caught on pretty quickly that I didn't like the dog, and my emotional rejection of his gift hurt his feelings. This made me feel so guilty that, when he offered to find another home for the wretched animal, I assured him that he shouldn't even consider doing such a thing — although it was a solution I would have been glad to embrace.

That was the way matters stood when, one day, I came home from the university, opened the front door, and braced myself to ward off Luke's usual well-meant but unwanted assault. But only Teddy was there to greet me, Willie being still at work. With growing concern, I looked all through the house. No Luke. It was impossible. An almost full-grown Great Dane, large even by the standards of his kind, couldn't just disappear.

Finally, when I'd gone into the study for the third time, I eyed the closed door on its far side. It gave access to a small storeroom that was also used as a spare guest bedroom in a pinch. The room was rarely entered, its door was always shut. No sound came from it. Still, it was the only place I hadn't looked.

When I opened the door, I stepped back in shock. Blood was everywhere, soaking into the carpet, the bed, an overturned chair. And in the middle of all the gore sat Luke, feebly wagging his tail, gazing at me with an expression in his eyes that upset me almost as much as the injury he had done himself.

I could only surmise that the door had been left slightly ajar, that he had nosed it open, then somehow managed to bump it shut behind him. But no guesswork was needed to figure out what had happened next. A second door to the little room, opening onto the garden, had two narrow glass panes in its upper panels. Luke had evidently become claustrophobic, and in his usual blundering way, had put a paw through one of the panes in a futile effort to get out. The glass had cut a main artery in his right front leg; and when I found him the blood was still spurting out. I suppose if he'd been a person, he'd have been white as a sheet.

He just went on sitting there, tail thumping, giving me that same strange, stricken look. I fetched a handkerchief and a towel and squatted down beside him. "By God," I told him fiercely, "I've put up with you this long; I'll be damned if I'm going to let you die on me now."

While he tried to give my ear a mournful lick or two, I tied the handkerchief tight above the gash and wrapped the towel around his leg, then rushed him to the vet, where he was speedily stitched up. After examining him, the doctor assured me that he hadn't lost quite as much blood as I had feared, and would be as good as new in no time at all. And indeed, robust brute that he was, he was his usual self again in a couple of days.

But I was not, at least not in my relation to him. I remembered the way he had gazed at me that afternoon, sitting there in his own blood. He'd known that he had really screwed up bad this time, that now there was no way he was ever going to get me to like him. He had looked at me as though he expected to be punished, not rescued.

At that moment I understood how unfair I'd been to him. How I had constantly compared him to Schaeffer when there were no comparisons to be drawn. He was an altogether different animal; a klutz, to be sure, but a well-meaning one, with a big heart and a desperate hunger for attention and love.

And he was still a pup, I reminded myself. With a little more training, he would no doubt shape up. He just needed someone to look after him and build up his ego a bit. Someone to make him feel wanted.

Faced with that look of pure misery in his eyes, I resolved that that someone would be me.

24

The boy who
loved horses

The passing years did little to mellow Joker. He still tried to break into a sudden gallop or slam me against a tree whenever he thought my guard was down. But we had come to an understanding on some matters, among them the fact that no matter where we were headed when we started out on a ride, we would take a turn around the waterless Big Pond on the way home. Once it finally registered with him that he wasn't going to get me off his back or receive his undeserved reward of Purina dog food until he cooperated, he usually took this last detour without an argument.

Over the years I had become reconciled to the Big Pond's failure to hold water. This was because the bare, cratered expanse where the pond ought to have been, but wasn't, served instead as a tabula rasa on which any passing creature could leave the imprint of its paw or hoof. Here, more than anywhere else on the Place, I could indulge my passion for reading tracks.

That was what I was doing on an April morning in 1977. I had dismounted and was peering closely at a spot where the trails of a deer, a wild turkey, and a raccoon had coincidentally intersected in the sand, which was still moist from a rain three days earlier. The unusually large, splayed tracks of the deer, quite possibly a buck, were so fresh that crumbled dirt still formed a finely crenelated edge around each indentation. The raccoon's were a day or two older, already faintly blurred where the breeze had dusted them. Those of the turkey dated from just after the rain had let up. The large three-toed tracks — easily distinguished from a heron's, the only other bird large enough to have made them, by the absence of a spur mark at the heel — were clotted with the waterlogged sand that had sagged into them as soon as they were made.

For going on three years, not trusting to memory, I had been keeping a record of the presence of wild turkeys on the Place — the tracks, the unmistakable gobble of a courting male, the infrequent sightings of the birds themselves. Turkeys were rare in the vicinity; a flock of more than three or four was almost unheard of. But for some time I had had the impression that the hard-pressed local population was making increasing use of the property, thanks in all likelihood to the improved condition and diversity of its woodland habitats. This morning's track was one more bit of evidence that I was right.

I was still hunched over, studying this welcome message in the sand, when Joker suddenly whinnied and tried to pull away from me, almost jerking the reins out of my hand.

A horseman was coming toward me along the outside of the boundary fence. Even at a distance, I could see that the horse, a sleek roan, quite outclassed my hammer-headed Joker. The rider was young, wearing torn jeans, a T-shirt with something printed on it, and a rather moody smile of recognition. A thin black beard sprouted on his chin, and thick black hair hung almost to his shoulders. Not all that many years earlier a fellow would have been asking for trouble, exhibiting that much hair around here; but nowadays, the appropriate interval of cultural lag having elapsed, hirsuteness was much in vogue among the sandhills' younger set.

I mounted and rode up to the fence.

"Didn't have nothin' to do," the young man said, "so I figured I'd come over, see what you was up to. Reckon you don't remember me, do you?"

His shirt announced that he was Born to Be Bad.

"I'm afraid not," I said.

"Been goin' on seven or eight years," he said. "Just 'fore Camille. You ain't changed, but I was just a kid. My name's Lonnie. We talked once." He waved back in the direction he had come from. "Over there, on the road goin' into your place. About horses." He eyed Joker noncommittally. "I see you got one now."

Then I did remember him.

He had been a scrawny, rather waifish youngster, at most twelve years old, when we met one spring day on the entrance road. He had been sitting under a tree when I came along, his knees pulled up to his chin, staring so earnestly into space that I was almost abreast of him before he noticed me.

"I got out of school early," was the first thing he said.

"Okay," I said. It was about one in the afternoon.

He seemed to want somebody to talk to, so we talked. He was one of the numerous Janier clan, though apparently no near kin to Roddy Ray. When I asked him the inevitable question about how he was getting on in school, he said forthrightly, "I'm doin' real good. Just ask my teachers. I don't drink and smoke and run with wild girls like most of them other fellas do. Couple of nights ago, the priest caught two of 'em with a girl stripped down to her waist right behind the church." He shook his dark head disapprovingly. "Now me, I like nice girls."

When I asked him, again inevitably, what he wanted to be, he said it was his ambition to become a basketball coach someday. "I'm goin' to go to college. I got plenty of uncles will help me through. I got this one uncle, he says he'll pay for two years."

Almost as an afterthought, he added, "Of course what I really love is horses. I used to want to be a jockey, but I'm growin' too big." He asked me if I had a horse. I told him no, but that I might get one later on.

"I had a horse," he said. "I was raised with him, y'know. He was the best horse you could ever ask for. His name was Joey.

He'd know just what you wanted him to do. You could put a baby on him, he was that gentle. But if you wanted him to run, boy, he'd go like the wind. I'm tellin' you, you don't hardly find them like that nowadays!"

"You don't have him now?"

He shook his head. "Last year, when I was at school, he jumped the fence and runned off. He got all the way to the highway. When I got home my folks told me a truck had hit him, one of them big trailer trucks."

"What a rotten shame," I said.

"Yeh," he said, looking down at his feet. "It really tore me up."

After that, we covered a number of other subjects — snakes, dogs, teachers good and bad. Then, suddenly, he asked: "Do you really think it could have happened the way they say?"

"The horse? Well, I guess so."

"Joey never jumped the fence before. And he wouldn't'uv run off two miles to the highway. My ma said this man she didn't know came to tell 'em about it. But then my stepbrother said it was him that told 'em."

He paused. "You know what I really think? They sold him. They got a good price so they *had* to sell him. My daddy promised they never would. But we needed the money, I guess."

"Did you ever ask your folks about it?"

"Sure. I asked and asked. I kept after my ma, but she just kept sayin' they didn't sell him, that he was killed. . ."

No doubt I looked sympathetic since that was the way I felt. But I couldn't think of anything to say.

After a while he sighed, "I keep hopin' I'll meet someone who'll know, who'll tell me the truth. I was really in touch with that horse, y'know? I mean, I was raised with him. . ."

I complimented Lonnie on the fine-looking horse he owned now and asked him over to the house for a beer. When we reached the compound, he had comments to make about the house: "Never seen one with so many trees"; about Luke: "You could put a saddle on him"; about the guineas: "You don't much see them round here anymore"; about the pond: "Bet you get some good fishin' out of there."

But about Willie, when he came outside to be introduced, Lonnie had nothing to say. He must have heard of him; at any rate, he didn't seem surprised to see him there. In fact, until Willie was right in front of him, he didn't seem to see him at all. When Willie extended his hand, I sensed the fraction of a second's hesitation on Lonnie's part before he took it. Willie picked up on it too. Unruffled, he turned off his welcoming smile, said he had work to do, and left us. I watched him walk away, wishing I could do the same.

But I'd offered Lonnie a beer, so a beer he must have. He settled himself on the porch with the air of a man who means to sit a spell. As on that afternoon years earlier, he wanted to talk; and although his reaction to Willie had made me a less willing listener than I had been back then, once he got started, I became interested in what he had to say.

He told me he had dropped out of school when he was fifteen and soon after moved away to live with one of his uncles at Raysville, about eight miles north of the Place. He made that minuscule roadside community, indistinguishable from a hundred others in southern Mississippi, sound as though it were in another country. "Folks are different up there, y'know? They got their own ways of sayin' and doin' things. And they're ignorant! You can't talk to them about nothin'. After a year I couldn't take it no more, so I come back here to live."

The reason for the move to Raysville was that he had gotten a local girl in trouble. "Yeh," he said, "we grew up together. When I was a kid I used to pray to God every night that I'd get to marry her someday. She was a real nice girl back then. But she changed, y'know? It's funny how people change. Even after she was beginnin' to show, I was willin' to go ahead with marryin' her. But she kept throwin' it up to me that I didn't have no money or anythin'. And then one day we was at a dance; she was talkin' with some of her girlfriends, and when I came up, she said I should get the fuck away. So I told her that was just what I was goin' to do, I was goin' to get the fuck away from her for good!" He shook his head. "I'm sure as hell glad I didn't marry the bitch. Not that I'm like most of them others, though. At least I owned up to bein' the father. I pay a little on raisin' the kid now and then, even though I don't have to."

He asked if he could have another beer. When I brought him one, he said, "I reckon you don't have some weed, eh? Well, it don't matter. I don't need it. I ain't gettin' into dope the way some do around here. You can't do that and still expect to make somethin' of yourself. I got my own trailer now, y'know. I'm just down the road about a mile. It's a good enough spot, but I don't much like some of the ones movin' in near me, mentionin' no names. One of them — he's a cousin of mine — stole my still; and my own uncle — he's alcoholic, but that ain't no excuse — was the one told the sonuvabitch where it was hid. It weren't but a little home-use outfit, y'know. There ain't no ways to make a profit on bootleggin' anymore, now the whole state's goin' wet; even ol' Hovit's give it up. But that don't mean they had the right to steal it."

He fell silent, staring moodily at the compound fence where our horses were tethered, nursing the wrong his kin had done him along with his beer. When he went on, he said, "Around here, folks don't forget nothin', not ever. They get to drinkin', and they'll start bringin' up somethin' that happened ten years ago, like: 'I remember you tryin' to make out with my ol' lady,' or somethin' like that. They never forget. And I gotta admit it, I'm the same. Somebody fights with me, hits me with a lead pipe, it don't matter that they help me out later on and do me some favor, I ain't never gonna forget. Same with that cousin that stole my still. Same with my uncle. I ain't never gonna forget what they done."

Another silence. Then, perhaps feeling that all this badmouthing of kith and kin might give an outsider like me the wrong impression, he added, "They're friendlier, though, folks around here, than they are down on the Coast, I will say that. Even the ones that'll steal from you; if you need help, they'll give you the shirt off their back. Course everything's sort of changed; but folks hereabouts are still friendlier than anywheres else I know of.

"My trouble is, there ain't no jobs. I'm even thinkin' of movin' down to Slidell, get me a job at the textile mill. There's lots more opportunities down there for makin' somethin' of yourself than there is up here."

He didn't sound too sure of himself as he said this, however; Slidell was forty miles away.

Our attention was drawn to the horses. I had unthinkingly hitched Joker right next to Lonnie's mare, and now he was loutishly nudging her in a half-amorous, half-belligerent way, while she did her best to ignore him. "I can see he's a real pistol," Lonnie said. "Lots of get-up-and-go."

It was the most that anyone could say for Joker; not much, but enough to turn the subject to horses and give Lonnie a chance to extol the virtues of his own pretty mare. "She's a real sweetheart," he said, his voice suddenly softening. "That's what I call her: Sweetheart. Got some thoroughbred in her; you can see it in her head and neck. And she's smart! It don't take but the lightest touch and she knows what I want her to do. She really knows me, y'know? I'm tellin' you, I think the world of that horse. More'n I do of anybody. I don't let nobody ride her but me. I've had plenty of offers, but I wouldn't never sell her, not for a thousand dollars."

He finished his beer, absently tossed the can into an azalea bush, and got up to leave. "I don't know why I remember us talkin' that day, but I do. It was a long time ago."

"I remember too."

"It sure is funny how things work out."

"Yes."

"Y'know," he said, "every once in a while I still ask my ma what really happened to Joey — tryin' to catch her off guard, you might say. But she just gets angry. If she lives to be a hundred, she ain't never goin' to tell me the truth about that day."

25

A betrayal

It's been my experience that as long as you don't do something to rile them, people who live in the country really do tend to be more friendly and helpful than their urban and suburban counterparts, just as Lonnie Janier claimed. You might not want the shirts off their backs, but it's a comfort to know that if your car slides into a ditch on a muddy back road, even the no-accounts among them will stop to offer a helping hand.

Nevertheless — whether the locale happens to be the sandhills of Mississippi, the backwoods of Maine, or the rangelands of Montana — there is no getting around the fact that the country is wasted on most born-and-bred country people. At best, they are indifferent to the natural landscape in which they live; at worst, they see it as the place where they can dump their garbage, set fires, ride dirt bikes, trespass at will, allow dogs and cats to roam unchecked, and blast away at any wild bird or animal large enough to make a decent target. That's the way their daddies learned them, by God; and they don't want any outsider trying to persuade them to change their ways.

If that sounds a bit cranky, not to say elitist, I'm sorry, but it's the truth; and if you aren't prepared to deal with it, you may be letting yourself in for a mild case of culture shock when and if you decide to restore some forlorn piece of rural real estate to its former health and beauty.

In our case, the culture shock cut both ways. I couldn't always keep my mouth shut on the subject of environmental ethics when talking with neighbors, which tended to make the conversational tone a bit tense at times. But it was in the arena of our own woods, especially in the early years, that differences of opinion and attitude between the local people and us sometimes became downright adversarial. A good many of them regarded our private wildlife reserve as their private hunting preserve, and felt they had the right to trespass whenever they thought we weren't around. Needless to say, Willie and I didn't share that view.

It wasn't only us. One day when I stopped by Hovit's, a crony of his, a deputy game warden no less, was telling him about the "fancy-lookin' sign" that an elderly couple had put up at the entrance to their property. "It was real polite," the deputy chortled, "sayin' how their place was a refuge and *please* not to hunt there!" Of course he had taken the plea as a challenge, to which he responded by shooting out a covey of their quail. While he was boasting to Hovit about this exploit, he noticed the way I was looking at him. With a none-too-friendly grin, he said flatly, "That's what quails is good fer" — his hunter's credo in a nutshell.

I was new to the sandhills at the time, so all I said was that I doubted the elderly couple would have agreed with him. Before long, however, I began to be less discreet. As far as I was concerned, trespassing hunters were thieves, robbing the Place of its most prized possession, its wildlife; and I resolved to do what I could to stop them.

There are some fairly effective ways of coping with slob hunters, but posting signs that appeal to their sense of decency is not one of them. The system that Willie and I developed was to put up store-bought Posted, No Trespassing signs at thirty- or forty-yard intervals around the perimeter of the Place. Then, at every point where intruders who ignored those signs were likely to

enter the property, we nailed up others a short distance inside
the boundary. These were hand-painted in lurid colors — blood
red on pale blue or white — and they bore pithy messages such
as Trespassers Will Be Prosecuted, or just a simple warning: Stay
Out.

That sort of no-nonsense posting often has the desired effect
on the less hardened types among would-be trespassers, if only
because they realize the signs have been put up not by some im-
personal government agency or timber company but by a landowner who is dead serious about keeping interlopers off his or
her property. However, if you mean to deter the really hard cases,
you must be psychologically primed to back up what the signs
say. Not with pistol drawn, of course, or a homemade citizen's
arrest warrant gripped in your quaking hand. What you'll need is
a terse, firmly worded script composed and memorized beforehand so you won't be at a loss for words when it becomes necessary to face an intruder down.

During our first years at the Place I became pretty practiced
at using mine. The scenario was always the same: An early morning shotgun blast resounding in the Hollow or the Brainch. Me
jumping into pants and a loud shirt, running at full speed in the
direction from which the shot had come. The figure of some
slack-jawed youth or paunchy adult standing in among the trees,
holding a shotgun in one hand, a dead woodcock or squirrel in
the other, gawking at me as I rushed toward him. In the background, the stir of hounds or bird dogs snuffling in the thickets,
wanting to get on to the next quarry.

Willie didn't at all like the idea of me going out alone on these
forays; but when I argued that his presence might introduce a
racist element into a situation already likely to be tense enough,
he had to admit I had a point. I did consider bringing Schaeffer along for support, and later, Luke. But in coloring and size,
Schaeffer looked so much like a deer and Luke so like the legen-

dary local panther that I feared an overexcited hunter might shoot them before noticing that I was just the length of a leash behind.

Even alone and unarmed, however, I knew I had the edge in these confrontations. In a coldly controlled (if somewhat panting) voice, I would deliver my lines: "You wouldn't like me trespassing on your property, would you? So why are you trespassing on mine?" And: "It gets a little old, having to worry about getting shot if you take a walk in your own woods." And: "I'm like most Americans; I enjoy seeing *my* wild animals alive rather than dead!" (I felt that "like most Americans" was a nice extra touch, making my preference seem vaguely patriotic.)

The trick in all this was to be firm without sounding downright insulting. Invariably, the trespasser's part of the dialogue would consist of a sullen, muttered claim that he hadn't seen the posted signs. Then would come the retreat, me watching but not following, as the intruder slouched with studied slowness toward the boundary of the Place.

I've found that even narrow-minded, rather aggressive people will usually back off if you take the high ground and stand up to them. They may not understand ecology or good sportsmanship, but they don't like feeling on the defensive. And word does get around. Nowadays I still find an occasional spent shotgun shell in the Hollow, the souvenir of some poacher who checked to see that the Place was unoccupied before he started blasting away; but it's been several years since I last had to deliver the offended-property-owner spiel to some culprit caught in the morning woods.

I still remember my lines, though.

There was only one time when the usual script didn't serve. This was in the late '70s, when we had been at the Place for ten years.

It was the night before Christmas Eve. Two days earlier, Willie and I had deposited Santa Claus's bottle of vodka on Vera and

Wilbur's doorstep and exchanged gifts with Hovit and Lurlee and with Roddy Ray's family before heading for New Orleans to get the city house ready for the holidays. But then the weatherman forewarned that a hard freeze was on its way to southern Mississippi, and since we had had trouble with the pipes the preceding winter, I decided to drive back to the Place to do a better job of insulating them. Which was how I came to be there when everyone in the neighborhood thought me gone.

In the gray dusk I went down to the Big Pasture to see how the cows were doing. Its two halves, divided by a cross fence, had both been planted in winter rye grass, with the cows being rotated every three or four weeks from one to the other. At that moment the herd was in the pasture at the upper end of the slope, and when I dumped a couple of Christmas bonus sacks of feeder pellets in their trough they crowded around as usual. I scratched Bully's curly forehead and for a while watched them — dim black shapes now in the descending darkness — contentedly munching away, indifferent to the cold. When I turned back to the house I was thinking that it was too bad I hadn't been able to get to the Place while there was still enough light to see the whole of the Big Pasture clearly. Usually the deer didn't come out to feed on the rye until it was full dark, but there was always the chance that an impatient doe or yearling might break the daytime curfew.

When I got back to the house I spent a cold couple of hours under the house with a flashlight, sheathing and taping pipe. Then I made a fire, had a couple of martinis, ate dinner out of cans, and, dead tired, went to bed.

Maybe two hours later I came out of a deep sleep with such violent suddenness that I was half dressed before I realized what I was doing. Yet I already knew what had happened. The shotgun blast was echoing over and over in my head even though I had no conscious memory of having heard it fired.

Some years earlier — in fact, not long after that young drunk had come to the house in the middle of the night, wanting me to rescue him and his unlovely date from their muddy quandary — I had yielded, with a little urging from Willie, to the Great American Temptation to buy a gun, in this case a single-barreled twelve-gauge shotgun. It wasn't a question of paranoia. By that time we were pretty much over our earlier jittery reactions to inexplicable stirrings in the country night. But we were isolated, after all; and the World Out There was becoming more unstable, more screwed up with every passing year. We figured a shotgun was like a fire extinguisher: not something one planned to use, but worth having around, just in case.

I never had used it. But now, almost as a reflex, I grabbed it as I ran for the Ford pickup that a couple of years earlier had replaced our terminally exhausted Volksbus. With the gun on the seat beside me, I tore along the rutted entrance track, through the open gate, around the curve where the widow woman's house had stood, down the alley of oak forest, and out onto the long, level stretch that led in a straight line to the county road. To my right, at a distance down the slope, lay the Big Pasture, swallowed up by the night. But on its far side, where it was paralleled by the county road, I could make out through the intervening grid of midnight pines the distant beam of headlights, first withdrawing as the vehicle they belonged to backed up, then swinging in a half arc, then moving off down the road away from me. Moving fast! Whoever was behind the wheel had seen my lights before I saw his.

By the time I reached the county road and turned right, I had just time to see the red brake lights of the fleeing vehicle flash on at the crossroads almost half a mile away. Then all the lights were suddenly off. The driver was making the turn in the dark so I wouldn't see which direction he had taken!

Someone who knows what he's doing, I thought. Someone who's had practice outrunning the law. Like a moonshiner, for instance. I covered the distance to the crossroads at 80 mph, no mean feat on a dirt and gravel road. There I hesitated a second. To the left the road led to Vera and Wilbur's shack; to the right, it passed Roddy Ray's new house and, farther on, Hovit's place.

Like a moonshiner, I had thought. I hauled on the wheel, turning the pickup to the right.

Cursing the light rain that had fallen a couple of days earlier — there might otherwise have been a dust trail hanging in the air — I swung around the sharp turn beyond which lay Roddy Ray's little spread. A floodlight under the eaves illuminated the bare space between house and road. I was about to roar past when a movement in the carport caught my eye — a figure holding open the kitchen door.

"Belina," I yelled, turning into the driveway and pulling up behind Roddy Ray's pickup. I jumped out, and Roddy Ray's pretty second wife hurried forward into the harsh glare of the floodlight. I liked Belina; she had made Roddy Ray happy, and she was a wonderful mother to Baby Gladys as well as the son she and Roddy Ray had had together; but her usual cool efficiency intimidated me a little, so I hadn't ever felt quite as close to her as I had to poor Eloise.

"I was just about to —" she started to say, and then stopped. The look on my face must have frightened her; she actually drew back a little as though I might strike her.

"Did you see anyone?" I demanded. "Anyone driving by just now?"

"No!" she stammered. "I — I just this second stepped outside to —"

I didn't wait for her to finish. Cursing the lost minutes, I dashed back to the pickup and drove on to Hovit's; but I already knew I had lost the race.

Except for the porch light, Hovit's house was totally dark, as though no one were at home. I wanted to rush up to the door and bang on it; but if anyone answered — and it would probably be

Lurlee, not Hovit — what could I say? What could I prove? I turned around in the driveway, the yard dogs barking at me as I drove away.

Heading back to the Place, I felt literally sick with rage. This was different from catching some yahoo squirrel hunter in our woods. For the first time in my life, I understood in my gut and heart what the victims of thieves and vandals meant when they spoke of feeling violated. For the first time in my life, I knew what it meant to actually want to kill someone.

Jacklighting is the most repulsive and the most popular form that illegal hunting takes in the United States; and I knew with absolute certainty that a deer had been jacklighted and shot in the Big Pasture that night. And the worst of it was that it had been in effect *baited* — by the rye grass that I myself had planted. Any wild animal is utterly vulnerable when it is approached upwind in the dark. Shine a bright light in its eyes and it will just stand there, mesmerized — as a deer had stood in the pasture that night — waiting to be slaughtered.

Shaking more with anger than with cold, I went down to the Big Pasture as soon as I got back to the Place. At first the flashlight didn't pick up anything but the golden eyes of the ruminant cows; but as I waded deeper into the rye, the beam reflected back a lone point of light shining through the grass. I was almost on top of it before the outline of a doe's head materialized around that shining eye. The animal lurched unsteadily to her feet and made for the fence. The first time she attempted to jump it — an easy hop for an uninjured deer — she snagged herself and fell back. On the second try, she managed to clear it and disappeared in the darkness of the Hollow.

After a sleepless night I went back to the Pasture at dawn, and there I found the whole story written in the flattened, blood-smeared grass. There was some dried blood where the wounded doe had been lying, but a lot more nearby, where another deer had obviously been shot and killed. Its body had been dragged to the fence and heaved across, and the wire was bent down where the poacher had hurriedly climbed over. On the far side the ground was marked by a large brown stain where the deer had apparently been left to lie for a considerable time. Beyond, less easy to trace among the young pines, the trail of the dragged carcass went on to the county road, to the spot where, from the entrance drive, I had seen the headlights of a car backing up.

Now everything fell into place. I saw again the pickup in Roddy Ray's driveway; if it had been an animal, it would have been panting. And I saw Belina, usually so self-assured, shrinking away from me as though I might hit her.

There could be no doubt. I had been betrayed by a friend whom I had absolutely trusted. Roddy Ray knew how I felt about the Place's wildlife, yet he had come into the pasture in the middle of the night, jacklighted one deer and killed it, and incidentally wounded another that had been standing behind it. When he saw my headlights caroming along the entrance drive, he had signaled Belina, waiting in the pickup, to clear out, which she had, flicking off the headlights at the crossroads in an attempt to lose me. However, she hadn't quite gained enough time to get into the house before I had come tearing by; and for a brief moment she must have thought that I knew the truth. And I would have known, I suppose, if it had crossed my mind to suspect her and Roddy Ray.

He, of course, had remained crouched in the dark woods with the dead deer until I finished searching the Big Pasture. Much later, after I had called it quits for the night, Belina had come back for him.

Last night's cold wind was still blowing from the north, soughing through the pines, sweeping across the winter rye. I stood there by the county road for a long time, bleakly wondering how many other deer Roddy Ray had killed over the years, how many others I had set up for him.

I walked the half-mile to his house. The pickup was gone, the house silent. The carport showed traces of dampness where it had been hosed down; but Roddy Ray's blood-covered boots lay where he had left them beside the back steps.

That night, on my way back to the city, I stopped by the house again. Roddy Ray opened the door and greeted me with a nervous smile, unsure of what I might or might not have figured out. He had just time to say, "Why hey, Don, I thought —" before I cut him short. For this encounter I didn't need a script. I told him what I thought of slob hunters and false friends. I told him, almost meaning it, that I would kill him if he ever set foot on my land again. Not forgetting the season, I told him I hoped he choked on his Christmas venison.

He just stood in the doorway, not saying anything. When I drove off, he was still standing there.

Occasionally during the following two years Willie and I would see Roddy Ray or Belina outside their house as we drove by. Sometimes they would raise a hand in a half wave. To my annoyance, Willie, after a while, started giving them a half wave back. I never did.

We still visited Cora now and then. Since Roddy Ray had remarried, she lived alone in a little house not far from the crossroads. Sad to say, she was no longer as cheerful and outgoing as she had been when we first knew her. Eloise had been more a daughter than an in-law, and Cora had never really gotten over the younger woman's tragic death. She was particularly haunted by something that an eyewitness to the accident had told her and even years later, out of the blue, she would bring it up: "I'd thought it was real quick for her, y'know; but this fellah said she was still alive when they pulled her out of that wreck! They put her by the side of the road, and she was *movin'!* Oh Don, I wish I hadn't been told about that. I'd give anythin' not to been told that!"

Whether because she felt that no one else could measure up to Eloise, or because Belina had a personality as strong-willed as her own, Cora sometimes seemed less than thrilled that Roddy Ray and her new daughter-in-law got on so well. She rarely visited them; yet that did not prevent her from being much troubled by the estrangement between her son and us. On more than one occasion, she broadly hinted that it wasn't Roddy Ray himself who first conceived the idea of shooting a deer in our pasture.

That argument left me unmoved. Indeed, I was a little surprised at just how unforgiving I could be. My anger eventually wore itself out, but that didn't make Roddy Ray's betrayal any easier to excuse. Yet I hated to see Cora getting upset about the situation. After she had told Willie and me for the twentieth time how Roddy Ray was "really hurtin'" over our lost friendship, and Willie, as usual, was um-umming and nodding sympathetically about what a shame it was, I finally said, in a moment of weakness, that I, too, regretted what had happened.

Maybe it was that little lapse, relayed with suitable embellishments by Cora to her son. Maybe it was just the passage of two years. In any case, a few days later, Roddy Ray and Belina showed up at our doorstep unannounced. Somewhat nervously, they exclaimed about all the things we had done around the Place since they had last been there. I was pretty stiff and distant at first. But Willie, who would have forgiven Satan himself for that bit of trouble he caused in Eden, had decided that enough was enough. Right off, he ushered our uninvited guests into the house, talking and smiling, getting them Cokes, generally making them feel welcome. Warmed by his goodwill, Roddy Ray and Belina began to relax, and my chilly reserve began to thaw. Before long we were all behaving almost as though the two years of alienation had never been. Almost.

None of us referred to that night before Christmas Eve, then or later on. But although Roddy Ray could not apologize, he did, I believe, give up jacklighting. At any rate, he made a point of remarking to me more than once that, by his own example, he was raising his son to be "an honest hunter."

As far as Roddy Ray was concerned, bygones were bygones and we were all back on the old familiar footing. Willie took the same view; but I had not his generosity of spirit. Maybe, after all, I was becoming a sandhiller. I was glad enough to be on friendly terms with Roddy Ray again. But what young Lonnie had said of the folks hereabouts was true of me as well. I wasn't going to forget. Not ever.

26

Subtractions and additions

For a couple of years after the jacklighting episode, Willie and I went on raising cattle, even though it became more than ever a losing proposition. Once we knew that at least one deer, and quite possibly several, had been attracted to our winter pasture only to be killed there, we felt obliged to give up planting it in rye grass. Roddy Ray might have learned his lesson, but I figured that sooner or later other poachers would use the pasture as a killing ground when we weren't there — if they hadn't been doing so already. To compensate for the loss of winter grazing, we tried increasing our production of hay; but to do that, we had to take the cattle off both sections of the Big Pasture in midsummer in order to have the Bahia grass tall enough by October for our hired baler to mow it. Even after we had reduced the herd by selling off the three oldest animals, we still ended up buying more hay than the Big Pasture produced. Unless we turned another ten acres of the Place into pastureland, which we weren't about to do, there was no way the arithmetic could add up. Raising livestock was becoming a very expensive hobby indeed.

In the end, however, money wasn't the deciding factor. By the early '80s, both Willie and I were making pretty decent salaries and I was earning some extra money as a writer, so we were actually feeling downright affluent for the first time in our lives. The real problem was that, between being a full-time professor and moonlighting as a writer, I had less time — and energy — to spare for the Place. Less time to do my share of disking pastures or loading bales of hay or repairing fences or dipping the cows or stocking up on feeder pellets or fertilizer. Or pausing long enough to savor the contentment of looking at contented cattle.

So the doleful day finally came when, in a rented cattle trailer, we carted Bully the Second and all his lowing wives and children off to auction. We had made the same trip at least half a dozen times before, using our own pickup to transport two or three yearlings or, more recently, the senior members of the herd; so by now we were pretty used to parting with individual animals. The Master Plan, after all, required that we periodically should. But this time it was the herd itself to which we were bidding farewell; and with it, my fond idea that the ecological healing of the Place and its utilitarian use could be compatible objectives. The concept itself had been sound enough. But the combination of jack-lighting poachers and my own busyness had defeated it.

The busyness reached its peak in 1982 when I was often away from home on writing assignments, and burning the midnight oil at my desk when I wasn't. After that, I began to be more sensible and less ambitious, and things eased up quite a bit. But during that hectic — and, as time would prove, fateful — year, Willie and I were lucky if we got to the Place a couple of times a month. Given that sort of schedule, we were no longer able to care properly for Joker and Big Jim, which meant that with them, as with our cattle, there must come a parting of the ways. Fearing that our aging mounts would end up as dog food if we sold them at auction, we practically gave them away to the owner of a riding stable with the understanding that, in keeping with their gift-horse status, not too much would be expected of them.

Although neither Joker nor Big Jim seemed all that moved, we said goodbye to them with heavy hearts. Well, to be honest, mine wasn't all that heavy, but, rather guiltily, I assumed that Willie's was — until, that is, an afternoon a couple of months later when we took a walk over to the Big Pasture. The pole gate was wide open. The gray boards lining the chute and the corral seemed already to be sagging. In the pasture itself, the ungrazed Bahia grass was up to our knees. We stood there for a while, surveying all that verdant emptiness. Then Willie turned to me and said, "Don't take this wrong, Don, but in a way, after more than ten years, I can't help thinking it's sort of a relief."

"Oh, Willie," I laughed. "I wish you'd told me sooner. It's what I've been thinking too."

Willie and I may have moved into the 1980s with some money to spare, but we soon found a way to spend it. The absentee owner of the forty acres adjoining the Place on the north died, and his two heirs each put their respective twenty acres up for sale. One parcel encompassed all the land along the winding entrance track that was not already part of the Place, and the other a stretch of piney woods on the far side of the county road. Happily, neither had been logged during the years we had lived at the Place.

We knew that we would have to buy these tracts now that they were on the market. Increasingly, the sandhills were being built up. Every back road in the vicinity of the Place was being uglified by more and more little cleared-off plots with trailers parked on them — sometimes two or three deep as children and grand-children settled in. It was unthinkable that "our" entrance road should suffer that sort of defacement. Or that, as Willie remarked, "Somebody who don't like blacks, like that Lonnie fellah, might move in next door."

Yet even if there had been no compelling need to create a buffer zone for the Place and ourselves, Willie and I would have gone into hock, if we'd had to, to buy that land. It was beautiful for one thing. For another, it belonged ecologically to the land-scape of the Place. The belt of hardwoods through which the entrance road wound its way was a continuation of our Hollow and Oak Grove, and its drainage system fed our Brainch. Moreover, it was a "highway" for wildlife. It extended to the county road and even beyond, though on the far side it soon changed character and became a shallow brainch. When deer, foxes, and wild turkeys crossed the road, they displayed a marked preference for this corridor of hardwoods. Acorns and other types of mast could be found there; but, even more crucially, the hardwoods provided better cover than the more open pine woods to either side. Once we acquired the quarter-mile of frontage on both sides of the road, the crossing would be lastingly secured against human development.

Like the Oak Grove, but unlike the Hollow where many different types of hardwoods grew, this belt, the most dry and upland section of the hardwood forest, was dominated by live oaks. One of the world's most beautiful trees, the live oak is often thought of as slow growing, but here in the Deep South nothing could be further from the truth. It does, however, tend to grow *out* as much or more than it grows *up;* and before its beauty can begin to manifest itself, it must, like a Rubens Venus, put on some weight. Which is what the oaks on the land Willie and I planned to annex were doing with quite wonderful success. The lordly Sherwood Forest that we had pictured in our minds some fifteen years earlier had now become a reality — and soon it would be ours!

At the heart of this live oak forest was the tree that was its centerpiece, the fulfillment of everything that all the oaks around it were in the process of becoming. By any standard except an economic one, it alone was worth the price of the property on which it grew. It was the most splendid specimen of its splendid species I had ever seen growing in the wild (as opposed to parks or plantations where competition from neighboring trees is minimal). Without question it was the oldest tree, as well as the oldest living thing of any kind, to be found for miles and miles around. A hundred times since first seeing it, I had wished that it had chosen to root itself just twenty-five or thirty yards south of where it grew, on our side of the boundary fence. A hundred times I had detoured from a walk along the entrance road to present myself to it, just wanting to look at it and, in some vague, inarticulate way, pay it homage. It was a real presence, creating its own atmosphere, its own world — albeit one that was now somewhat in ruin. In places, patches of the black furrowed bark had fallen away, exposing the gray wood underneath; elsewhere, the massive trunk wore a thick patina of moss and lichens. The heavy, hurricane-battered boughs, some dead or dying, were hung with wisps of Spanish moss and matted with gardens of resurrection fern — so named because the small fern fronds, brown and shriveled during a dry spell, spring to emerald life after even the smallest rain.

I didn't indulge in a gosh-if-a-tree-like-that-could-only-talk sort of reverie. Not quite. But I did a lot of wondering about that oak. I wondered why it was still there, for one thing. It had to be well over a century old; closer, probably, to two. It had begun its life when this part of the sandhills was still a wilderness presumably dominated by vast barrens of longleaf pine. How then, during its early vulnerable years, had it withstood the fires that were said to have swept through this region, unimpeded by roads or firefighters? Unless, of course, it had been sheltered from the flames by the pine and grass excluding shade of oaks already mature when it was young. In which case, what had happened to those older trees? Had they, like the longleafs, been felled during the years of the Big Cut? And if so, how had this one oak, already mature by the early 1900s, escaped the same fate? It wasn't near enough to the widow woman's home site for her to have spared it as a shade tree. Had the loggers themselves erected their shelters under its wide canopy, or sought its shade during breaks in their hard labors?

There were no certain answers to these questions, but the Oak did have a thing or two to tell me. Clearly, it must be the progenitor of the oak forest that surrounded it, of which our Oak Grove was now a part. Its offspring had been able to take root in spite of annual fires, no longer set by lightning storms or Choctaws, but by the likes of Hovit and Roddy Ray, and their fathers before them. The first seedlings must have survived by growing in the Oak's own shadow, and later generations had sprung up in theirs, protected from the combustible winter grasses and showers of dead pine needles that would have turned them into torches whenever a fire came through. Even before Willie and I had come along to keep the fires out, some of those trees, notably those in our Oak Grove, had outgrown the reach of the flames. Although we had accelerated the process of expansion, to some extent it would have occurred in any case. The Oak's offspring were, in fact, reclaiming what had once belonged to them. The Oak itself would not have been there unless live oaks had occupied this particular ridge when the sandhills were a wilderness. Its presence was a vindication, if we had felt we needed one, of our headstart policy for underprivileged hardwoods.

We jumped too quickly, I expect, at the chance to buy those forty acres. Property in the sandhills, as everywhere else, had appreciated considerably during the '70s, but even granting that, we paid through the nose for the two tracts. Fortunately, a great friend of ours, Arlan — he who had contributed the soap-bubble magic to our raising-the-roofbeam celebration — offered to buy ten acres of the twenty on the far side of the county road. He had no particular plans for the land, but he loved the Place, and this investment was a way of buying a share in it. If he ever had to sell the ten acres, he said, it would be to us.

In late 1983, with the cattle and horses gone, the new land purchased, and the workload considerably reduced, Willie and I were able to turn our energies to new projects. This translated into an urge to start building again. Enough years had elapsed for us to conveniently forget the mashed thumbs, sore muscles, and frayed tempers that our earlier construction efforts had cost us. Our fiefdom had been enlarged, and it seemed only right and fitting that our castle should be too.

Willie started us off by complaining about the narrow galley kitchen; how there wasn't enough room for him to set things out or move around while he was fixing one of his culinary extravaganzas. That led me to a consideration of the upstairs loft. It was a perfectly good place to sleep as long as we didn't have overnight guests, but when we did, it became a dormitory. The more I thought about all the times we had had to lie awake listening to our friends' snores (during the intervals when they were not lying awake listening to ours), the more appealing the idea of a private bedroom became.

So we set to work. First we braced and walled in the half of the downstairs and upstairs porches that fronted on the kitchen and the area of the loft directly above it. Then we tore out the original exterior walls, put windows into the new ones, and relocated the sink, stove, and water heater in the kitchen. Upstairs we built interior walls that divided the loft into two bedrooms, one for us, one for guests. We took such great pains hanging and floating the sheetrock that only Brian, our architect friend, seemed to notice that the jointing between the original rooms and the additions was a bit uneven. Notwithstanding his quibbles, we were vastly pleased with the results of our labors: a kitchen almost double its original size, and a snug, well-insulated little bedroom with a view of the pond and Schaeffer's Hill.

We were so pleased, in fact, and so relatively unscarred by all that sawing and hammering, that we decided to press on. To compensate for the foreshortened porches, we built a deck at the side of the house the size of a handball court, furnishing it with benches made of treated wood, a cable spool table, a couple of trees growing through holes cut in the planking, and old cow skulls found in the woods. Our resident lizards were delighted with the new addition, as was a descendant of the Downstairs Armadillo, who dug a den underneath it as soon as it was finished.

In effect, we now had a large, open-air living room that the wind would sweep and the rain would mop. We spent a lot of time out there when the deer flies weren't acting up too badly, defleaing Luke and Teddy, drinking Cokes, watching guineas and cardinals and squirrels at the feeders, cleaning bass caught in the pond, filing the chain on the chain saw, or, quite often, doing nothing at all.

But it was not in my nature to leave well enough alone. I felt that, in visual terms, there was something missing. The far end of the deck was just there, pointlessly jutting out over the low, box-like structure that contained the pump for our well. It somehow looked unfinished. It didn't *lead* to anything.

Then, one day while I was sitting there staring at that Something that was missing, the idea came to me.

"I know what we need," I said to Willie.

He looked up from the peas we had been shelling. "So do I. A microwave oven. And a VCR."

"A tower!" I said.

"And a washing machine," he went on. "We could really use a washing machine."

But pretending not to hear was just Willie's way of reserving judgment. Once I explained what I had in mind, he was as excited as I was. "Kind of like a tree house," he said approvingly.

"That's it exactly!" I exclaimed. "A tree house tower!"

The not very towering tower I was visualizing would be a two-story structure somewhat like the one I had planned for our first house, but it would be surmounted by a railed platform — a sort of widow's walk, not a steepled roof. The first floor would be a pump and storage room. The second story, a little above the level of the deck, would be a ten-by-ten study and extra bedroom, with wide windows taking up most of three walls. On the fourth wall, facing the house, would be a glass doorway, raised a couple of steps from the deck. The height of this room would elevate the platform above it to within touching distance of the limbs of the live oak on the pond side of the house. Sitting on that deck, we would be roofed by the oak's branches, shaded by its leafy canopy. A tree house indeed!

Access to this miniature Falconhurst would not be from the room below or from an outside stairway, but via an extension of the main house's second-story porch. For some reason, this little bridge struck both Willie and me as the perfect final touch in the tower's design.

It took us three months, but the day finally came when the four removable sections of the platform deck (painstakingly angled to take into account the roof's slight slant for drainage), were assembled, the tower railings were nailed into place, and the job was done. That same evening, after trotting back and forth across the eight-foot bridge half a dozen times, Willie and I took possession of our embowered aerie. The evening star was overhead. A wind was singing in the pines. The nearby red oak, but not the live oak, was showering down its leaves. It was pretty cold, but we didn't care. With a celebratory bottle of champagne on the little table between us, we sat there quietly until the light had entirely faded, enchanted by this new, more encompassing view of compound and pond, Schaeffer's Hill and the autumn woods beyond, the garden, the leafless fruit trees, the pines on the index ridge backed by the Hollow's gray-green wall — the whole calm and smiling aspect of our beloved Place smiling calmly back at us.

27

The controlled burn

Late in February 1985, just before the Deep South spring was ready to once again unfold, Willie and I reversed our long-standing policy of banning woods fires and undertook a couple of controlled burns at the Place, one on Schaeffer's Hill, the other on the lower slope of the index ridge. Both areas were grown up in pines, most of which were now tall enough to withstand even a very hot fire with little harm done.

We discovered — the hard way, as usual — that preparing a controlled burn was a lot more work than we had thought. We could have hired the Forest Service people to do the job, but, cost aside, they would have used trench plows to gouge out the fire breaks, and we had seen enough of the ugly eroded scars those things left on the land to not want to use them if we could avoid it.

Our environment-friendly fire lanes were eight-foot-wide swaths, each encircling some eight or nine acres for a combined total length of at least half a mile. First we did some preliminary clearing, wielding bushwhackers to cut back the gallberry and cypress weed. Then we raked. And raked some more. The lanes ran mostly through pine woods, including our now well-established slash pine plantation, and after more than fifteen unburned years, the pine straw underneath the trees was layered so thickly that we could almost have used pitchforks to scoop the stuff up.

When that job was finally done, we mowed. Our lawnmower had a rough enough time of it just working the compound, what with the lurking pine cones, half-exposed roots, and other excrescences that were the byproducts of our deliberately shaggy landscaping. But even by that harsh standard, those fire lanes, clotted with thick clumps of aptly named wire grass, were a lawnmower's Golgotha. The machine with which we began the job broke down before we were halfway through; and by the time we finished, its brand-new replacement was a palsied wreck.

Mowing done, we raked again, this time scraping up all the cones, dead grass, and powdery, highly inflammable pine duff that we hadn't been able to get the first time around. Lastly, we used the rototiller to disk a two-foot-wide ridge down the middle of the lanes — enough to halt any low fire that might inch out into the short, mowed grass of the lanes when the flames reached the edge of the fire breaks. The width of the lanes, we confidently assumed, would prevent the fire from jumping from the area it was supposed to burn to areas it wasn't.

That was the plan, and I had so much faith in it that I drove over to Cora's and asked her to phone her Forest Service friend at the fire tower — we had no phone ourselves — so he would know he needn't come to the rescue if he saw a woods fire burning up our way.

The wind was the only wild card in the deck. In late February and early March it can spring up from any direction at a moment's notice and, giving full value to the term "variable," blow this way and that with considerable force. However, this otherwise unreliable wind had one fairly reliable trait: it was a late riser, not likely to get really gusty until midmorning at the earliest. With that in mind, Willie and I started the first burn, on the index ridge, at the crack of dawn.

So much for relying on fairly reliable traits. We had no sooner set the tinder-dry grass and pine straw on the index ridge ablaze along one side of the area to be burned when the sleeping wind came suddenly and mischievously awake. For a moment we just stood there, stunned. Amateurs that we were, we hadn't fully realized how combustible our woods had become after so many years of being fire-free. The annual ground fires we had fought on the much-burned lands outside the Place were weenie roasts compared to this one we had started ourselves. Even without benefit of a wind, it would have been rather more of a conflagration than we had bargained for. As it was, with 25 mph gusts to fan it, we had an eight-acre bonfire on our hands. Yaupon, waxmyrtle, huckleberry — fifteen feet high and thickly wrapped in an excelsior of dead pine needles — exploded into flames that reached up into the crowns of the pines themselves, setting some of them ablaze. When the wind shifted direction for a minute and came at us, the wave of heat it drove before it scorched us like a blowtorch.

"Holy shit," I said.

"Backfire," said Willie. Which struck me first as a comment on the way things had worked out, and then as a good idea.

Willie was already on the move. Over his shoulder he said, "You stay on this side till the fire's burned away from the lane, then come help me."

"Right," I said, as he bounded toward the roaring wall of fire and elegantly jumped through it at a place where the flames were not too high.

He had no sooner disappeared when the wind, which had been generally blowing westerly, toward the far side of the burn area, suddenly changed direction again. A veritable Vesuvius of burning pine needles swept past me and into the woods outside the fire lane's perimeter. There, a mixed stand of pines and oaks, interspersed with dense thickets of young hardwoods, created a transition zone between the pine woods we had meant to burn and the Hollow, which we emphatically had not.

A wraith of smoke rose from the dead grass on this "safe" side of the fire break. Then another and another.

During the lively ten minutes that ensued, I carried on like a dervish with a hotfoot. Luckily, the wind had almost immediately swung back to the west again. But even so, I had my work cut out for me. Soon as I had subdued one small blaze with my boot or the rake, another would flare up a dozen yards away. I'd reach it just before it began to spread — but even as I was stomping on it, a third blaze would spring to life back where I'd put the first one out.

By the time the last of these unauthorized fires had been extinguished, the authorized one had swept across most of the area it was supposed to burn and was advancing toward the fire break on the opposite side — and Willie's backfire — like the fiery equivalent of a tidal wave bearing down on a foot-high seawall. I ran across the blackened, smoking expanse and when I caught up with it, jumped half over, half through the swirling flames into a swath of unburned ground, only a few yards wide, that still separated the fire behind me from the one Willie had set to meet it. I knew that when the two collided, as they would in a matter of seconds, there would be a mini-firestorm. So I jumped again — and again and again, since the backfire, burning more slowly against the wind, made for a wider wall of flames to get through.

When I had finally dodged around the roaring pyres of pine straw we had so painstakingly raked up and stumbled into the fire lane on the far side, my face and hands felt as though they'd been barbecued, and my feet were fairly sizzling in my boots. But even worse was the inescapable, lung-searing smoke that now enveloped me. *Poor Willie!* I thought; for I realized that, except when the wind had turned around toward me for an occasional minute or two, the smoke had been blowing in his direction all the while.

I found him farther up the lane, on hands and knees, his face just inches from the ground. A little beyond him, a thicket of yaupon was in flames — on the wrong side of the fire break. "You got to get down here to breathe," he said in a choking voice. He looked done-in, as well he might — eyes bloodshot, dark skin and black hair gray with ash. His backfire had worked, in the sense that it had prevented the fire we had originally set from reaching the fire break, which it would have easily jumped all along the line. But the backfire, fanned by the obstreperous wind, had itself jumped the lane in several places, so that Willie, too, had been desperately trying to put out one flare-up after another — with the difference that he had been working in the midst of choking clouds of smoke. He nodded toward the burning yaupon. "I got 'em all," he said, "except that one."

The wind was swiftly driving the flames toward the ravine below the House Pond. This little tributary brainch, which fed into the pitcher plant bog at the bottom of the ridge, boasted particularly dense thickets of yaupon laden with clusters of bright red berries, as well as the largest stand of young cypress on the property. Too young, I knew, to survive a fire as hot as this one.

Willie and I made a last desperate attempt to beat the fire back. We positioned ourselves in an area where the brush was not too thick; and when the fire came at us, we attacked it from either end, flailing frantically with our rakes. But the wind was too strong, the smoke too thick, the woods too dry. And we were half suffocated and totally spent.

"It's no use," I croaked.

Which was when Willie, whose all-time favorite movie was *The Ten Commandments*, decided to do a Charlton Heston number. I'd never seen him so thoroughly exasperated, not even when he'd found the dismembered rats in the freezer. Coated in ashes from head to toe, he stepped in front of the fire, facing the wind, righteous as Moses when he came down from the Mount to find the Israelites partying and worshiping false gods. He shook his rake. "Stop it!" he hollered. "Right now, you hear me? *Stop it!*"

These late-winter winds, along with their other erratic ways, are subject to sudden lulls, so the timing was probably coincidental. What is certain is that, when Willie spoke, the wind died down.

Willie gave me a smug Charlton Heston smile. I looked suitably awed. Then, fueled by a final surge of adrenaline, we attacked the fire again. By the time the wind revived, we had it licked.

Afterwards, too tired to climb the blackened ridge to the house, we sat in our much-breached fire lane for quite some time, blending in nicely with the smoldering ashes all around us.

"I've had it," I said in a charred voice, "I vote for hiring the Forest Service to do the burn on Schaeffer's Hill."

But Willie, basking in the afterglow of his unofficial miracle, wouldn't hear of it. "We'll fool that wind yet," he said. "We'll get up and start the fire even earlier, while it's still dark. You'll see; this time everything will work out just right."

And it did. In the hour before dawn, the second burn moved steadily across Schaeffer's Hill, came obediently to a halt at our arduously constructed fire lane, and burned itself out — just minutes before the wind, furious at being outsmarted, began sweeping back and forth across the scorched ridge.

"We were in luck this time," I remarked to Willie. He nodded politely, but I could tell from his look — Moses, after the children of Israel had gotten through the Red Sea and Pharaoh's army hadn't — that he felt there was a little more to it than that.

28

Luck runs out

e did those controlled burns in the hope that they would entice our gopher tortoises back to the Place.

The tortoise that had settled in our vegetable garden hadn't stayed for long. Perhaps there were not enough tender leafy greens to keep him interested; or he felt inconvenienced because I sometimes took the dogs out for a prebedtime walk just when he was gearing up to do some roaming of his own. Whatever the reason, he left. But that was all right. Pulling up stakes was his decision, and when he did, he didn't move far; his new burrow was only a few dozen yards beyond the compound fence. He was still our luck.

During the next ten years or so, I very occasionally saw him or one of his relatives plodding across the entrance road at night; and now and then I noticed the telltale mound of freshly excavated dirt where one of them had dug a new den. But although I loved knowing the gophers were out there, it never occurred to me to keep close tabs on them. I took it for granted that they had always been part of the Place and always would be. The land, after all, was in better shape now than it had been when we first acquired it, so they should be more content than ever to stick around.

But then, one summer day in the very early '80s, Willie and I saw a curious sight that should have alerted us that something was not quite right in tortoiseland. We were just arriving at the Place, and I had gotten out of the truck to unlock the fence gate when I saw a tortoise emerge from its burrow a few yards from the drive. Without so much as a look around, he descended the burrow's apron of red dirt and shouldered his way into the surrounding stand of gallberry bushes. It seemed odd enough that he should be active in the middle of a hot, sunny day when tortoises were almost never abroad. But even more I was struck by the forthright manner of his departure. I somehow knew he wasn't just out foraging. He was leaving home.

Yet close to three more years would go by before Willie and I would realize that the Place was entirely bereft of tortoises, our excuse being that during that too-busy period, the Place was so often bereft of us. It wasn't until Willie happened to notice that all the burrows in the vicinity of the house were obstructed by brush, their entrances clouded by cobwebs, that we became concerned enough to check other burrows around the Place and found that all of them had been deserted for a long time.

This unhappy discovery coincided with a larger one that many naturalists were documenting at the time: In much of their relatively narrow Deep South range, but especially in Alabama and Mississippi, gophers were on their way out. And now that I belatedly made a point of learning more about them, I realized that I may have unwittingly done my small part to push them into the "threatened" category of the Endangered Species List.

In fairness, there wasn't that much information available concerning the lifestyle of gopher tortoises until they started doing their vanishing act. Their decline has since been attributed to a number of causes, including disease; the conversion of their preferred habitat into pastureland, plantations of slash pine, and housing developments; and the growing popularity of such grotesque community diversions as rattlesnake roundups, which encourage people to gas tortoise dens because they are a favored hiding place of diamondback rattlers. Worse yet, even in areas where tortoises remain fairly common, few juveniles are being seen. The gopher's reproductive rate, which is naturally low, seems to be falling below the replacement level for reasons that are still not fully understood.

What is known is that fire is a key element in tortoise ecology. The natural habitat of the species is the dry sandy hills of the longleaf pine belt, where frequent woods fires keep the forest floor clear of brush, allowing the tortoise to move around comfortably inside its cumbersome carapace, feeding on such forbs, berries, and wild grasses as are favored in a fire-dominated ecosystem. However, the national forests and the vast privately owned timberlands in the Deep South have been increasingly managed as commercial tree farms where fire is suppressed during the first seven or eight years after clear-cuts have been planted in seedling slash pines — time enough for such areas to become inhospitable to gophers.

My own intentions in excluding fires had been different, of course. I had wanted to help reestablish the hardwoods that were as native to the sandhills as the pines, and to generally create a greater diversity of wildlife habitats on the Place; but as far as our tortoise colony was concerned, my plans were as disastrously conceived as those of the most profit-oriented forester. Except for the Big Pasture, which we had been disking and planting for years, and the small wild meadows we kept open on the index ridge and Schaeffer's Hill, the Place had become very woodsy and thickety indeed, with not many brush-free areas left in which a tortoise could maneuver and find something to eat.

To complicate life even further for our displaced gophers, by the early '80s they had nowhere else to go. The commercial timberlands around us were being managed as fire-free tree farms, and most small private holdings like those belonging to Roddy Ray and Hovit had either been converted into cattle pastures or bestrewn with the trailers of their owners' offspring and in-laws.

Gopher tortoises weren't the only losers. A good many other

species partial to brush-free pine woods and open meadows had also been affected by our ban on fire. The coveys of bobwhites that came to the feeders in winter were smaller now, and we only occasionally heard their plaintive springtime calling on the ridges, where the grassy openings they liked were being usurped by gallberry bushes and young trees. This successional change also explained the growing scarcity of nighthawks, mockingbirds, and that most beautiful of woodpeckers, the red-headed, as well as the total disappearance of kingbirds, meadowlarks, and the unlamented cowbird (which lays its eggs in other birds' nests). Nor did I doubt that other less conspicuous creatures, such as certain species of snakes and rodents and meadow-loving butterflies, were losing ground as well.

The exclusion of fire had also affected the pitcher plant bogs in a negative way, a fact that worried me all the more because, like the tortoise, this highly specialized ecosystem was becoming threatened throughout its range. During the early years when Willie and I drove the roads to the Place in spring, every low, damp spot in the pine woods had been bedecked with the nodding, weirdly beautiful blooms of yellow pitcher plants. Now these little bogs were almost all gone, displaced by pastures and lawns, or drained to make way for stiff rows of artificially planted slash pines.

In our pitcher plant bogs, a good many slash pines had planted themselves, albeit with some unintentional help from us. Of all the Southern pines, slash is the most tolerant of wet soils, although it also thrives on high, dry ground. It is an aggressive, fast-growing species, and, given the chance, often takes over on upland slopes where longleaf forests have been eliminated. However, the young trees are much more vulnerable than the longleaf to fire. Silviculturists theorize that back in the days when fire was a natural phenomenon, the slash pine's range was restricted to the damp edges of bogs and brainches, which were not likely to burn so hotly or so often. However, the slash pine was rarely

successful in invading the bogs because the poverty of their soils
— so unnutritious that some bog plants have evolved as insecti-
vores — slowed its normally rapid growth significantly. Thus, the
trees were rarely able to attain sufficient height and girth to
survive when, in the course of a drought, a hot fire did sweep
through.

The pitcher plants and other species native to our bogs were
adapted to such periodic scorchings. What they couldn't handle
was the invasion of vegetation that fire was supposed to keep out
but hadn't, thanks to our no-burn policy. The result was that,
poor soil notwithstanding, some of the slash pines had grown tall
enough to be unaffected by any fire we might set now. Indeed, in
the smaller of the two bogs, it seemed that a critical stage in the
successional process had been reached. A dense thicket of swamp
gallberry, a tall, waxy-leaved shrub, had anchored itself at the base
of each of the taller pines in the bog, evidently finding the ever-
so-slightly elevated ground that the pine roots had been thirstily
draining a good place to take root. From these anchorages they
were sending out runners, colonizing the bog and draining it of
moisture as swiftly as the pines themselves.

It had been such a gradual, subtle process! The pines had
seemed so spindly and innocuous; even now, the pitcher plants
and pogonia and white-topped sedge and young cypress still
appeared to be unaffected by the gallberry and the new crop of
seedling pines springing up in their midst. Indeed, it wasn't until
more than a year after we did those first controlled burns, from
which the bogs had been excluded, that it finally dawned on me
that they might be in trouble. I resolved that come March of next
year — 1987 — it would be their turn to be torched.

Meantime, I set to work with chain saw and axe. The pines
were easy. I girdled those that were of any size, leaving them to die
standing up, so woodpeckers could make the most of them as
cafeterias and nest trees; and I mowed down the smaller ones
with the saw. The swamp gallberry, on the other hand, took an

exasperatingly uncooperative attitude toward my attempts to do it in. It grew in thick clumps of many-branched stems, with no main trunk — the stems being too thick to be cut by a hedge trimmer but too thin and springy for the chain saw to sink its teeth into. When I tried the latter approach, the chain promptly snagged, jumped the guide bar, and would have chewed my hand up if the handle guard hadn't blocked it. So, by default, the axe was my weapon of choice, although it didn't work very well either. All those dozens of supple branches, bellying out from the central root in every direction, offered no target for a proper swing; the axe blade simply glanced off the pliant stems, which then sprang back, often as not catching me a retaliatory slap across the face. The only way I could get the best of them was to press each branch separately to the ground and hold it there firmly with my foot while I whacked it as close to the center of the bush as its interfering fellow branches would allow.

Demolishing gallberrys still ranks right up near the top on my list of least favorite types of physical labor; but it was just as well that I hacked back those unruly bushes when I did, for it would be a long time before the pitcher plant bogs got the burn I had promised them.

I bitterly regretted that we had expelled our tortoises and placed the pitcher plant bogs in jeopardy by not setting controlled burns sooner than we had. And I missed the sweet calling of the quail, the meadowlark's song, the bonk of dive-bombing nighthawks. Yet, for all my remorse, I couldn't honestly repent the original decision to protect the Place from fire. Granted its importance in the natural functioning of sandhills ecology, it had never been meant to eat away, year after year, at land that for decades had been unnaturally despoiled by its human exploiters. We had given the land a breather, a chance to accelerate if not actually restart the processes of successional regeneration. The sandhills were meant to be forested, after all, and on the Place, the forests, with amazing resiliency and speed, were coming back. The Oak Grove was now an oak forest, and the Hollow a textbook illustration of the natural relationship of forest types to elevation and moisture, light and shade — with dogwood, black cherry, red and turkey oaks gradually giving way to holly, swamp maple, water oaks, and yellow poplar on the descending slopes; and they, in the lowest elevations where Hollow merged with Brainch, to stands of cypress, tupelo, and sweet bay.

Yet, pervasive as these changes were, the Place still belonged, as it always had, principally to the pines. Most of the pine woods were a mix of slash, longleaf, and, in lesser numbers, loblolly; but on the far side of Schaeffer's Hill there was a pure stand of quite tall longleafs that set off, in its sunny openness, our lone grove of shortleaf pines, dense and dark, that grew nearby.

I've always loved visual contrasts, and the Place has a great many of them to choose from. But for me, none is more beautiful than that created by a regiment of Southern pines standing starkly at attention, each black trunk braided along one edge by the light of the setting sun, imposing a gridlike geometric pattern upon the billowing, rather blowzy backdrop of a hardwood forest. Perhaps more than any other prospect, this juxtaposition most typically represented what the Place was in the process of becoming; and with every turn in the slow-motion passage of the years, it gained that much more shape, texture, definition.

Viewed from an ecological rather than an aesthetic perspective, such a juxtaposition involves a lot more than first meets the eye. The interface between two different ecosystems often creates what is known in the parlance of wildlife managers as an "edge effect." Because they are composed of more diversified, overlapping types of vegetation, usually in a transitional stage, these areas of demarcation are the plant world's equivalent of free trade zones. In the States, at least, they are capable of providing more food and cover for a greater number of wildlife species than the more uniform habitats they intersect.

At the Place, hardwood thickets were the most obvious of these edges — not that they were all that obvious when we bought the property. At that time they were notable mostly for their tenacity: brushy little suckers sprouting up bravely from their root systems each spring only to be burned to the ground again the following year. With the ban on fire, however, all that had quickly changed. Around the Oak Grove and along the edge of the Hollow, mobs of young hardwoods, intermixed with shrubs and shrub trees such as yaupon, waxmyrtle, chinquapin and sassafras, vied with seedling pines to see who would outgrow whom. On lower, wetter ground, along the edges of the brainches and the bogs, swamp gallberry, catbrier, and titi (a marvelous honey plant) took over, forming walls of vegetation so dense that in some places the only way to get through them was to crawl on one's belly. Where they were penetrable, however, the transition from one ecological zone to another, especially in summer, was like stepping through the looking glass: from the blazing hot, thinly shaded pine woods on the slopes, through a thick hedge of broad-leafed plants, into the solipsistic, mysteriously beautiful world of the bottomland woods, free of underbrush and as damply cool as a cave.

I've already ruefully admitted that the encroachment of the thickets on the Place's open meadows and stands of young pines worked to the detriment of some wildlife species. But overall, these transitional zones between hardwood forests and piney woods seem to have attracted more wild creatures than they've repelled. As they mature into woodlands, the thickets increase the territories of barred owls, pileated woodpeckers, gray squirrels; they have even provided an acceptable nesting habitat for wild turkeys and a pair of Cooper's hawks. At an intermediate stage, they offer sanctuary to a long list of birds, from everyday species such as cardinals, towhees, and thrashers, to more secretive or less common ones like the wood thrush, yellow-billed cuckoo, black-and-white warbler, summer tanager, and orchard oriole. Moreover, for the last fifteen years or so, the deep thicket scrub at the lower edges of the Hollow has served as nursery for several whitetail fawns. If recent studies of the whitetail's breeding behavior can apply to the sandhills, where deer rarely live long enough to acquire much seniority, these animals may be related in a matriarchal hierarchy, with the senior daughter of an experienced doe claiming the fawning territory closest to her mother's, while junior offspring make do with territories more removed.

Willie and I were reguarly amazed at how effectively wild mothers conceal their young, and this was never more true than in the case of those whitetail does. Often enough we would find the quarter-size toe prints of the fawns, along with their mothers', not far from the compound, and sometimes the mother herself would come out to feed on Schaeffer's Hill at evening; yet only once did we see a fawn in its first few weeks of life, and then only with the inadvertent help of the dogs.

It was August, and Willie and I were taking Teddy and Luke with us on an evening stroll down to the pitcher plant bogs, where we hoped to find a few leopard lilies and yellow fringed orchids in bloom. Luke, five years old at the time, had really shaped up. He had never altogether outgrown his klutziness, but he was devoted and gentle-hearted and reasonably well behaved. Now that I thought so much better of him, he seemed to think better of himself, though he still allowed Teddy, whom he could have swallowed whole, to push him around a good bit. Although I had promised him and myself that I wouldn't compare him to Schaeffer, I was glad to notice that he did have one trait in common with his predecessor, namely, a general disinterest in the local wildlife. Regrettably, the same could not be said of Teddy. Though small in size, he was as bold as Sammie had been timorous, and he was fast on his feet and had a keen nose. Let him catch a whiff of a rabbit or a coon, and, given the chance, he was off like a shot. So whenever Willie and I took the dogs with us for a walk we put him on a leash, whereas Luke was free to wander at will, although, in practice, he rarely left my side.

As we often did, instead of heading straight down the index ridge, we took a roundabout path that led through the Hollow and then the thicket at its southern edge. While we were making our way along the tunnel-like passageway we had cut through the thicket, a rabbit started up ahead of us, and Teddy made a lunge for it as it ran off. Willie, caught unawares, let the leash slip from his hand, and in a trice both rabbit and dog disappeared. For a minute or so, we could hear Teddy's noisy progress as the rabbit wove him in and out of the maze of tangled undergrowth, but then the noise abruptly stopped.

Willie was alarmed, "He's got his leash hooked on something," he said. "We got to find him before he chokes himself!"

I doubted the choking part, but it did seem likely that the little mutt had snagged the leash and would have to be rescued. I turned to Luke and told him, "Find Teddy," not really expecting him to understand. But he obediently headed off in the direction Teddy had taken through the thicket, with us blundering along behind, sometimes hunched over, sometimes on hands and knees, and sometimes, where the catbrier was really bad, crawling on our stomachs. Luckily, we hadn't far to go before Luke came to a halt, poking his nose bemusedly at a furry brown rear end and a vigorously wagging tail, which was all that could be seen of Teddy. The rest of him was thrust into the bowels of a rotted tree trunk under which the rabbit had taken refuge. Not in the best of moods by this time, I grabbed the end of his leash, which in all that wilderness of snags hadn't snagged on anything, and unceremoniously hauled him out. Teddy looked surprised but unapologetic, shook some of the dirt off his face, sniffed around for a bit, and then sat down. Luke did the same, while Willie and I caught our breath and tried to figure out the least difficult way to disentangle ourselves from the tangle we were in.

We were still doing that when Willie said softly, "Look." He was staring at a cluster of royal ferns growing alongside the rotted log ten feet from where Teddy had been rooting, less than that from where we and the dogs were gathered now.

"What?" I whispered.

"Look," he insisted.

And then I made it out, my eyes focusing, separating the spotted fur from the spotty texture of leaves and earth and bark into which it blended so perfectly: the fawn, probably not more than a few days old, curled up on itself, head down, legs tucked in, not budging, seeming not to breathe. Yet it was watching us, its eyes bright with fear.

I had heard of this behavior in very young fawns — how, along with their near absence of a scent, this "freezing" enabled them to escape predators that would otherwise easily make a meal of them. But even so, that concentrated, instinctive immobility was a wondrous thing to see.

To get back to the tunnel-path, we had to move even closer to the fawn's hiding place than we already were; yet as we passed, it didn't so much as twitch an ear, and the dogs remained oblivious to its presence. During our noisy progress, with Teddy's leash now getting hooked on every clutching vine and shrub, I could imagine the little creature's mother, perhaps no more than a couple of dozen yards away, anxiously waiting for us to be gone.

The expanded Hollow, the Cooper's hawks, the fawn nursery, the whole more verdant aspect of the Place — I congratulated myself on all the welcome changes that our ban on fire had helped along. But I couldn't shake a feeling of uneasiness about those vanished tortoises. I kept seeing that old fellow by the gate making his final exit, and I wished a hundred times over that we had understood the problems he and his kin were facing before they decided to abandon the Place, and us.

Not that I was ready to believe they had given up on us for good! During the year after we did the controlled burns, I often scouted the slopes of the index ridge and Schaeffer's Hill, hoping to find the fresh burrows that would indicate that some of them had moved back home. I searched the Big Pasture as well, thinking one or two might have settled there even though it was already thickly colonized by blackberry and sumac and hundreds of seedling pines. But I had no luck.

It was that, having no luck, that really bothered me. Certainly I wanted the tortoises back because they belonged to the Place, because they were part of its wildlife community, because they were a threatened species. But there was no denying that animistic superstition had a part to play in my almost obsessive desire to reclaim them. Ever since that day when one of them had moved into our vegetable garden for the second time, the tortoises had become for me a sort of totem animal. I truly felt that they were the luck of the Place. *Our* luck.

Next year I resolved that I would not only burn the bogs, but expand the burns on the ridges. Then there would be lots of open ground, lots of grasses and legumes springing up under the pines. Surely that would convince them to return.

There was no way I could know, back then, that it was too late. That our luck had already run out.

29

The coven of crows

One evening in the autumn of 1985, over by the Big Pond, I had the chance to spy on a council of crows. The setting sun was exiting in style. The western horizon was massed with piled-up clouds edged in a lava flow of vermilion and molten gold, and the sky overhead was a color chart of delicate pastels ranging from pink to lavender to a whole range of blues. Against this backdrop loomed the skeleton silhouette of a lone tall pine that had been struck by lightning the previous year. And assembled in this tree were the crows.

I swear there must have been two hundred of them, every dead branch loaded end to end with birds. That they were gathered in anticipation of an imminent migration was obvious enough. What was mysterious, at least to me, was their uncrowlike conduct. These normally loudmouthed, pushy birds were being absolutely silent and well behaved; except for the quiet alighting of occasional new arrivals who somehow found perching space where there seemed none to spare, they hardly moved.

It made for a beautifully eerie scene, that black tree and its freight of black crows outlined like a shadow painting against the lurid western sky. Eerie and expectant; for all those hushed birds seemed to be waiting for something to happen. And, just when I was wondering if I might have stumbled into a scene in a Stephen King novel, something did. The King Crow began to speak. I know it sounds anthropomorphic to describe his behavior that way, but there it is: from the topmost snag of the dead tree, he began croaking in an unusually low crow voice as though he really were holding forth to the assembled throng. Whatever he was lecturing about — regulations pertaining to migration, the beauty of blackness, the significance of omens — all the other crows kept quiet and listened respectfully. When he finished — it was not a long oration — he shook his feathers in a dismissive, self-satisfied way and settled down for the night.

I stuck around until the light had almost drained from the sky and the tree and its coven lost their sharp edge, and then headed back to the house. It was irrational, I knew, but I wished that the birds had chosen somewhere other than the Place to hold their meeting.

Notwithstanding my vague forebodings concerning that somehow ominous council, or the more persistent disquiet about our gophers' disappearing act, the spring and early summer of 1986 turned out to be one of the happiest periods of my life, and Willie's too. True, poor Luke had died the previous winter of one of those peculiar ailments, a kidney disorder, that afflicts dogs that have been bred to be overlarge; but apart from that loss, we could actually believe that we had it all, everything we had ever hoped for. I had retired from the university at the earliest allowable date — not that I didn't love teaching and the academic life, but I'd had that, and now I wanted more time to write and live at the Place. And Willie was able to semi-retire too. Thanks to the cooperation of his boss, a good friend of ours, and his high standing as a floor sander, he now worked only when there was a special job requiring his skill and experience, or when he wanted to earn some spending money — an arrangement which usually left him free, on average, three weeks out of four. For the first time since we had owned it, we could live practically full-time at the Place.

Although we were furnished with most of the modern amenities and in touch periodically with the city and our friends, I suspect that a person living a hundred years ago would have been more in tune with the rhythm of our lives than were most of our contemporaries. Simplify, simplify, Thoreau had said, and so we did, not through any conscious intent, but because the day after day routines of a secluded country life dictated that we should. Often a week or ten days would pass without our seeing any face except each other's. Many times we lost track of what day of the week it was.

Still, there was no lack of things to do. We gave the house a new coat of barn-red paint, repaired the compound fence, filled potholes in the entrance road with gravel. Willie built more cabinets for the enlarged kitchen and got the spring garden under way, and I began an ambitious excavation at the rear of the House Pond. I had taken it into my head that we must have a pond in two sections — a duplex pond — with the new rear section separated from, and elevated above, the existing pond by a dam composed of the dirt I was digging up. It was simple grunt work that left my mind free to wander. I knew that before long there would come an interruption, albeit an agreeable one, in the life we were now living. I had just signed a contract to write a book about the Yucatán Peninsula; and while I shoveled away, I planned and replanned my itinerary, all the more pleased with the prospect of the upcoming journey because this time Willie would be able to come along.

Meanwhile, there was the Place itself, a presence that encompassed ours. We no longer had to look to its promise to appreciate its beauty. In the course of that fine spring and early summer, it was composing itself into what I regarded, not too extravagantly, I think, as a medieval vision of Eden, a green and golden tapestry crowded with more exquisite detail than the senses could take in. It was all there, all we could have wished for: thick-limbed oaks casting their deep shade along the entrance road, colonnades of pines soughing in the wind, an embroidery of white dogwood stitched across the Hollow's green brocade, the piping of daytime birds and nighttime frogs, a doe on Schaeffer's Hill, the crabapples spilling their sweet scent, irises and daylilies flowering in turn along the pond's dark edge, the languid evenings and star-bright nights, still not too hot, sliding into summer.

On one of those evenings, Willie and I were sitting on the tower, drinks in hand, Teddy dozing at our feet. Willie was telling me stories about his two favorite aunts, now long dead, who had looked after him during his early years. "They was such nice aunts," he sighed. "I wish they was still alive. I wish I could see them again."

"They'll be in Heaven," I said dutifully. "You'll see them there."

"That's true," he said. "That is, if I get in."

"Oh, you will," I said, "believe me! But let's not rush it, okay?"

He grinned, "Don't worry. I'm in no big hurry. I'm happy just the way things are."

"That makes two of us," I said.

A little later, when he got up to check on whatever he had roasting in the oven, I noticed that in the fading light the shadows around his eyes and under his high cheekbones seemed deeper than they should have been. "You need to start eating more," I said. "You're getting too thin."

"It's just the warm weather coming on," Willie shrugged. "In summer I always lose weight."

But it wasn't just that. A month later, a doctor sat us down in his office and somberly explained that Willie was HIV positive, and that his weight loss probably indicated the onset of AIDS. It came out that at a certain moment during the early '80s, when I had been too busy, too often away from home, Willie had contracted the virus. Now, after years of lying dormant, it was bent on killing him. Ironically, the ignorance of the medical profession at that time regarding HIV and AIDs shielded Willie from the true bleakness of his prognosis. For a while longer there was only his weight loss to contend with; but in October, he began to have fevers and other flu-like symptoms. From private consultations with his doctors, I knew the truth; but between Willie and me it was understood that the "flu" was a consequence of his damaged immune system, not a symptom of AIDS. I encouraged him to believe that the disease could be held at bay until the recently discovered "miracle drug," AZT, became available in time to save him. Willie coped gallantly with the fevers and night sweats but, always the optimist, he didn't want to be told that there was no hope for him. In the waking nightmare that our lives had now become, the one mercy granted was that, before he ever had to face that fact, the circuits in his brain began to disconnect.

Willie's dying and death had their setting in the city where we spent those last months, never far from the pharmacies, the offices of specialists, the laboratories where T cells are counted and vital signs are checked. However, during the nightmare s final stages, there was one moment that belonged to the Place.

The new year, 1987, had just begun. After weeks of seemingly endless gray, the sun was out, the air was almost warm, and Willie, except for being very weak, was in no great discomfort. When I suggested that we might overnight at the Place for what I knew would be the last time, Willie responded with an enthusiastic, if somewhat dreamy, "Oh, yes!" So we set off in the middle of a shiny bright Sunday afternoon, driving slowly, reaching the Place an hour before the winter dark set in.

During the preceding months I had come up alone several times just long enough to fill the corn bins for our remaining poultry before heading back to the city again. On one of these brief visits I had told Roddy Ray to help himself to the chickens, which he had done. On their own initiative, the mallards, sensing our neglect, had flown away to the Big Swamp where they were briefly observed by one of our neighbors before they disappeared for good. Now only the geese and guineas remained to greet us when we arrived, their numbers much reduced by some human or animal predator I hadn't had the time or inclination to discover. The geese honked complainingly as I helped Willie out of the car; the guineas, feral, unusually quiet, swirled restlessly back and forth across the untended, leaf-strewn lawn.

After we had eaten a simple meal of fresh vegetables, we sat for a couple of hours in front of the fire, staring at the flames. Sometimes Willie was entranced and far away; when he wasn't, we talked about the coming spring and all the projects we would undertake once his health improved.

But that night, as often happened now, he had a dreadful fever during which he moaned and tossed but didn't wake. After a while I went downstairs, took the shotgun from the place where I kept it, and loaded it with two OO shells. When I came back to the bedroom, I stood over Willie for some time with the barrel pointed at his head. At this stage in the nightmare's course, I had only one wish: to put an end to it for both of us. I still believe that I would have done so, but for one thing: I couldn't bear the thought of the bloody damage a shotgun blast would do to Willie's person. Thinking about that, my resolve weakened and I finally put the gun away.

The next morning, the weather had turned morosely gray again. While Willie still slept, I wandered around the compound. The camellias, Willie's favorite flower, were in full bloom. I picked one, put it in a jar, and set it beside his bed. It was the first thing he saw when he woke up. He wasn't all there, but the sight of that velvety, blood-red flower seemed to fascinate him, as though it were something magical, something he had never seen before.

Later, when it was time to head back to New Orleans, I wrapped him in a blanket and settled him in a folding chair on the deck while I loaded the car with the few things we had brought with us. But when I went to fetch him, the chair was empty. He had decided to take a walk.

From a little distance I watched him make his way across the compound slope, passing under the leafless crabapple and the dark green oaks, his thin body silhouetted against the gray of the sky reflected in the quiet pond. He was like a sleepwalker, moving in slow motion; but I could see he was taking it all in: the crabapple, the oaks, the guineas gathered at the replenished feeders, a cardinal flying by. And he knew where he wanted to go. Slowly, with a drifting, loose-limbed grace, he moved up the slope to where the camellias grew among the pines. When he reached them, he cradled one of the flowers in his long fingers. Then he tried to break the stem, but he couldn't.

I crossed the slope at a run, took the stem, and snapped it for him. He held the flower to his face, and as he did so, he gave me that incredibly radiant smile of his, as though I had presented him with the most magnificent of all possible gifts. He was in a dreamlike fugue, somewhere where I couldn't follow him; yet he recognized me, and he was really happy, really pleased. Of all the smiles with which he brightened my life, that is the one I will best remember as long as I live.

30

Afterwards

Willie died in New Orleans, in his own bed, on January 20, 1987. He would have been pleased to see how many people came from near and far to attend his memorial service.

When all that was over, I took some of his ashes to the Place, meaning to scatter them in the Oak Grove, the Hollow, and our other favorite places. But when I was faced with the prospect of actually doing that, I changed my mind and buried them on Schaeffer's Hill — not under the oaks where Schaeffer and Sammie and Luke were buried, but among the pines on the slope near the compound fence, a spot that offered a fine view of the house and pond. I was later glad that I did this, for during the desolate months and years that were to follow I always had this place to come to. To mark the site, I piled several heavy granite paving blocks, brought long ago from the city, into a sort of cairn.

Nothing in my rather fortunate existence had prepared me for what had happened. The fixed point of the compass was gone, and with it all sense of meaning and direction in my life. Before this I had never envied anyone; now I felt that I would willingly trade places with anybody who was not me. For the first time in my life I knew what it meant to be seriously, inescapably depressed. It's difficult, probably useless, to try to describe this condition. I think, perhaps, that only people who have experienced a truly catastrophic personal loss can know what it is like.

I'm not sure how I would have made it, had it not been for two things: the almost relentless attentiveness of friends, and the abiding solace of the Place.

After I had dealt with the practical matters pertaining to Willie's death, I moved to the Place and settled in. For months afterwards I rarely ventured into the city; but friends took turns descending on me for visits. What with my gloomy state and the palpable sense of Willie's absence lying heavy on the Place, they could hardly have enjoyed these expeditions, but they insisted on coming anyway; and when they left there was usually a week's worth of meals in the freezer. At the time this steady show of sympathy and support touched me not at all; only later on would I realize how sustaining it had been.

With the Place it was much the same. I lived there utterly unmoved by the onset of what would have been, if Willie had lived, the twentieth spring we had witnessed there. There was no question of attempting a garden, but in a fitful sort of way I undertook some of the usual chores, clearing rain gutters, raking up the live oak leaves that fell in March and early April, dragging mattresses and pillows out of the house to air on the decks, sweeping dead wasps from the windowsills, throwing a little more dirt up on the dam of the duplex back pond. However, in the middle of these tasks I would sometimes suddenly stop and sit down wherever I happened to be, paralyzed by an awareness that what I was doing had no purpose. Late at night I would spend hours on the tower, unable to sleep, rerunning in my mind the last months, days, hours of Willie's life.

Teddy, though not an especially soulful or perceptive little dog, understood that everything was changed. Partly for that reason, partly because he was no longer as young and larky as he had once been, he spent most of his time dozing in Willie's chair, almost as insensible as I was to the allure of the surrounding woods. As for the poultry, by this time only a single guinea hen was left. Previously, guineas would have been the last creatures in the world I would have thought of as being emblematic of anything except silliness; but this last survivor didn't strike me as silly now. She was so pathetically lonely that she actually sought me out for company, even following me into the house, putt-chukking softly, if I left the sliding screen door open. When the whatever-it-was that had taken the others came for her after a week or so, I was relieved for both our sakes.

One morning when I had been shut away at the Place for a couple of months, I looked out at the pond and saw that a bird of some sort, half hidden by a screen of irises, was swimming close to the near bank, trailing a wake like those the mallards used to make. Just as it was coming into view, it slipped under the surface — again as a mallard might, except that it stayed underwater for what seemed a long time. When it finally reappeared, bobbing up like a miniature duck made of balsa wood, it was on the opposite side of the pond. It quickly dove again, but not before I'd had a good look at it and recognized it as a pied-billed grebe — the first I had ever seen at the Place.

Not all that long ago, this unlikely and momentous sighting would have had me dancing up and down, yelling for Willie to come look. Now, however, its only significance was that it had none. I might as well have been staring at a pigeon in Jackson Square.

It may be that this small incident represented a turning point of sorts. At any rate, I remembered just then a comment made by a friend who had come to visit not long after Willie died. This was the same woman who had been our hostess at the dinner party twenty years earlier when Willie and I announced to our friends that we had bought the Place. Halfway between then and now, her much-loved husband had died of a heart attack, so she had spoken from firsthand experience when she said, "You never really get over it, you know. But it does get better, a little bit better, every day." When I didn't reply, she had given me a shrewd sidelong glance and added, "*If* you let it. If that's what you want."

It hadn't been what I wanted. By being unalive myself I had felt, not unreasonably, that I was keeping faith with the dead.

Only now — seeing that grebe and not caring that I had — I consciously understood for the first time that, after having already lost so much, I was going to lose it all if matters kept on as they were going.

From then on, I started taking walks that led me farther afield than Willie's grave. On pleasant afternoons I sat for hours in the Hollow, losing myself as I had only occasionally done in years gone by. Sometimes I stretched out on my stomach in the leafy mold, courting chigger bites, but also in some primitive way inviting the familiar maternal earth to lend me what strength and comfort it could. Once, a black racer slid around the arm on which my chin was propped. I was just one more obstruction on the branch-littered forest floor.

In a way, my friend was not quite accurate in saying that each day it gets a little better. At least not at first. What does happen, once you want to get on with your life, is that each day you become a little bit more alive. That, I learned, can be an anguishing process, as when an amputee learns to walk with an artificial limb. The depression doesn't go away; but it begins to alternate with a lot of more active feelings like frustration, anger, pain.

And guilt. One night, when one of those rowdy summer storms came up out of nowhere, knocking out the electricity, shaking the house with rolls of thunder, I paced back and forth, upstairs and down, from one sliding door to another, holding frightened Teddy in my arms, looking out at the compound lit up almost continuously by flare after flare of lightning. I felt stirred up, unexpectedly excited by the storm's raw energy. For a while there I found myself positively reveling, in a Heathcliffean way, in the tumult going on outside. But then, as was bound to happen, there flashed through my mind the long-ago image of Willie, standing drenched to the skin in the waters of the Brainch, scared out of his wits but determined to rescue me from a summer storm as wild as this one.

In the barrage of flashing lightning, I could see his grave on Schaeffer's Hill, the rain streaming down the stones. While I'd been prowling around the house, enjoying myself in a weird, apocalyptic way, I had forgotten he was out there, all alone, beyond any hope of human rescue.

At the moment I realized this, I wished — no idle phrase — that I was dead.

But I wasn't; and there was no way to escape the fact that, for a few moments, I had been happy.

Eight months after Willie's death I finally headed for the Yucatán to gather material for the book I had contracted to write a year and a half earlier. My incredibly patient and understanding publishers would still have a long wait before the book went to press; but for me this was the first step, which I took with much trepidation, toward living actively again in the world outside the Place. That long journey was no cure — there is no absolute cure for an amputee — but it was an important stage in the process of adjustment and acceptance that had begun at the Place and that still goes on. I could finally begin to believe in what my friend had promised: that it does get better, a little bit better, every day.

31

The reserve

In 1990 the absentee owners of the 160-acre tract that adjoined the Place on its northwestern and western borders were persuaded by a Gulf Coast real estate agent to sell the entire property to her at a bargain-basement price. Years earlier I had tried to buy the forty acres on the northwest side of the Place, which straddled the county road, but at that time the owners had been unwilling to subdivide the land. Now the new owner, having assured me that although she was a real estate agent, she was "a good Christian woman and not at all greedy," offered me the forty if I could meet her price, which was very steep indeed.

In the three years that had passed since Willie's death, the tide of development that had been spreading into the sandhills from the Coast for more than a decade had greatly accelerated, and almost all the land in the region that was not held by timber companies and banks was being subdivided into smaller and smaller parcels. It was obvious that unless I acted fast, the real estate agent's northwest forty would suffer the same fate. So, although I could ill afford it, I decided that I would have to buy it to protect the ecological integrity of the Place.

After Willie's death I had made a new will bequeathing the Place to the Nature Conservancy, a private organization dedicated to protecting rare and endangered species and ecosystems.

At the time, I had been too depressed to care much about my own preservation, much less that of the Place; so according to the terms of the bequest, the Conservancy was free to sell the property if it wished and use the proceeds to buy land elsewhere in the Deep South that it considered to be more ecologically valuable.

Since then, my attitude had changed. I now wanted very much to preserve the Place, both for its own sake and as a memorial to Willie. The problem was that the Conservancy, the only reliable custodian I could think of, was pretty fussy in determining the importance of any property it took on as a nature reserve, and for a time I hadn't been sure the Place would qualify. However, with the ecological diversity of the sandhills vanishing at the rate of thousands of acres a year, it seemed likely that few, if any, other places of comparable size still survived in which virtually all of the area's representative ecosystems were so conveniently concentrated. And its diversity would be further enhanced by the acquisition of the real estate agent's forty acres, which consisted mostly of a flat expanse of pine woods, a fairly rare landscape feature in the sandhills' undulant topography.

After a good many weeks of circling around a decision that rather scared me, I finally made up my mind. If the Nature Conservancy would agree to preserve the Place for posterity, I would hand it over to them now instead of waiting until I kicked off. Indeed, it seemed to me that I was offering the organization such a good deal that they might be willing to help me buy that additional forty.

I had had dealings with the Nature Conservancy some twelve years earlier. Dave Morine, then the director of the Conservancy's land acquisition program, had hired me to write about the organization, with particular emphasis on a complex and daring real estate transaction that had successfully protected the Pascagoula, the largest remaining bottomland swamp in Mississippi.

In the course of researching the project, I had been much impressed with the Conservancy's way of doing business. Unlike most environmental organizations, which rely on political lobbying and legal action to get results, the Conservancy was into land brokering. While its cadre of scientists compiled a vast data bank on endangered flora and fauna, its field staff concentrated on "doing deals" with individual and corporate landowners, working out tax breaks and other incentives as a way of acquiring threatened ecosystems and essential habitat for endangered species. What I had particularly liked about the organization was its pragmatic attitude: These were people who could have been very successful developers and real estate brokers, yet in contrast to that unlovely tribe, they were using their wheeler-dealer skills to save, rather than destroy, the natural world.

In the late spring of 1990, I contacted the Conservancy's recently opened office in Jackson, Mississippi. A week or two later its young director and I spent a day crisscrossing the Place's hills and dales, the director casting an appraising eye at this or that landscape feature while I hovered over him, boasting and blathering, as fidgety as a parent trying to convince the headmaster of an exclusive prep school that his little darling is worthy of admission.

As it turned out, the director didn't need much convincing about the Place's ecological worth. The one little hitch was that his fledgling Mississippi chapter was already in hock for a reserve it had just acquired, and his board of directors was in no hurry to take on another project. The upshot was that the idea of preserving the Place was put on hold, and I had to buy the north forty myself.

There matters rested for two years. Then one day I had a call from a fellow who had bought eighty acres abutting the Place on the west from the same agent. Seems that he was having some financial disagreements with the lady, who held the mortgage on the land. So he suggested that I might want to take all of the tract off his hands except the ten-acre parcel on which his house stood.

At his invitation, I explored every nook and cranny of the property — no easy task considering the condition in which I found it. Topographically at least, it was pretty much an extension of my own land. The drainage creek that wound through it was a continuation of the Place's Brainch, but wider, thanks to the additional runoff it accumulated as it made its way to the western boundary of the tract. There it was joined by another brainch, flowing southward — the two of them forming an elbow curve that conveniently cradled most of the property's broad high ridge of uplands. At the base of this ridge, where the brainches met, lay the Big Swamp — the very same where Hovit, who had recently died at a ripe old age, had so often observed the carryings-on of hog bears, black panthers, and bushy-tailed bobcats while taste-testing the product of his stills.

Unfortunately, the present owner had allowed the real estate agent to remove all the salable timber from the property before he bought it. Which apparently, in her book, meant removing all the timber, period. Even in the much-abused sandhills, I had rarely seen a more brutally sloppy clear-cut. The high ridge and its drainage slopes had been stripped of every pine big enough for a chain saw to slice through without snagging; and even the Brainch had been torn apart in a determined effort to get at whatever marketable timber it contained. At least at first glance, the prospect that now presented itself — a landscape of flattened brush and smashed treetops — did not exactly recommend itself for inclusion in a Nature Conservancy reserve, even if the Conservancy should decide, which it so far showed no sign of doing, to preserve the next-door Place.

However, the land had one ecological feature that was truly impressive — a bog that was larger than both of those on the Place put together — almost ten acres of blood-red and chartreuse pitcher plants growing in dense profusion. Being virtually treeless, it had escaped the destruction inflicted on the rest of the tract. From studying NASA's most recent aerial maps of the area, I knew that this bog and the two on the Place were the only remaining links in what had once been a whole chain of hillside bogs paralleling the brainches in this watershed, all the others having been sown to slash pine. I also knew that the Mississippi Nature Conservancy had given a very high priority to preserving pitcher plant bogs. So I thought, What the hell, it was worth a try.

Once again I contacted the Conservancy. By this time the Mississippi chapter had some funds to spare, and after their botanists discovered a couple of species of bog button and yellow pipewort that were endangered in the state, and attested to the overall ecological value of the Place and the adjoining seventy acres, the director's interest in the project was revived. It helped, of course, that I had already added the forty acres of piney flatwoods at my own expense, and now indicated that, if I absolutely had to, I would chip in on the purchase of the seventy-acre tract to the west. Negotiations, which unfortunately involved the mortgage-holding real estate agent, were resumed in earnest. They would drag on for half a year; but the day finally came when all the interested parties were gathered in a lawyer's office on the Coast, documents were signed, registered checks were handed over, and the deal was closed. The Conservancy ended up buying thirty acres of my neighbor's land, including the pitcher plant bog, while I bought the other forty, consisting mostly of the clear-cut uplands. This I promptly handed over to the Conservancy along with all the other lands that now comprised the Place. For its part, the Conservancy guaranteed me a life tenure on the original eighty acres Willie and I had bought twenty-five years earlier, and committed itself to maintain the land in perpetuity. It was also agreed that when I bowed out, a full-time caretaker or custodian would look after the reserve.

A few months later, the tract, now amounting to 240 acres

(including the ten that Arlan owned and was bequeathing to the Conservancy in his will), was officially dedicated as the Willie Farrell Brown Nature Reserve.

Although the negotiations leading to the establishment of the reserve had often been frustrating, not to mention financially draining, planning for the reserve's management proved to be great fun. I had tried to be a good custodian of the land, and I had learned a lot as I went along. But it gave a very different twist to things, now that I had to start thinking — along with the Conservancy's people — of land restoration as a process that would extend far beyond my lifetime. The question was no longer "What will the Place be like in another decade or two?" but, "What will it be like a hundred, even two hundred years from now?" In the fullness of time — that phrase I had been so fond of — was taking on a whole new meaning!

More than anyone else, Mickey Webb, the likable and earnest forestry consultant to the Nature Conservancy's Mississippi office, would bring that large perspective home to me. He belonged to a new breed of Southern silviculturists who had made themselves apostles of the longleaf pine. For generations, foresters in the Gulf states had been promoting loblolly and slash pine as replacements for the original stands of longleaf cut down early in the century, even though the longleaf was the superior tree in terms of its commercial value. The problem was that silviculturists, lacking an understanding of the longleaf's reproductive ecology, had found it difficult to propagate commercially. When artificially reared, infant longleafs are quite choosy about the conditions under which they will consent to flourish. It took researchers decades to discover that their taproots have to be significantly thicker and longer than the slash's or the loblolly's before they can be moved from tree farm nurseries to the field;

and that once moved, longleafs must be protected during their first critical years from the shading effect of grass and shrubs — to which they are very susceptible — by controlled burns that would kill a slash or loblolly at the same tender age. Careful management is required to time this fire regimen correctly; but once established, the longleaf soon demonstrates why, under natural conditions, it dominated the Deep South's piney woods. It is highly resistant to fire and to the attacks of the voracious Southern pine beetle; and on the dry, inhospitable ridges of the sandhills it grows to more towering heights than any other pine.

Given his evangelistic bias in favor of longleafs, Mickey regarded the clear-cut that the real estate agent had inflicted on the west seventy not as a disaster but an opportunity. He assured me that once a controlled burn had cleared the ground a bit, it could be planted in longleaf seedlings; and that with the proper allocation of fire over the next couple of years, and some judicious thinning later on, these shorn and battered slopes would look, in a mere fifty years or so, much as they had before the Big Cut. This vision so entranced me that, after only a little hesitation, I decided that the several acres of slash pine Willie and I had planted on the lower slopes of Schaeffer's Hill should be harvested, and that land also consecrated to the renaissance of the longleaf pine.

There is no such thing as a tidy-looking clear-cut, but the one on Schaeffer's Hill was carried out with a decent regard for environmental considerations, and Mickey took pains to see that the smattering of longleafs and oaks growing among the slash should be spared. A year and a half later, the slope looked much as it did when Willie and I first saw it; except that in among the gallberry and wild grasses (already scorched once and soon to be scorched again), hundreds of charming little longleafs reared their tufted, bright green heads.

Much of the rest of the Place, including all three of the pitcher plant bogs, will undergo trials by fire during the coming years. There will be trained personnel and heavy machinery on hand to ensure that these controlled burns really are controlled. No more lane-jumping conflagrations like the one that would have gotten the better of Willie and me if Willie hadn't made the wind stop blowing.

Even without benefit of fire breaks, there is little chance now that fire would make much headway in the damp and shadowy depths of the Oak Forest and the Hollow, which become more lordly and imposing with each passing year. As for the Big Pasture, for a while at least, a bush hog, a machine that mows shrubs the way a lawnmower mows grass, may be used to maintain it as it is, which is to say, in a halfway stage between the pasture it once was and the mixed woodland it is trying to become. With its impenetrable blackberry brier patches, its brushy tangles of waxmyrtle, ilex, young pines, and yaupon, it is the ultimate thicket — such a welcoming habitat for songbirds, deer, snakes, and small game that I can't resist the ecologically incorrect urge to halt the natural successional pattern. At least, as I say, for a while.

This leaves the many acres of maturing pine woods — longleaf, slash, and loblolly — growing side by side on the index ridge, the northwest forty, the far side of the county road. Where the trees had become so crowded together they had stopped growing, they have been selectively logged. But I suspect that Mickey would like to go further than that, clear-cutting most of these areas so that they, like the tracts already planted, could one day be transformed into pure stands of longleafs. On this point, however, I am more catholic than he. Why not, I argue, let the different pine species fight it out among themselves — as they sometimes must have, once upon a time, before we humans messed things up? In theory, if controlled burns are applied at irregular intervals to simulate the cycle of wildfires, the slash and loblollies will be disadvantaged in their reproductive efforts, at least on the dry uplands, and the longleafs will eventually prevail. But no one can say for certain that that is how matters would shake out. So why not put the theory to the test in a long-term field experiment that has never been attempted before? And what better place than the Place to try it out?

I admit that my enthusiasm for such a project isn't altogether disinterested. With Willie, I watched most of the pines that now dominate the Place's hills grow from spindly, hurricane-battered adolescents into tall and stately trees; so it is natural, I suppose, that, regardless of species or silviculturists' theories, I should hate to see too many more of them cut down, even to make way for something as engaging as an additional crop of baby longleafs. Ultimately the decision on whether to clear-cut or not to clear-cut will belong to the Conservancy people; but while I'm still around, I intend to take advantage of their policy of being nice to me to press my case.

Epilogue

Of all the projects that I talked about with the Conservancy's director and Mickey Webb, there was one that was dearer to my heart than any other. I still longed to bring gopher tortoises back to the Place. Without them, I felt, Willie's reserve was incomplete. I had given up hoping that the animals would return on their own — there seemed no place left from which they could emigrate — but now that the land was officially a reserve, I figured it wouldn't be that difficult to have two or three of them transferred from somewhere else. Indeed, once the clear-cuts and the first controlled burns were accomplished, there was enough suitable habitat to keep ten times that number happy.

It all seemed so simple and easy. I asked the Conservancy director for help and he said he would do his best. I approached a friend who had contacts with the Audubon Zoo in New Orleans and she promised she would do what she could. I talked to a landowner who had a healthy colony of gophers on his property, and he said he would consider giving me a couple. I called the appropriate official in Jackson and he assured me that, although the state management policy for tortoises called for maintaining surviving populations in their present locales, he would put me at the top of the list if any stray animals were collected from highways or wherever.

For a year and a half I pestered these and other people; but nothing came of these efforts. Finally, I gave up.

That was where matters stood a month ago on a mild overcast day in October — the twentieth, to be exact. At the time, most of the first draft of this chronicle was written, and I was much preoccupied with the common literary problem of how to end it in a neat and fitting way. At noon, as I always did, I left the tower office and took off on a nature walk that was also an antipoaching patrol. I decided I would stroll along the entrance road for a ways, then head down to the overgrown Big Pasture. However, when I reached the shady curve where the old widow's homeplace had been, some serendipitous impulse turned me in the opposite direction, and I found myself walking instead along the trail that led into that level tract of pine woods, the north forty that I had bought some four years earlier. After running a few hundred yards due west, the trail made a sharp right turn toward the county road, and there I stopped, debating whether to follow it or keep on in the direction I was going, which would eventually bring me to the west seventy clear-cut.

I was still standing there when, some twenty feet away, the gallberry bushes beside the trail were stirred by something that was not the wind. Quietly, I moved forward a few steps. As I did so, the bushes parted and a black wizened face emerged into the sunlight, its old eyes peering up at me in mild surprise.

There was no use even trying to guess where that tortoise had come from. The small miracle was that I had chanced to meet him when I did. The big one was that he was there at all after almost fifteen years' absence. Plainly, he was in a peregrinating mode, traveling purposefully and in broad daylight toward Schaeffer's Hill and the heart of the Place.

Normally, gopher tortoises are wary creatures and will hurry off when they see a human. But this one must have come a long way; he appeared to be tired, and more put out than frightened to find me standing in his way. He lugged his large carapace out on the trail, plunked it there like a piece of heavy luggage, and extended his head and leathery front legs to their full length, all the while staring at me as though he wished I would just go away. I thought I heard him sigh.

Or maybe I just heard myself. I was elated of course; but it is all too true, what the poet said: how, in the very temple of delight, veiled melancholy has her sovereign shrine. I remembered how our luck had left us. And I wondered briefly if it could still matter to me that now it had come back.

However, this was not the time to pursue these ambivalent musings. For the moment, Willie's reserve was no longer gopherless, but it was by no means a sure thing that our wayfaring tortoise had come back to stay. It was imperative that he should keep on going in the direction he was headed — which meant that I had better stop standing there like an idiot, blocking his path!

For a moment I was tempted to pick him up, as I had once before all those years ago, and cart him over to Schaeffer's Hill. But I knew that wouldn't do. The tortoise would have to make up his own mind about where his home should be.

I left him alone to do that, with only a couple of over-the-shoulder glances before I hied myself out of sight. Back at the house, I spent the rest of that day and the following night fretting about whether he might have turned around, or, just as bad, crossed Schaeffer's Hill, the Hollow, the Big Pasture — the whole breadth of the Place — and kept right on going.

I needn't have worried. The next morning — the weather had turned colder overnight — I found his freshly dug burrow on the slope of Schaeffer's Hill, not far from Willie's grave. He is still holed up there as I write this. For the rest of the winter, at least, it seems likely that he will stick around.